THE PRACTICE OF TRANSLATING

HELPS FOR TRANSLATORS SERIES

TECHNICAL HELPS:

Old Testament Quotations in the New Testament

Section Headings for the New Testament

Short Bible Reference System

New Testament Index

Orthography Studies

Bible Translations for Popular Use

*The Theory and Practice of Translation

Bible Index

Fauna and Flora of the Bible

Short Index to the Bible

Manuscript Preparation

Marginal Notes for the Old Testament

Marginal Notes for the New Testament

The Practice of Translating

HANDBOOKS:

A Translator's Handbook on Ruth

A Translator's Handbook on the Book of Amos

A Translator's Handbook on the Book of Jonah

A Translator's Handbook on the Gospel of Mark

*A Translator's Handbook on the Gospel of Luke

A Translator's Handbook on the Gospel of John

A Translator's Handbook on the Acts of the Apostles

A Translator's Handbook on Paul's Letter to the Romans

A Translator's Handbook on Paul's Letter to the Galatians

A Translator's Handbook on Paul's Letter to the Philippians

A Translator's Handbook on Paul's Letters to the Colossians and to Philemon

A Translator's Handbook on Paul's Letters to the Thessalonians

A Translator's Handbook on the First Letter from Peter

A Translator's Handbook on the Letters of John

GUIDES:

A Translator's Guide to Selected Psalms

A Translator's Guide to the Gospel of Matthew

A Translator's Guide to the Gospel of Mark

THE PRACTICE OF
TRANSLATING

DRILLS FOR TRAINING TRANSLATORS

by

Jacob A. Loewen

UNITED BIBLE SOCIETIES

London, New York,
Stuttgart

17552

PRINTED IN THE UNITED STATES OF AMERICA

Books in the series of Helps for Translators
that are marked with an asterisk (*) may best
be ordered from

    United Bible Societies
    D-7000 Stuttgart 80
    Postfach 81 03 40
    West Germany

All other books in the series may best be
ordered from

    American Bible Society
    1865 Broadway
    New York, N.Y. 10023
    U.S.A.

ISBN 0-8267-0028-4

ABS-1981-1,500-CM-1-C#08560

CONTENTS

[v]

ABBREVIATIONS USED IN THIS VOLUME

Translations Quoted:

AB   The Amplified Bible, 1965
ASV   American Standard Version, 1901
BE   The Basic Bible, 1950
Beck   W. F. Beck, The Holy Bible, an American Translation, 1976
Br   Hans Bruns, Die Bibel, 1964
Brc   William Barclay, The New Testament, 1969
Ch   Chichewa from Malawi, a new popular language translation in preparation
Co   Concordant Literal New Testament, 1966
Em   Empera, an unpublished translation from Panama
GeCL   Die Gute Nachricht, a common language translation into modern German, 1971
Gk   The Greek New Testament, United Bible Societies, 1968
GNB   Good News Bible (see TEV)
Hb   Hebrew Old Testament
JB   The Jerusalem Bible, 1966
KJV   The King James Version, often called Authorized Version
Knox   Monsignor Knox, The Bible, 1955
LB   Kenneth Taylor, The Living Bible, 1966
Mft   James Moffatt, New Testament, 1934
NAB   The New American Bible, New Testament, 1970
NAS   The New American Standard Version, 1971
NEB   The New English Bible, 1970
NIV   The New International Version, New Testament, 1973
NRT   A Translation for New Readers, United Bible Societies, 1972
PCL   A Biblia na linguagem de Hoje, O Novo Testamento, a common language Portuguese translation, 1975
Phps   J. B. Phillips, New Testament in Modern English, 1959
RSV   Revised Standard Version, 1952
RV   Revised Version, 1898
SpCL   Dios Llega al Hombre, Version Popular, a common language Spanish translation, 1970
TEV   Today's English Version (the Good News Bible), 1976
TNT   The Translator's New Testament, 1973
Wn   Waunana, an unpublished translation from Panama
YL   Your Language, refers to the language spoken by the translator-in-training
Zink   Jörg Zink, Das Neue Testament, 1965
ZT   Zambian Tonga, a new popular language translation now in preparation

Note: Biblical quotations in New Testament drills come from the Eight Translation New Testament, Tyndale House, 1974, unless otherwise indicated.

Books of the Bible:

1,2 Chr	1,2 Chronicles
Col	Colossians
1,2 Cor	1,2 Corinthians
Dan	Daniel
Deut	Deuteronomy
Eccl	Ecclesiastes
Eph	Ephesians
Est	Esther
Exo	Exodus
Ezek	Ezekiel
Gal	Galatians
Gen	Genesis
Hab	Habbakuk
Hag	Haggai
Heb	Hebrews
Hos	Hosea
Isa	Isaiah
Jer	Jeremiah
Josh	Joshua
1,2 Kgs	1,2 Kings
Lam	Lamentations
Lev	Leviticus
Mal	Malachi
Matt	Matthew
Neh	Nehemiah
Num	Numbers
Phil	Philippians
Prov	Proverbs
Psa	Psalms
Rev	Revelation
Rom	Romans
1,2 Sam	1,2 Samuel
Song	Song of Solomon (Song of Songs)
1,2 Thes	1,2 Thessalonians
1,2 Tim	1,2 Timothy
Zech	Zechariah
Zeph	Zephaniah

SPECIAL USAGES AND SYMBOLS

*   The asterisk is used to identify a translation which the author of these drills prepared in order to illustrate a point.

[ ]   Square brackets are used for two purposes:

        (a) to mark important information that the author has added or inserted into the text

        (b) to mark words that are in the quoted text but are not included with the words that are important for the particular drill

Gr   is an abbreviation for Graded. It marks drills that use specially selected materials in a suggested teaching order.

Italics are used for three purposes:

        (a) to mark a translation into English from another language

        (b) to mark words that are originally in italics in the passage quoted

        (c) to give emphasis to words occurring in a phrase or clause that is underscored

HOW TO USE THESE DRILLS EFFECTIVELY

The Purpose of This Book. This book has been prepared primarily for people in the Third World who want to learn how to translate the Bible in dynamic equivalent style. It uses very simple English because it is written primarily for people for whom English is a second language. Native speakers of English who use this book should remember this.

However, this book can also be used by pastors, translators, and others who want a quick way to evaluate a new or unknown translation. One simply fills in the "Your Language" (YL) blank with the appropriate passage and compares it with the other translations given. If one compares a dozen or so passages under each of the principles of translation treated in the book, one should have good evidence about the nature of the translation one wants to check. However, the main purpose of the book is that of training mother-tongue speakers to translate into their own language.

The Reasons for the Drill Approach. The idea of using drills in general, as well as the development of many specific drills, has grown out of the problems I met during my years of service as a translations consultant with the United Bible Societies. These problems include the following:

1. At translators' institutes (called "TI's") translators-in-training often complained that the specific lectures in the morning were not related to the practical work on passages of scripture in the afternoon. So I began to develop drill exercises to go with specific lectures for TI's in Meshed (Iran), at Lumko (South Africa), etc.

2. When I visited the translators after a TI, I found that many of them could still recite the translation principles they had learned; but again and again I noticed that they were not applying them in their work. They needed help in putting the theory and principles of translation into practice. First, they needed help in recognizing the contexts in which a particular principle should be used, and then they needed practice in using that principle when translating. Drills in which trainees applied the same principle over and over again seemed to help them.

3. Now that we are no longer training missionaries as translators, but are training mother-tongue speakers to be translators, we must adjust the training to the needs of those whom we train. Just as nations at war often have to train emergency workers in practical medical skills because they do not have enough physicians available, so we now have to train practical translators who have learned the skills of translation, but who perhaps are not always able to explain why a translation principle should be applied. To train a person in a practical skill, one usually makes him repeat the same task over and over until he has mastered the skill. This book wants to apply the same method in training Bible translators.

4. More than ever, common language translations are now becoming available in the major languages of the world. Some translators make the mistake of doing a literal translation of these versions because they can understand them so much more easily. While a literal translation of a common language translation is usually better than a literal translation of a King-James-Version-type translation, it still is not good enough. For example, many Hebrew figures of speech in the Old Testament cannot be translated literally

into common language English, but they may be normal speech in common language Bantu. In such a language a literal translation of the TEV would result in losing unnecessarily many valuable biblical expressions. The drills in this book train the translators to always look at two texts—the one (RSV) preserving more of the form of the original, and the other (TEV) preserving more of the meaning of the original. One hopes that the two-text habit will become so fixed that translators will never again be tempted to translate a single text literally.

5. Sometimes one finds that translators are already using several translations in their work. But often they just select those phrases that are easy to translate from the different translations, and when they fit those phrases from several sources together into one translation, they sometimes end up translating the same kernel idea several times while other ideas are omitted completely. The emphasis of this book on discovering how many kernels the text contains helps the translators to avoid this kind of translation error.

However, it can be helpful to study other translations. If translators compare a variety of translations carefully, they will learn some important things:

(a) They will see that not all translations into English are equally good; in fact, some of the translations are not even good English. The translators who study different translations and then discover that some ways of translating a passage are good while others are not good, are more likely to remember this than if they had merely heard the same information in a lecture.

(b) They will see how easily a translator can unintentionally introduce changes in focus and in emphasis into his translation.

(c) They will see more quickly whether a translation has followed the translation principles as it should.

(d) They will develop a feeling about whether or not a translation is prejudiced.

6. Many people who translate into their mother tongue have had their formal education in a second language. As a result they have often learned to respect and admire too much the idioms and other characteristics of that language. When they see many English translations and discover the problems they contain, the translators will be less likely to respect the form used in English and will look for the meaning instead. The reason for adding YL in each drill is to make sure that the trainee applies the principle in his own language again and again. This will make him more aware of those areas in which his language is different from English, Greek, or Hebrew, and it will also make him aware of the beautiful ways in which his language can express the exact meaning of the original.

How to Use This Book in Training Translators. This book can be used by a translator who cannot get any formal training in the techniques of translating, but it has really been prepared for training sessions in which a translations consultant guides the translator-in-training. The consultant is expected to select the specific drills as well as the order in which the drills or their parts are to be practiced by the trainee. Different languages present different kinds of translation problems and therefore need different kinds of drills.

In my own work I often use parts of section A, dealing with form and meaning, when addressing a church gathering that is considering the need for a new translation. It introduces the idea of dynamic equivalent translating, and at the same time it reassures church people about the faithfulness of dynamic equivalent translating by stressing the manner in which a translation should handle biblical form.

I prefer to train translators in a series of four or five programs, each program lasting one week. Such programs are held every three or four months over a fifteen-month period, and the trainees have to complete translation assignments during the time between programs. Only those who do their assignments satisfactorily and in time are invited to the next session. In this way we remove slackers from the program. Only really committed individuals tend to remain faithful to the end. Because it is necessary to review the principles of translation each time the translators return for a training program, they seem to learn to understand and to use the principles more effectively than after a single four-week training session.

A typical first-week training program will spend one day on each of the following: (a) form and meaning, (b) breaking down of text into kernel sentences, (c) implicit information, (d) components of meaning, (e) figurative usage. The material for the first week is also available on prerecorded cassettes. Therefore, while the mornings are usually spent in meetings between the consultant-teacher and the translator trainees, in the afternoons and evenings an assistant helps the trainees with specific follow-up drills or in listening to the prerecorded lectures. Usually the trainees are more likely to ask questions of an assistant than of the consultant-teacher. During the listening the assistant stops the cassette recorder at any point where the trainees have questions, and he then discusses their questions and clarifies anything they have not fully understood.

For the programs that follow, the training may be done in two ways. First, the group may review the translations they have made. Each time someone has shown good use of a principle, or when someone has failed to use it, this can become the opportunity for a lesson. The drill book then provides a selection of additional examples. Frequently one member is asked to state the principle to a second person in his mother tongue, while a third person is asked to listen carefully to make sure the explanation is correct and complete. This gives the trainees experience in explaining the principles in their own language. Even the trainees themselves often use the drill book as a source of examples to which they refer during such free discussions.

A second way is to have a lecture-and-drill session. When certain problems appear again and again in the translations, the class leaves the review and instead has a lecture-and-drill session on the problem. During such a session the teacher may review materials already covered or he may use new drills on which the trainees have not yet worked. The trainees should not merely memorize the answers to the examples in one drill. This is why using a new drill is often best.

[3]

Toward the end of the training program the greater part of one week is used to strengthen the translator's skill in recognizing and translating figurative language, because figures of speech usually create some of the most serious problems for the translator.

When a translation program is in progress, I have found it helpful to have the book of drills on hand, so that one can review or emphasize any point that arises.

No two people will use the materials in exactly the same way. For a carefully planned program it may be possible to duplicate only certain selected drills on separate pages. But usually it is best for each translator to have the complete book in his hands. Then the teacher can use it for reinforcing certain translation solutions and for additional lessons as the need arises.

In addition, if the translator learns to refer to the workbook frequently, he will learn to use it as a kind of handbook which he consults when he faces difficulties in his own translation. However, it is important to remember that this workbook in no way replaces Bible dictionaries and commentaries. In fact, the instructions will ask the translator to look for definitions and explanations in Bible dictionaries and to get exegetical help from good commentaries.

Finally, it is important to notice how the graded drills have been prepared (they are marked "Gr"). In them the easier problems are presented first and the more difficult ones follow. In all the other drills the problems appear in their biblical order. Of course, the biblical order is not always the best teaching order. Each teacher must choose those examples that best suit his purpose and arrange them in the order that is best for him and his students.

As for the ungraded drills, it is important to remember that not all the problems presented are illustrations of only that point which the lesson teaches. Some of them illustrate various other kinds of problems. They are good examples of the sort of problem the translator will actually find in the biblical text. A single problem may include textual differences, differing interpretations, and the figurative function of part or of all of a construction. For example, hardness of heart in PEQR analysis looks like a Q-R-P construction, but it actually is a figure of speech and does not refer literally to the heart as a part of the body. Such examples are introduced (a) to make the translator aware of the fact that not all items that look alike do in fact function alike, and (b) to prepare him to function adequately with the normal biblical text which contains all these problems and more.

Old Testament and New Testament Supplementary Drills. The drills in this book have been divided into Old Testament and New Testament. This allows a New Testament project to use only New Testament drills during the training program. Likewise an Old Testament training program can use only Old Testament drills. Sometimes trainees may require additional practice materials. Supplementary drills are available for sections A through F. The available drills are listed in parentheses in the Table of Contents of this book; for example, "Drill A-2 Old Testament (SA-1 to SA-3)" says that there

[4]

are three additional Old Testament drills available. Supplementary drills are available at cost in xeroxed form. They come in separate Old Testament and New Testament volumes. Supplementary drills should be ordered from The Translations Department, United Bible Societies, 1865 Broadway, New York, N.Y. 10023, U.S.A.

A Note of Thanks. Several colleagues have encouraged me in writing this book and have given technical help and valuable suggestions. However, on a more practical level, the stimulus for the completion of this work comes from my wife Anne, who has given herself unstintingly to assembling drills, typing and retyping pages, checking and editing already typed materials, etc. Her personal courage and perseverance in this rather formidable task cannot be overestimated.

J.A.L.

A. FORM AND MEANING

1. LEARNING TO DISTINGUISH FORM AND MEANING

Purpose. In this section we want:

(a) to learn to distinguish two aspects of a message: its form, and its meaning or content. By form we mean the specific words chosen and the way they have been put together to express an idea,[a] and by meaning we refer to the content of the message or to the idea itself. Essentially the same idea (meaning) can often be expressed by several different forms even in one language. For example, in English we can speak about the death of someone and say: he died (simple statement), he passed away (euphemism), he kicked the bucket (slang), he gave up the ghost (KJV church language), he expired (obsolete), the deceased (formal high-level language), etc. The translator must be fully aware of these two aspects of the message because different languages often must use very different forms to express the same idea. For example:

English: How are you?
Spanish: Cómo está Ud.? (literally: How are you?)
German: Wie geht es Ihnen? (literally: How goes it to you?)
Tonga: Mwabonwa? (literally: Are you seen?)
Waunana: Pöd si? (literally: Are you sitting?)

(b) to develop awareness that the translator's first responsibility is to communicate faithfully the meaning of the original. In some instances it may be possible to parallel the original form, but this should never be done at the expense of the meaning nor at the expense of natural dynamic language.

Method. For the first few sets of drills we will use the Hebrew and Greek to illustrate that the RSV usually preserves the Hebrew or Greek form in English. As a result, of course, it often fails to communicate the meaning of the original. Thereafter we will use the RSV (sometimes KJV) as our substitute for the original text.

The TEV, sometimes another version, or a translation prepared for these drills and marked with an asterisk (*), will be used as an example of a translation that communicates the original message faithfully in clear, simple English.

Other translations are introduced to provide practice in identifying whether they have focused upon the form or the meaning.

Instructions

(a) Study the underlined word or expression in order to identify both its form and its meaning. If you know Greek or Hebrew, use the original language; if not, use the RSV as your substitute for the original language. If you need help on the exegesis of a passage, be sure to consult a commentary.

(b) Compare the various versions listed to see whether they have focused primarily on the form, on the meaning, or whether they adequately represent both.

(c) If there is a translation in your language, see what it has done about the form and the meaning of the expression in the translation.

---

[a]A more scientific statement of our use of form should include at least three dimensions: (1) grammatical, including word classes, word order, etc.; (2) rhetorical, including parallelisms, chiasms, under- or overstatements, etc.; (3) semantic, relating to the use of central (literal) versus peripheral or figurative meanings.

(d) Make a simple popular language translation into your language which clearly expresses the meaning of the passage. (For more information on popular-language translation, see W.L. Wonderly, Bible Translations for Popular Use.)

Procedure. It usually will be best to do each of the above steps separately. Steps (b) and (c) can be combined, but writing in class often takes too much time. Furthermore, experience has shown that reinforcement is greatest when steps (c) and (d) are combined and assigned as homework, which is then thoroughly discussed the next day. If several local languages are involved, it may be necessary to separate into language groups to allow for adequate discussion. Separation, however, prevents cross-fertilization, that is, the sharing of ideas between the groups for helping one another improve.

Examples

Matt 7.16

Form: Gk ἀπὸ τῶν καρπῶν αὐτῶν ἐπιγνώσεσθε αὐτούς
           RSV you will know them by their fruits

Meaning: TEV you will know them by the way they act

    (a) The form is fruit, but what is the real meaning of that form? Is it fruit of a tree? Is it offspring? Is it appearance? Is it the fruit a person is carrying, eating, or selling? It is none of these. Fruit refers to how people act or behave, and it is translated accordingly in the TEV.

    (b) Compare the following versions:

NIV by their fruit you will recognize them
      [has retained the form and lost the meaning]

NEB you will recognize them by the fruits they bear
      [has retained the form and introduced a new ambiguity in the word bear,
      which could mean "produce fruit" or "carry."]

LB   you can detect them by the way they act
      [has translated the meaning but has introduced a component of secrecy or
      spying that is not present in the original.]

    (c)

YL   _____

    (d) After each person has made a popular-language translation, discuss the
      different translations proposed in your language and formulate the best.

John 5.25

Form: GK ἀμὴν ἀμὴν λέγω ὑμῖν
           RSV truly, truly, I say to you

Meaning: TEV I tell you the truth

    (a) The form involves a repetition of the word truly, but the repetition
      really means that truly is emphasized.

    (b) Compare the following versions:

NIV I tell you the truth [states the simple meaning]

TNT in very truth I tell you [restates one truly as emphatic]

NAS truly, truly, I say to you [repeats the original form]

NEB in truth, in very truth I tell you [retains the doublet, but introduces
      emphasis]

    (c)

YL   _____

    (d) Discuss the proposed translations.

---

1. Matt 2.20
   Gk   οἱ ζητοῦντες τὴν ψυχὴν τοῦ παιδίου
   RSV   those who <u>sought</u> the child's life[a]
   TEV   those who <u>tried to kill</u> the child
   Compare:
   Co   they...who are seeking the <u>soul</u> of the little Boy
   NIV   those who were trying to <u>take</u> the child's life
   NAS   those who sought the Child's life
   NEB   the men who threatened the child's life
   LB   those who were trying to kill the child
   YL   _____

   [a]The TEV correctly avoids the old, obsolete form of the RSV and translates the meaning into simple English.

2. Matt 6.2
   Gk   ὅταν οὖν ποιῇς ἐλεημοσύνην, μὴ σαλπίσῃς ἔμπροσθέν σου
   RSV   when you give alms, <u>sound no trumpet</u> before you[b]
   TEV   when you give something to a needy person, do not make a big show of it
   Compare:
   NIV   when you give to the needy, do not announce it with trumpets
   NAS   when...you give alms, do not sound a trumpet before you
   NEB   when you do some act of charity, do not announce it with a flourish of trum-
          pets
   LB   when you give a gift to a beggar, don't shout about...blowing trumpets
   YL   _____

   [b]In current English <u>sound no trumpet</u> functions as an idiom. Thus the TEV translates the meaning with a different figure of speech. However, in many African societies where the horn is still used for announcements the form can be kept.

3. Matt 11.10
   Gk   ἰδοὺ ἐγὼ ἀποστέλλω τὸν ἄγγελόν μου πρὸ προσώπου σου
   RSV   behold, I send my messenger <u>before thy face</u>
   TEV   here is my messenger, says God; I will send him ahead of you
   Compare:
   NIV   I will send my messenger ahead of you
   NAS   behold, I send my messenger before your face
   NEB   here is my herald, whom I send ahead of you
   LB   a messenger to precede me
   YL   _____

4. Matt 20.3
   Gk   ἐξελθὼν περὶ τρίτην ὥραν εἶδεν ἄλλους ἑστῶτας ἐν τῇ ἀγορᾷ ἀργούς
   RSV   going out about the <u>third</u> hour he saw others standing idle in the marketplace
   place
   TEV   he went out again to the marketplace at nine o'clock and saw some men stand-
   ing there doing nothing
   Compare:
   NIV   about the third hour he went out and saw others standing in the marketplace
   doing nothing
   NAS   he went out about the third hour and saw others standing idle in the market
   place
   YL   _____

5. Matt 20.33
   Gk Κύριε, ἵνα ἀνοιγῶσιν οἱ ὀφθαλμοὶ ἡμῶν
   RSV Lord, let our eyes be opened
   TEV Sir...we want you to open our eyes
       Compare:
   NIV Lord...we want our sight
   NAS Lord, we want our eyes to be opened
   NEB Sir...we want our sight
   LB Sir...we want to see
   YL _____

6. Matt 21.25
   Gk τὸ βάπτισμα τὸ ʼΙωάννου πόθεν ἦν; ἐξ οὐρανοῦ ἢ ἐξ ἀνθρώπων;
   RSV the baptism of John, whence was it? From heaven or from men?
   TEV where did John's right to baptize come from: from God or from men?
       Compare:
   NIV John's baptism—where did it come from? Was it from heaven or from men?
   NAS the baptism of John was from what source, from heaven or from men?
   NEB the baptism of John: was it from God, or from men?
   LB was John the Baptist sent from God, or not?
   YL _____

7. Matt 27.4
   Gk ἥμαρτον παραδοὺς αἷμα ἀθῷον
   RSV I have sinned in betraying innocent blood
   TEV I have sinned by betraying an innocent man to death
       Compare:
   NIV I have sinned...for I have betrayed innocent blood
   NAS I have sinned by betraying innocent blood
   NEB I have sinned...I have brought an innocent man to his death
   LB I have sinned...for I have betrayed an innocent man
   YL _____

8. Mark 14.36
   Gk καὶ ἔλεγεν, Αββα ὁ πατήρ
   RSV he said, "Abba, Father,..."
   TEV "Father," he prayed, "my Father!"
       Compare:
   NEB 'Abba, Father,' he said
   JB 'Abba (Father)!' he said
   Phps "Dear Father," he said
   LB "Father, Father," he said
   NIV "Abba, Father," he said
   YL _____

9. Luke 1.64
   Gk ἀνεῴχθη δὲ τὸ στόμα αὐτοῦ παραχρῆμα καὶ ἡ γλῶσσα αὐτοῦ
   RSV immediately his mouth was opened and his tongue was loosed
   TEV at that moment Zechariah was able to speak again
       Compare:
   NIV immediately his mouth was opened and his tongue was loosed
   NAS at once his mouth was opened and his tongue loosed
   NEB immediately his lips and tongue were freed
   LB instantly Zacharias could speak again
   YL _____

1. Gen 3.7
   Hb וַתִּפָּקַחְנָה עֵינֵי שְׁנֵיהֶם וַיֵּדְעוּ
   RSV then the eyes of both were opened, and they knew
   TEV they were given understanding, and realized
   Compare:
   LB suddenly they became aware
   NAS then the eyes of both of them were opened and they knew
   NEB then the eyes of both of them were opened and they discovered
   YL _____

2. Gen 4.1
   Hb וְהָאָדָם יָדַע אֶת־חַוָּה אִשְׁתּוֹ
   RSV now Adam knew Eve his wife
   TEV then Adam had intercourse with his wife
   Compare:
   LB then Adam had sexual intercourse with Eve his wife
   NAS now the man had relations with his wife Eve
   NEB the man lay with his wife Eve
   Br *but Adam fellowshipped with his wife*
   YL _____

3. Gen 4.5
   Hb וַיִּפְּלוּ פָּנָיו
   RSV and his countenance fell
   TEV and he scowled in anger
   Compare:
   LB his face grew dark with fury
   JB Cain was...downcast
   NAS and his countenance fell
   NEB and his face fell
   YL _____

4. Gen 6.11
   Hb וַתִּמָּלֵא הָאָרֶץ חָמָס
   RSV the earth was filled with violence
   TEV violence had spread everywhere
   Compare:
   NEB and the whole world was...full of violence
   NAS the earth was filled with violence
   JB the earth...filled with violence
   AB the land was filled with violence (desecration, infringement, outrage, assault, and lust for power)[a]
   YL _____

[a]This translation demonstrates the false idea that a word carries all its meanings in every context.

5. Gen 30.2

Hb   אֲשֶׁר־מָנַע מִמֵּךְ פְּרִי־בָטֶן
RSV God, who has withheld from you the fruit of the womb
TEV he is the one who keeps you from having children
      Compare:
JB   it is he who has refused you motherhood
LB   he is the one who is responsible for your barrenness
NAS God, who has withheld from you the fruit of the womb
NEB God, who has denied you children
YL   _____

6. Gen 33.4

Hb   וַיִּפֹּל עַל־צַוָּארָו וַיִּשָּׁקֵהוּ
RSV and fell on his neck and kissed him
TEV threw his arms around him and hugged him and kissed him
      Compare:
JB   took him in his arms and held him close
LB   and embraced him affectionately and kissed him
NAS and fell on his neck and kissed him
NEB he threw his arms around him and kissed him
YL   _____

7. Exo 14.3

Hb   סָגַר עֲלֵיהֶם הַמִּדְבָּר
RSV the wilderness has shut them in
TEV they are closed in by the desert
      Compare:
JB   the wilderness has closed in on them
LB   are trapped now, between the desert and the sea
NAS the wilderness has shut them in
NEB and are hemmed in by the wilderness
YL   _____

8. Lev 5.2

Hb   אוֹ נֶפֶשׁ אֲשֶׁר תִּגַּע בְּכָל־דָּבָר טָמֵא
RSV if anyone touches an unclean thing
TEV if someone unintentionally touches anything ritually unclean
      Compare:
JB   or else he touches something unclean
LB   anyone touching anything ceremonially unclean
NAS if a person touches any unclean thing
NEB if a person touches anything unclean
YL   _____

9. Num 5.22

Hb   וְאָמְרָה הָאִשָּׁה אָמֵן אָמֵן
RSV the woman shall say, 'Amen, Amen'
TEV the woman shall respond, "I agree; may the LORD do so"
      Compare:
NEB the woman shall respond, 'Amen, Amen'
JB   the woman must answer: Amen! Amen!
Beck the woman should say, 'Certainly, so be it!'
Mft 'So be it,' shall the woman say, 'so be it'
LB   the woman shall be required to say, 'Yes, let it be so'
YL   _____

2. ADJUSTING THE BIBLICAL FORM TO THE RECEPTOR LANGUAGE

Purpose. In this section we want to learn how we can handle the biblical form when its meaning clashes with the usage of the receptor language or is entirely unknown in it. The first step is to identify the generic class or family of things to which the unknown form belongs. For example, a denarius is "money" or a "coin." The translator now has several choices: first, he can use the generic word alone, as in "they brought him a coin" (Matt 22.19), or "after agreeing with the laborers for a sum of money" (Matt 20.2). If the generic form alone is too broad, its meaning can be limited in a number of ways:

(a) by adding the transliterated biblical form, as in "each of them received a coin called denarius" (Matt 20.9).

(b) by adding a local comparison, as in "each of them received a coin like a shilling."

(c) by adding a descriptive expression, as in "each of them received a coin, the usual day's wage."

Classifying the Biblical Form by Means of a Generic Expression

Instructions. Classify the following biblical words generically in both English and in your own language. If there is a translation in your language, see whether a classifier has been used. Would a classifier have made it more understandable to non-church people?

If you need help regarding the meaning or the function of any item in the drill, consult a good Bible dictionary.

Examples

denarius (Matt 20.13) can be generically classified as "money" or as a "coin"
YL _____

fig tree (Matt 21.19) as a "fruit tree"
YL _____

wine (John 2.9) as a "fermented drink"
YL _____

dragon (Rev 12.3) as a "giant creature," "fierce creature," or "legendary creature"
YL _____

amethyst (Rev 21.20) as a "precious stone" or "jewel"
YL _____

A-3 New Testament: Classifying Meanings Generically

1. camel (Matt 3.4) English _____

YL _____

2. devil (Matt 4.1) English _____

YL _____

3. angel (Matt 4.11) English _____

YL _____

4. disciple (Matt 5.1) English _____

YL _____

5. wolf (Matt 7.15)   English_____

                           YL_____

6. leprosy (Matt 8.3)   English_____

                           YL_____

7. centurion (Matt 8.5)   English_____

                           YL_____

8. cummin (Matt 23.23)   English_____

                           YL_____

9. trumpet (Matt 24.31)   English_____

                           YL_____

A-4 Old Testament: Classifying Meanings Generically (Instructions as for Drill A-3)

1. bdellium (Gen 2.12)   English_____

                           YL_____

2. bronze (Gen 4.22)   English_____

                           YL_____

3. ark (Gen 6.14)   English_____

                           YL_____

4. altar (Gen 22.9)   English_____

                           YL_____

5. bracelet (Gen 24.22)   English_____

                           YL_____

6. veil (Gen 24.65)   English_____

                           YL_____

7. sword (Gen 34.25)   English_____

                           YL_____

8. sheaf (Gen 37.7)   English_____

                           YL_____

9. grape (Gen 40.10)   English_____

                           YL_____

Limiting a Generic Expression by a Local Comparison

Instructions. Express the comparison in both English and in your own language on the lines given.

Examples

denarius (Matt 20.13)   English   a coin like a shilling or a coin like a peso

                        YL _____

fig tree (Matt 31.19)   English   a fruit tree that has a fruit with many seeds
                                  like a guava

                        YL _____

wine (John 2.9)   English   a fermented drink like chicha, moa, etc.

                        YL _____

dragon (Rev 12.3)   English   a creature like a giant crocodile; a mytho-
                                  logical creature like he (a Waunana legendary
                                  water dragon)

                        YL _____

amethyst (Rev 21.20)   English   a precious stone like red or blue quartz; a
                                  red or blue jewel similar to an emerald

                        YL _____

A-5 New Testament: Limiting a Generic Expression by a Local Comparison

1. camel (Matt 3.4)   English _____

                         YL _____

2. devil (Matt 4.1)   English _____

                         YL _____

3. angel (Matt 4.11)   English _____

                         YL _____

4. disciple (Matt 5.1)   English _____

                         YL _____

5. wolf (Matt 7.15)   English _____

                         YL _____

6. leprosy (Matt 8.3)   English _____

                         YL _____

7. centurion (Matt 8.5)   English _____

YL _____

8. cummin (Matt 23.23)   English _____

YL _____

9. trumpet (Matt 24.31)   English _____

YL _____

A-6 Old Testament: Limiting a Generic Expression by a Local Comparison (Instruc-
    tions as for Drill A-5)

1. bdellium (Gen 2.12)   English _____

YL _____

2. bronze (Gen 4.22)   English _____

YL _____

3. ark (Gen 6.14)   English _____

YL _____

4. altar (Gen 22.9)   English _____

YL _____

5. bracelet (Gen 24.22)   English _____

YL _____

6. veil (Gen 24.65)   English _____

YL _____

7. sword (Gen 34.25)   English _____

YL _____

8. sheaf (Gen 37.7)   English _____

YL _____

9. grape (Gen 40.10)   English _____

YL _____

10. chariot (Gen 41.43)   English _____

YL _____

11. almonds (Gen 43.11)   English _____

YL _____

12. balm (Gen 43.11)   English _____

YL _____

13. bitumen (Exo 2.3)   English _____

YL _____

Limiting a Generic Expression by a Descriptive Phrase
    Instructions. Write both English and your own language on the lines provided.

Examples		
denarius (Matt 20.13)	English	a coin equal to a day's wage, or a silver money piece equal to a peso
	YL	
fig tree (Matt 21.19)	English	a tree with fruit that has many small seeds
	YL	
wine (John 2.19)	English	a fermented drink made from the juice of fruit
	YL	
dragon (Rev 12.3)	English	a big, dangerous creature with a long tail, or a legendary monster that spits fire
	YL	
amethyst (Rev 21.20)	English	a precious stone which is red or blue in color
	YL	

A-7 New Testament: Limiting a Generic Expression by a Descriptive Phrase

1. camel (Matt 3.4)   English _____
                          YL _____

2. devil (Matt 4.1)   English _____
                          YL _____

3. angel (Matt 4.11)   English _____
                          YL _____

4. disciple (Matt 5.1)   English _____
                          YL _____

5. wolf (Matt 7.15)   English _____
                          YL _____

6. leprosy (Matt 8.3)   English _____
                          YL _____

7. centurion (Matt 8.5)   English _____
                          YL _____

8. cummin (Matt 23.23)   English _____
                          YL _____

9. trumpet (Matt 24.31)   English _____
                          YL _____

1. bdellium (Gen 2.12)

    English _____

    YL _____

2. bronze (Gen 4.22)

    English _____

    YL _____

3. ark (Gen 6.14)

    English _____

    YL _____

4. altar (Gen 22.9)

    English _____

    YL _____

5. bracelet (Gen 24.22)

    English _____

    YL _____

6. veil (Gen 24.65)

    English _____

    YL _____

7. sword (Gen 34.25)

    English _____

    YL _____

8. sheaf (Gen 37.7)

    English _____

    YL _____

9. grape (Gen 40.10)

    English _____

    YL _____

10. chariot (Gen 41.43)

    English _____

    YL _____

11. almonds (Gen 42.11)

    English _____

    YL _____

12. balm (Gen 43.11)

    English _____

    YL _____

13. bitumen (Exo 2.3)

    English _____

    YL _____

3. RESTATING DIFFICULT BIBLICAL FORMS BY MEANS OF DESCRIPTIVE PHRASES

Introduction. We have just learned how to classify difficult forms by means of a generic word, and how to limit such a generic definition by means of local comparisons, a description of the form, or an explanation of the function. Since there are a number of kinds of forms that often are difficult to transfer to the receptor language, we now want to focus on several different classes of forms and their adjustment in translation.

For example, in the case of most unknown cultural objects it is important to tell the receptor to what class of objects the item belongs, how or of what it is made, and how it is used; for example, sword is a "long, double-edged weapon used in war." Here weapon gives the generic class to which sword belongs, long, double-edged is the description of its shape, and used in war refers to its function.

On the other hand, strange or unknown events require a description of the action plus a statement of the cultural meaning of the action; for example, kiss in many Old Testament contexts must be rendered as greet with a kiss. The form kiss is retained, but its cultural function as a greeting has been made explicit.

Restating the Meaning of Cultural Items by Means of Descriptive Phrases

Instructions. Restate the meaning of the following cultural items found in the Bible by means of descriptive phrases both in English and in your language. The phrase may describe what the object looks like, what it is made of, how it is used, or a combination of these. Where necessary a picture can be put into the Bible to illustrate the item. Be sure to consult a good Bible dictionary for all unfamiliar words.

Examples

sickle (Mark 4.29)   is a curved knife used to harvest grain

YL _____

scroll (Rev 5.2)   is a roll of paper with writing on it, an early
                                      form of our books

YL _____

lyre (1 Sam 18.10)   is a stringed instrument like a harp

YL _____

helmet (2 Chr 26.14)   is a metal head protector used in war

YL _____

A-9 New Testament: Restating Names of Cultural Items

1. farthing (Matt 10.29 KJV)   English _____
                               YL _____

2. boat (Matt 14.22)   English _____
                               YL _____

3. phylacteries (Matt 23.5)   English _____
                               YL _____

4. sword (Matt 26.51)   English _____
                               YL _____

5. cross (Matt 27.32)   English _____
                               YL _____

6. net (Mark 1.19)   English _____
                               YL _____

7. altar (Luke 1.11)   English _____
                               YL _____

8. bier (Luke 7.14)   English _____
                               YL _____

9. chain (Luke 8.29)   English _____
                               YL _____

A-10 Old Testament: Restating Names of Cultural Items (Instructions as for Drill A-9)

1. gold (Gen 2.11)   English _____
                               YL _____

2. gum (Gen 37.25)   English _____
                               YL _____

3. flax (Exo 9.31)   English _____
                               YL _____

4. hyssop (Exo 12.22)   English _____
                               YL _____

5. scurvey (Lev 22.22 KJV)   English _____
                               YL _____

6. frontlets (Deut 6.8)   English _____
                               YL _____

7. unicorn (Deut 33.17 KJV)   English _____
                               YL _____

8. loom (Judges 16.14)   English _____
                               YL _____

9. ephah (Ruth 2.17)   English _____
                               YL _____

Restating the Meaning of Class Names by Means of Descriptive Phrases

Instructions. Restate the meaning of the following class names by means of a phrase describing their form, their function, or both, in the space provided. Long descriptions should be put into a glossary. Check the translation in your language to see if it has been properly translated. If not, write a correct translation on the line marked YL. Be sure to consult a good commentary or Bible dictionary.

Examples

Nephilim [giants] (Gen 6.4)   are giants who were believed to be of super-
                                     natural origin

YL _____

Stoics (Acts 17.18)   are members of a school of philosophy which
                                     stresses that happiness is to be free from
                                     both pleasure and pain

YL _____

idol (1 Kgs 15.12)   is a man-made figure worshiped as a god, or a
                                     man-made image of a god

YL _____

A-11 New Testament: Restating Class Names

1. Gentile (Matt 12.21)   English _____
                                 YL _____

2. proselyte (Matt 23.15)   English _____
                                 YL _____

3. scribe (Mark 2.6)   English _____
                                 YL _____

4. Caesar (Luke 2.1)   English _____
                                 YL _____

5. tetrach (Luke 3.1)   English _____
                                 YL _____

6. Zealot (Luke 6.15)   English _____
                                 YL _____

7. Levite (Luke 10.32)   English _____
                                 YL _____

8. freedmen (Acts 6.9)   English _____
                                 YL _____

9. eunuch (Acts 8.27)   English _____
                                 YL _____

10. trustee (Gal 4.2)   English_____

                               YL_____

11. elemental spirit (Gal 4.3) English_____

                               YL_____

12. prophet (Eph 4.11)   English_____

                               YL_____

13. barbarian (Col 3.11)   English_____

                               YL_____

14. antichrist (1 John 2.22)   English_____

                               YL_____

15. archangel (Jude 9)   English_____

                               YL_____

A-12 Old Testament: Restating Class Names (Instructions as for Drill A-11)

1. cherubim (Gen 3.24)   English_____

                               YL_____

2. angel (Gen 19.1)   English_____

                               YL_____

3. chief butler (Gen 40.2)   English_____

                               YL_____

4. midwife (Exo 1.15)   English_____

                               YL_____

5. slave (Exo 12.44)   English_____

                               YL_____

6. satyr (Lev 17.7)   English_____

                               YL_____

7. medium (Lev 20.27)   English_____

                               YL_____

8. Nazirite (Num 6.21)   English_____

                               YL_____

9. Anakim (Deut 1.28)   English_____

                               YL_____

10. priest (Josh 14.1)   English_____

                               YL_____

11. teraphim (Judges 18.18)   English_____

                               YL_____

12. concubine (2 Sam 5.13)   English_____

                               YL_____

[22]

Restating Proper Names by Means of Descriptive Phrases

    Instructions. As a general rule personal proper names are transliterated according to the phonology of the receptor language. However, when a proper name has been given to a group of people or objects, it will be necessary to provide at least a generic classifier indicating to what class of things or people the name belongs; for example, Pharisees are a Jewish religious party. If necessary, the glossary can carry a fuller description. Thus, for Pharisees the glossary could have an explanation like the TEV: "Pharisees: A Jewish religious party during the time of Jesus. They were strict in obeying the Law of Moses and other regulations which had been added to it through the centuries." (GNB, Word List, page 361)

    Many proper names are not merely names; they carry meanings. Often the meaning of such a name is essential for understanding the message; for example, Onesimus means "useful," and Paul makes a play on the meaning of the name when he says "he was of no use to you but now he is useful" (Philemon 11). In such cases it is essential that either the meaning be added to the transliterated form, for example, Zoar, that is, "small" (Gen 19.22 NEB footnote), or a new name be coined containing the meaning, for example, Loruhamah (Hos 1.6 KJV) rendered as "Unloved" in TEV.

    Consult a Bible dictionary or commentary and find out whether the following proper names identify a generic class, or if they have a meaning, or both. Write your findings on the line marked English. Restate the definition in your own language and write it on the line marked YL.

Examples

Christ (Matt 2.4)   English   means "the anointed one," but anointing was also a ritual means of indicating that someone had been chosen for a special task, in this case, to be the savior of the world. Compare GeCL *you are Christ, the promised savior.*

         YL _____

Zeus (Acts 14.13)   English   is the name of the chief of the Greek gods. Thus TEV translates "the god Zeus" and in the Word List gives a fuller description.

         YL _____

A-13 New Testament: Restating Meaningful Proper Names

1. Satan (Matt 4.10)   English _____
         YL _____

2. Beelzebul (Matt 10.25)   English _____
         YL _____

3. Sanhedrin (Mark 15.1 JB)   English _____
         YL _____

4. Hades (Luke 16.23)   English _____
         YL _____

5. Calvary (Luke 23.33 KJV)   English _____
         YL _____

6. Paradise (Luke 23.43)   English _____

                                      YL _____

7. Messiah (John 1.41)   English _____

                                      YL _____

8. Golgotha (John 19.17)   English _____

                                      YL _____

9. Zeus and Hermes (Acts 14.12)   English _____

                                      YL _____

A-14 Old Testament Restating Meaningful Proper Names (Instructions as for Drill A-13)

1. Genesis   English _____

                                      YL _____

2. Exodus   English _____

                                      YL _____

3. Leviticus   English _____

                                      YL _____

4. Numbers   English _____

                                      YL _____

5. Deuteronomy   English _____

                                      YL _____

6. Molech/Moloch (Lev 18.21)   English _____

                                      YL _____

7. Baal (Num 22.41 KJV)   English _____

                                      YL _____

8. Ashtaroth (Judges 2.13)   English _____

                                      YL _____

9. Rimmon (2 Kgs 5.18)   English _____

                                      YL _____

10. Adar (Est 9.1)   English _____

                                      YL _____

Restating Event Words by Means of Descriptive Phrases

Introduction. Many languages do not have unit words for all the concepts expressed in the Bible. However, those same languages can express those concepts by means of descriptive phrases. Wherever such event words have additional symbolic meaning, the latter may also have to be expressed explicitly.

Instructions. Restate the following event words by means of descriptive phrases which describe the act, the objects associated with it, and its function. Write your findings on the line marked English. Now consult the Bible in your own language and see how this has been translated. If the translation is not clear, make a new translation and write it on the line marked YL. Consult a commentary or Bible dictionary for all unknown words.

Examples

anoint (Exo 29.7)   means "to pour on special oil" but it also has an additional symbolic meaning of "setting apart for God or for some other special religious purpose."

YL _____

crown (Rev 3.11)   sounds like a mere object, but in actual fact its primary reference is to the event of placing a wreath of leaves on the head of a person winning a contest. Continued usage then caused the meaning to be extended to the awarding of any prize to the person winning a victory.

YL _____

sacrifice (Exo 3.18)   to kill an animal as an offering or as a gift to the Lord. Usually the event implies that the animal is dying instead of the giver.

YL _____

A-15 New Testament: Restating Event Words by Means of Descriptive Phrases

1. sign [Greek: *semeion*] (Mark 8.11)   English_____
                                            YL_____

2. miracle [Greek: *dunamis*] (Mark 9.39 KJV)   English_____
                                                  YL_____

3. wonder [Greek: *teras*] (Acts 2.43)   English_____
                                           YL_____

4. grinding at the mill (Matt 24.41)   English_____
                                         YL_____

5. sealing the stone (Matt 27.66)   English_____
                                      YL_____

6. baptize (Mark 1.8)   English_____
                          YL_____

7. enrollment (Luke 2.2)   English_____

                                     YL_____

8. offering (Luke 5.14)   English_____

                                     YL_____

9. stewardship (Luke 16.2)   English_____

                                     YL_____

10. purification (John 2.6)   English_____

                                     YL_____

11. prune (John 15.2)   English_____

                                     YL_____

12. witness (Acts 1.22)   English_____

                                     YL_____

<u>A-16 Old Testament: Restating Event Words by Means of Descriptive Phrases</u> (Instructions as for Drill A-15)

1. circumcise (Gen 17.11)   English_____

                                     YL_____

2. shear (Gen 31.19)   English_____

                                     YL_____

3. sacrifice (Gen 31.54)   English_____

                                     YL_____

4. binding sheaves (Gen 37.7)   English_____

                                     YL_____

5. divine (Gen 44.5)   English_____

                                     YL_____

6. embalm (Gen 50.2)   English_____

                                     YL_____

7. thresh (Gen 50.10)   English_____

                                     YL_____

8. covenant (Exo 2.24)   English_____

                                     YL_____

9. passover (Exo 34.25)   English_____

                                     YL_____

10. tithe (Deut 14.22)   English_____

                                     YL_____

11. curse (Josh 24.9)   English_____

                                     YL_____

12. riddle (Judges 14.12)   English_____

                                     YL_____

Forms That Have Often Been Transliterated

Introduction. Certain Hebrew and Greek words have a long tradition of being transliterated, that is, of being transcribed with the sounds or letters of another language instead of being translated. As a result of the long usage, the meanings of many of these words are today fairly well known in English. Because of this, modern English translations vary greatly as to whether they have used the transliterated form or whether they have translated the word into modern English.

In other parts of the world where these transliterated words are relatively new and known only to some Christians, it is usually best to translate them.

It should be noted that certain technical words like *Selah* in the Psalms are not included in modern translations because they are considered marginal notes, not really a part of the text.

Instructions

(a) Study the meaning of each of the following underlined, transliterated words in a good Bible dictionary and write the real meaning in English on the line marked (a).

(b) Check the translation in your language and write it on the line marked YL. If the word has been transliterated, make a translation of it in your language and write it on the line marked (b).

Examples
Num 5.22   (a) "let it be so"
RSV Amen, Amen
TEV I agree; may the LORD do so   (b)
YL   _____

Psa 52.3   (a) a musical or liturgical marker
RSV *Selah*
TEV does not indicate it   (b)
YL   _____

A-17 New Testament: Frequently Transliterated Words

1. Matt 4.23   (a)
   RSV synagogue
   TEV synagogue   (b)
   YL

2. Mark 8.29   (a)
   RSV Christ
   TEV Messiah   (b)
   YL

3. Mark 14.36   (a)
   RSV Abba, Father
   TEV Father... my Father   (b)
   YL

4. CLASSIFYING GEOGRAPHICAL NAMES

Instructions. Classify the following geographical names as cities, rivers, etc. Uncommon names should always be classified in your translation to help the reader understand the message, even if the place name is unknown to him. Names appearing repeatedly need to be classified only the first time they occur in a chapter or section, but after a long gap they should be classified again. How many names and how often they are classified will depend on the needs of the audience. An almost totally Christian audience who has had the Bible for several generations will require much less classification than a first Bible for a largely non-Christian audience. Consult a commentary or a Bible dictionary for all unknown names.

Examples	
Endor (1 Sam 28.7)	town
Carmel (1 Sam 15.12)	mountain
Judea (Matt 4.25)	region

A-18 New Testament: Classifying Geographical Names

1. Jordan (Matt 3.13) _____
2. Arimathea (Matt 27.57) _____
3. Bethany (Luke 24.50) _____
4. Cana (John 2.1) _____
5. Siloam (John 9.11) _____
6. Galilee (Acts 1.11) _____
7. Cyrene (Acts 2.10) _____
8. Charran/Haran (Acts 7.2) _____
9. Mesopotamia (Acts 7.2 KJV) _____
10. Canaan (Acts 7.11) _____
11. Paphos (Acts 13.6) _____

A-19 Old Testament: Classifying Geographical Names (Instructions as for Drill A-18)

1. Ai (Gen 12.8) _____
2. Egypt (Gen 12.10) _____
3. Elam (Gen 14.9) _____
4. Shur (Gen 20.1) _____
5. Dothan (Gen 37.17) _____
6. Nile (Exo 1.22) _____
7. Elim and Sinai (Exo 16.1) _____
8. Arnon to the Jabbok (Num 21.24) _____
9. Bashan (Deut 1.4) _____
10. Horeb (Deut 1.6) _____
11. Hormah (Deut 1.44) _____

5. TRANSLATING BOTH FORM AND MEANING

Instructions. Many words (forms) have both a literal and a figurative meaning. When such words function as very important symbols throughout the Bible, it may be quite important to make a special effort to keep them in the translation, for example, blood, cross, lamb, etc. This often will require that both the form (F) or the literal meaning and also the figurative meaning (M) be given in the translation; or, to use our figurative description, we have to cross the translation river twice, once with the suitcase (the form or literal meaning) and a second time with its content (the figurative meaning). If it is impossible in a given language to give both the form and the meaning, it will be necessary to indicate the symbolic function of the form in a footnote or glossary (word list).

Translate both the form and the meaning of the underlined words in the following passages into YL and write your translation on the lines given. Then compare the translations given and discuss their treatment of the form and meaning.

Examples
Matt 26.39
Form: RSV let this cup pass from me
Form and Meaning: TEV take this cup of suffering from me (GNB)

   Compare:
JB let this cup pass me by
LB let this cup be taken away from me
TNT let this cup pass from me [the glossary then explains that cup is a metaphor which expresses the idea of suffering a bitter experience]
GeCL _let this cup of suffering pass me by_
YL _____
New Translation with F and M in YL _____

_____

Only TEV and GeCL "cross the river twice" with both form and meaning, but TNT gives the explanation in the glossary.

John 1.29
Form: RSV behold, there is the Lamb of God
Form and Meaning: *   here is the one whom God gave to be sacrificed as a lamb

   Compare:
TEV there is the Lamb of God
NEB look...there is the Lamb of God
NAS behold, the Lamb of God
GeCL _this one is God's sacrificial lamb_
Zink _look! There he is — the one whom God gave to the world for a sacrifice, as one sacrifices a lamb_
YL _____
New Translation with F and M in YL _____

TEV, NEB, and NAS have translated only the literal meaning (form) of lamb, leaving it to the context to suggest the figurative meaning. GeCL and Zink both introduce the figurative meaning of sacrifice, but only Zink makes the full meaning explicit and also translates the form.

1. Acts 20.28
RSV the church of the Lord which he obtained with his own blood
TEV the church of God, which he made his own through the death of his Son
   Compare:
NEB the church of the Lord, which he won for himself by his own blood
TNT the church of God which he won for himself by the death of his own Son
NIV the church of God, which he bought with his own blood
NAB the church of God, which he has acquired at the price of his own blood
* the church of God which he made his own through the blood, that is, the death of his own son
YL
New Translation with F and M in YL _____

2. 1 Cor 1.18
RSV for the word of the cross is folly
TEV for the message about Christ's death on the cross is nonsense
   Compare:
NEB this doctrine of the cross is sheer folly
LB I know very well how foolish it sounds...when they hear that Jesus died to save them
NIV for the message of the cross is foolishness
SpCL *the message about the death of Christ on the cross seems foolish*
GeCL *the message of the dying on the cross must seem like utter nonsense*
YL
New Translation with F and M in YL _____

3. Eph 1.7
RSV in him we have redemption through his blood
TEV by the death of Christ we are set free
   Compare:
LB he took away all our sins through the blood of his Son, by whom we are saved
TNT it is through Christ's death that our sins are forgiven and we are set free
NEB for in Christ our release is secured...through the shedding of his blood
* we are set free from our sin by the blood, that is, the death of Christ
YL
New Translation with F and M in YL _____

4. Eph 2.16
   RSV might reconcile us both to God in one body through the <u>cross</u>, thereby bring-
        ing the hostility to an end
   TEV by his death on the cross Christ destroyed the enmity; by means of the cross
        he united both races into one body and brought them back to God
        Compare:
   NEB this was his purpose, to reconcile the two in a single body to God through
        the cross, on which he killed the enmity
   JB   through the cross, to unite them both in a single Body and reconcile them
        with God. In his own person he killed the hostility
   Phps for he reconciled both to God by the sacrifice of one body on the cross, and
        by this act made utterly irrelevant the antagonism between them
   TNT he died on the cross to put an end to the hatred and bring us both back to
        God as one people
   SpCL *in this manner, by his death on the cross, Christ ended the antagonism there
        was between the two races, and put them at peace with God, making a single
        body out of them*
   GeCL *and by means of his death to reconcile both to God. In this way the enmity
        between man and God was to be wiped out once and for all*
   YL   _____
   New Translation and F and M in YL _____

5. Rev 5.12
   RSV worthy is the <u>lamb</u> who was slain
   TEV the Lamb who was killed is worthy
        Compare:
   NEB worthy is the Lamb, the Lamb that was slain
   TNT the Lamb who was slaughtered is worthy
   Phps worthy is the Lamb who was slain
   Zink *Christ, the Lamb, is worthy (because) he has suffered*
   SpCL *the Lamb who was sacrificed is worthy*
   GeCL *the lamb, who was offered as sacrifice, is worthy*
   YL   _____
   New Translation with F and M in YL _____

B. ANALYSIS OF THE TEXT

1. ANALYSIS I: THE PEQR FUNCTION OF WORDS

<u>Definition</u>. By PEQR we mean the following:

P: identifies people, objects, and tangible things that are involved in actions, conditions, or states, or have certain qualities.

E: identifies events, such as actions, happenings, states, etc.

Q:[a] marks qualities, quantities, and degrees. They can relate to P's, E's, and even other Q's.

R: marks relationals which serve as the "glue" or "mortar" that binds words together into phrases, sentences, paragraphs, etc.

In the book <u>The Theory and Practice of Translation</u> (hereafter abbreviated TAPOT) PEQR are marked OEAR and are called: Objects, Events, Abstracts, and Relationals, respectively. We are using labels different from TAPOT because PEQR are more easily translated into African languages. For example, P is usually rendered as he who, or that which, <u>participates</u> in an event. You will have noticed that P (O of TAPOT) sounds like what traditional grammar calls nouns, E like verbs, Q (A of TAPOT) like adjectives and adverbs, and R like prepositions, conjunctions, etc. However, you will soon discover that our kind of analysis shows that traditional nouns can actually function in all four categories. For this reason we must avoid the traditional labels which relate largely to the surface form, and use new labels which identify the actual basic function of words in the text.

<u>Purpose</u>. In order to make sure that the translator understands the full meaning of the biblical text, he must carefully analyze the surface structure, that is, the actual words and sentences he sees in the text. He must do so in several ways. One of these is to learn to recognize the PEQR functions of words. As we have already said, words, like chameleons, can appear in a variety of shapes in the surface structure. However, if we can identify their basic PEQR function in a given text, we will be able to reconstruct the simple kernel sentences that underlie the surface we see. Then by counting the number of kernel sentences we can know how many propositions, or complete ideas, are being communicated. In other words, PEQR analysis is a necessary step for discovering the kernel sentences that underlie the text we see. However, since PEQR functions are only one dimension of the analysis of surface structure, we will need to learn several more kinds of analyses before we can safely formulate all the kernels fully. But we will tentatively restate as kernels the individual text fragments analyzed in this drill. Later, when we come to the actual study of kernel sentences, we will, in a sense, be reviewing and putting together what we have learned from the various methods of analysis we will use in this section.

<u>Method</u>. First, we will begin with small fragments of text in learning to identify the PEQR functions of the words used. As we gain experience we will go to larger and larger chunks of text. Then in order to reinforce our learning we will compare several translations to see whether the words will apppear in essentially the same surface form as in the original, which for our purposes here is the RSV. Translations often show big differences in the surface form of the words used, but our analysis will show that in accurate translations only the same PEQR functions appear in the text.

---

[a]In some languages like Hebrew, Q's may function grammatically as statal verbs, but this does not change their basic PEQR function.

Instructions

(a) Identify the basic PEQR functions of the words in the RSV phrases presented below and mark them as P, E, Q, or R. English the and a, the definite and indefinite article respectively, should technically be classified as R's, but for practical purposes we will always treat them as part of the word with which they go in the text. Should you have any difficulty understanding a passage, be sure to consult a good commentary.

(b) Rephrase the words into a simple sentence and write the sentence on the line marked (b).

(c) Compare the various translations presented to see in what surface form they use the words. Note any similarities and differences with the form used by the RSV. Write your findings in the space marked (c).

Examples

Luke 11.32

	E	R	P

RSV [at the] preaching of Jonah

Compare:

TEV [heard] Jonah preach
NEB preaching of Jonah
JB [when] Jonah preached
NIV preaching of Jonah
Phps Jonah's preaching
YL

(b) Jonah preaches

(c) TEV and JB have the words in their basic PEQR function. All the rest do not make the E function of preach explicit.

ᵃSquare brackets within a biblical quotation indicate that the word or phrase is not part of the problem.

Ruth 2.11

	E	R	P

RSV the death of [your] husband

Compare:

TEV your husband died
NEB your husband's death
JB your husband's death
LB death of your husband
Beck your husband died

(b) husband dies

(c) TEV and Beck have the words in their basic PEQR function. All the rest do not express the basic E function of death in their surface form.

Eph 1.13

	Q	P	R	E

KJV Holy Spirit of promise

Compare:

RSV the promised Holy Spirit
TEV the Holy Spirit he had promised
LB Holy Spirit, who...had been promised

(b) [God] promised the Holy Spirit

(c) TEV contains the full kernel including the actor. JB with the passive voice uses two P's for Spirit. RSV has a full kernel once the implicit actor is added and promised is treated as an event.

1. Matt 27.56

RSV	the mother of James	(b)_____
	Compare:	
TEV	the mother of James	(c)
JB/LB	the mother of James	
NEB/Knox	the mother of James	
YL	_____	

2. Luke 12.16

RSV	the land of a rich man	(b)_____
	Compare:	
TEV	a rich man who had land	(c)
NEB	a rich man whose land	
JB	a rich man...his land	
NIV	the ground of a certain rich man	
YL	_____	

3. 2 Cor 3.3

RSV	tablets of stone	(b)_____
	Compare:	
TEV	stone tablets	(c)
NEB/JB	stone tablets	
YL	_____	

4. Matt 2.15

RSV	the death of Herod	(b)_____
	Compare:	
TEV	Herod died	(c)
NEB	Herod's death	
JB	Herod was dead	
NIV	the death of Herod	
YL	_____	

5. 2 Thes 2.9

RSV	the coming of [the law-less] one	(b)_____
	Compare:	
TEV	the Wicked One will come	(c)
NEB	the coming of that wicked man	
JB	the Rebel comes	
NIV	the coming of the lawless one	
YL	_____	

6. Acts 4.13

RSV	the boldness of Peter	(b)_____
	Compare:	
TEV	how bold Peter [was]	(c)
NEB	the boldness of Peter	
JB	the assurance shown by Peter	
NIV	the courage of Peter	
YL	_____	

B-2 Old Testament, Gr: Of-Phrases (Instructions as for Drill B-1)

1. Gen 4.23

   RSV you wives of Lamech   (b)_____
        Compare:
   TEV [his wives] Adah and Zillah (c)
   JB   Lamech's wives
   NEB you wives of Lamech
   LB   my wives
   YL   _____

2. Gen 29.10

   RSV the flock of Laban   (b)_____
        Compare:
   TEV Laban's flock   (c)
   NEB Laban's flock
   LB   his uncle's flock
   JB   the sheep of his uncle Laban
   YL   _____

3. Gen 2.16

   RSV tree of the garden   (b)_____
        Compare:
   TEV tree in the garden   (c)
   JB   trees in the garden
   YL   _____

4. Gen 23.16

   RSV the hearing of the Hittites (b)_____
        Compare:
   TEV the hearing of the people   (c)
   JB   hearing of the sons of Heth
   YL   _____

5. Hos 3.1

   KJV the love of the LORD   (b)_____
        Compare:
   TEV I [the LORD] still love   (c)
   RSV the LORD loves
   JB   Yahweh gives his love
   YL   _____

6. Psa 52.7

   RSV the abundance of [his] riches (b)_____
        Compare:
   TEV his great wealth   (c)
   NEB his great wealth
   JB   his own great wealth
   LB   their wealth
   YL   _____

7. Deut 2.14

RSV   men of war   (b) _____
     Compare:
TEV   the fighting men   (c)
JB   men fit for war
YL   _____

8. Psa 33.5

KJV   the goodness of the LORD   (b) _____
     Compare:
TEV   his constant love   (c)
NEB   his love unfailing
JB   Yahweh's love
YL   _____

9. Ezek 27.34

RSV   the depth of the waters   (b) _____
     Compare:
TEV   the ocean depths   (c)
NEB   in deep water
NAB   the watery depth
YL   _____

10. 1 Chr 11.23

RSV   a man of great stature   (b) _____
     Compare:
TEV   a huge man   (c)
NEB   a giant
JB   a huge man
YL   _____

11. 1 Sam 2.3

RSV   a God of knowledge   (b) _____
     Compare:
TEV   a God who knows   (c)
NEB   a God of all knowledge
JB   an all-knowing God
LB   the Lord knows
YL   _____

12. Jer 5.28

RSV   deeds of wickedness   (b) _____
     Compare:
TEV   evil deeds   (c)
LB   wicked deeds
JB   wickedness
YL   _____

Introduction. Possessive constructions[a] are very similar to of-constructions, except that the R is always expressed as part of the possessive adjective.

Instructions

(a) Identify the basic PEQR functions and mark them as P, E, Q, or R. Use a hyphen to show that the possessive has both a P and an R function in the surface structure.

(b) Rephrase the expression into a simple sentence and write it on the line marked (b).

(c) Compare the various translations to see in what surface form the words appear. Write your findings in the space marked (c).

---

[a]Translators should note that many languages have a different treatment for alienable possessions, that is, possessions you can sell, versus inalienable ones, that is, ones you cannot sell. They should also note that many of the so-called possessive constructions do not really express possession, but many other kinds of relationships.

Examples

Matt 6.18

	P-R E
(a) RSV	your fasting

Compare:

TEV	you are fasting
NEB/NAB	you are fasting
NIV/JB	you are fasting
LB	you are hungry
YL	_____

(b) you fast

(c) All of the translations use a present continuative form of the verb with the auxiliary verb to be which always functions as an R, but you and fast are the real basic PEQR functions. LB uses hungry which is really the result of fasting.

Rom 5.8

	P-R E
(a) RSV	his love

Compare:

TEV	he loves us
NEB	his love
JB	God loves us
NIV	his own love
YL	_____

(b) he loves [us]

(c) TEV and JB show the words in their basic PEQR function. Both have also made the implicit object of the verb explicit. NEB and NIV follow the RSV.

Psa 34.1

	P-R E
(a) RSV	his praise [shall continually]

Compare:

TEV	I will never stop praising him
NEB	his praise
JB	his praise
LB	I will constantly speak of his glories and grace
Beck	my mouth [will continually] praise him
YL	_____

(b) [I] praise him

(c) TEV, LB, and Beck are very close to the basic PEQR function. They also make the implicit I explicit. Beck uses a figurative expression to replace I. JB and NEB are like the RSV.

Matt 20.15

	P-R Q
(a) RSV	my generosity
Compare:	
TEV	I am generous
Phps	I am generous
JB	I am generous
NEB	I am kind
LB	I am kind
Beck	I'm generous
BE	I am good
YL	

(b) I [am] generous

(c) All translations except RSV keep the words in their basic PEQR function. The am functions as an R. LB and NEB use kind instead of generous, but BE's use of good is a little too general for an accurate translation.

Job 13.26

	P-R Q
(a) RSV	my youth
Compare:	
TEV	[when] I was young
NEB	my youth
JB	my youth
Beck	my youth
LB	my youth
BE	my early years
YL	

(b) I [am] young, or when I was young

(c) Only TEV shows the words in their basic PEQR function. BE uses a paraphrase for youth but follows all the other translations in keeping the possessive construction.

Luke 19.36

	P-R P
(a) RSV	their garments
Compare:	
TEV	their cloaks
BE	their clothing
JB	their cloaks
LB	their robes
YL	

(b) they own, wear garments

(c) All of the translations have the words in the same PEQR function.

B-3 New Testament, Gr: Possessives

1. Matt 2.6

RSV	my people
Compare:	
TEV	my people
JB/NEB	my people
YL	

(b) _____

(c)

2. Matt 13.30

RSV	my barn
Compare:	
TEV	my barn
JB/NEB	my barn
BE	my store-house
YL	

(b) _____

(c)

3. Matt 10.30

RSV	your head	(b) _____
Compare:		
TEV	your head	(c)
JB/NEB	your head	
YL	_____	

4. Matt 6.17

RSV	your fasting	(b) _____
Compare:		
TEV	go without food	(c)
NEB	you are fasting	
TNT/LB	you fast	
YL	_____	

5. Matt 11.5

RSV	their sight	(b) _____
Compare:		
TEV	the blind can see	(c)
NEB	their sight	
BE	the blind see	
JB	the blind see again	
YL	_____	

6. Matt 13.44

RSV	his joy	(b) _____
Compare:		
TEV	he...is so happy	(c)
NEB	the man...for sheer joy	
Phps	a man...overjoyed	
YL	_____	

7. Matt 24.3

RSV	your coming	(b) _____
Compare:		
TEV	your coming	(c)
Phps/NEB	your coming	
LB	your return	
YL	_____	

B-4 Old Testament, Gr: Possessives (Instructions as for Drill B-3)

1. Josh 1.14

RSV	your wives	(b) _____
Compare:		
TEV	your wives	(c)
JB/NEB	your wives	
YL	_____	

2. Gen 31.18

    RSV   his cattle   (b)_____
        Compare:
    TEV   his flocks   (c)
    JB   his livestock
    LB   Jacob's flocks
    YL   _____

3. 1 Sam 26.7

    RSV   his spear   (b)_____
        Compare:
    TEV   his spear   (c)
    JB/NEB his spear
    YL   _____

4. Josh 4.18

    RSV   its banks   (b)_____
        Compare:
    TEV   the riverbank   (c)
    LB   the banks of the river
    YL   _____

5. Jer 51.4

    RSV   her streets   (b)_____
        Compare:
    TEV   the streets of their cities (c)
    LB/NEB her streets
    JB   the streets of Babylon
    YL   _____

6. Psa 4.1

    RSV   my prayer   (b)_____
        Compare:
    TEV   I pray   (c)
    JB/NEB my prayer
    YL   _____

7. Job 31.24

    RSV   my trust   (b)_____
        Compare:
    TEV   I have...trusted   (c)
    NEB   my faith
    JB/LB   my trust
    YL   _____

8. Ezek 35.11
    RSV   your hatred   (b)_____
        Compare:
    TEV   your hate   (c)
    NEB   your hatred
    JB   you hated them
    YL   _____

9. Eccl 9.15

RSV	his wisdom	(b)	_____
	Compare:		
TEV	who was...so clever	(c)	
JB/NEB	his wisdom		
LB	he knew what to do		
YL	_____		

10. Psa 124.3

RSV	their anger	(b)	_____
	Compare:		
TEV	their furious anger	(c)	
NEB	their anger		
JB	their rage		
BE	their wrath		
YL	_____		

Words with Complex PEQR Structure

Instructions. We have already seen that possessive adjectives, such as "his" (P&R), have more than one PEQR function. We now want to become aware of the fact that many words can have several PEQR functions. It is important that the translator recognize this because his language may require that each function be represented by a separate word.

(a) Mark all the PEQR functions of the words given below.

(b) Write the kernel contained in each of the lines marked (b).

(c) Study the various translations listed to see in what surface form they use the words. Note any similarities or differences with the RSV usage. Write your findings in the space marked (c).

Examples All the examples will illustrate (a) and (b), but only example 5 will illustrate (c). Implicit participants are given in square brackets.

1.	E-P (P) teacher	(Luke 2.46)	(b) he teaches [someone]
	E-P (P) Savior	(Luke 1.47)	(b) he saves [someone]
	E-P (P) servant	(Luke 1.69)	(b) he serves [someone]
	(P) E-P (or E-P-Q) angel	(Luke 1.18)	(b) [God] sent someone who is supernatural
	E-P (P) tetrarch	(Luke 3.1)	(b) he rules [someone, in one of four parts of an area]
	P-E-P shepherd	(Luke 2.15)	(b) he herds sheep
	(P) E-P (P) gift	(Matt 2.11)	(b) [someone] gives something [to someone]

Notice that in teacher we can clearly see the event teach and the -er suffix indicating a person. The same is true of Savior. In servant it is not as clear, and in angel and tetrach there is no suffix or word part that specifically marks the P

---

[41]

function. Angel carries additional information about it being a supernatural or a spirit being, while tetrarch also tells us he is one of four equal rulers. In shepherd there is no special marker for the "doer" of the action, but in "sheep" (seen in shep- of shepherd) the P being herded is indicated. Compare the word "sheepherder," where both P's and the E are clearly visible. In gift there is an implicit P^1 as the giver who gives something to an implicit P^2. (See page 44.)

2.
      Q-E
    sanctify   (Exo 19.22 KJV)   (b) [someone] makes holy

      E-Q
    blaspheme   (1 Kgs 21.13 KJV)   (b) [someone] speaks evil

      E-Q
    bless   (Gen 27.34)   (b) [someone] speaks good, or does good

In sanctify the suffix -ify marks the E, and the first part sanct- indicates the Q. However, in blaspheme and bless in English we cannot identify the separate E and Q functions with specific parts of the word. In Spanish this is possible in *maldecir*: *mal* "evil" *decir* "to speak," and in *bendecir*: *ben* "good" *decir* "to speak."

3. We see even more complicated PEQR functions in the following word:

      P-E-P
    enemy   (Exo 23.22)   (b) he hates someone and usually this someone hates him

4. Notice that three P's are contained in the word:

      P-E-R-P-P
    mediator   (1 Tim 2.5)   (b) he stands, works, talks between two or more persons or groups

A mediator is a person who stands or works between two other people. In the Chulupi language in Paraguay he is called he-who-talks-between-two-people, and in this phrase-word all the PEQR functions are made explicit.

5. Heb 10.27

      P-E-P
RSV adversaries   (b) some people oppose someone
    Compare:
TEV those who oppose God   (c) Only TEV has separate words for each
NEB God's enemies   of the PEQR functions. NEB, BE, and
NAS adversaries   NIV make only one P [God] explicit.
BE   haters of God
NIV enemies of God
YL _____

B-5 New Testament: Single Words

1. Matt 13.55

RSV carpenter   (b)_____
    Compare:
TEV carpenter   (c)
BE   wood-worker
JB   carpenter
NAS carpenter
YL _____

2. Mark 2.18

    RSV [John's] disciples   (b)_____
       Compare:
    TEV the followers of John   (c)
    JB   John's disciples
    Phps the disciples of John
    YL   _____

3. Mark 3.29

    RSV blasphemes   (b)_____
       Compare:
    TEV says evil things against   (c)
    JB   blaspheme
    NEB slanders
    BE   says evil things against
    YL   _____

B-6 Old Testament: Single Words (Instructions as for Drill B-5)

1. Gen 14.20

    RSV   [your] enemies   (b)_____
       Compare:
    TEV   enemies   (c)
    NAS/JB enemies
    YL   _____

2. Exo 15.17

    RSV   sanctuary   (b)_____
       Compare:
    TEV   Temple   (c)
    NEB/JB sanctuary
    BE   building
    *   the holy house [you built for yourself]
    YL   _____

3. Josh 2.9

    RSV [all the] inhabitants   (b)_____
       Compare:
    TEV everyone in the country   (c)
    JB   all who live in this territory
    NAS all the inhabitants
    YL   _____

4. Job 9.15

    RSV [my] accuser   (b)_____
       Compare:
    TEV God my judge   (c)
    NEB my accuser
    NAS my Judge
    *   God who judges me
    YL   _____

2. ANALYSIS II: IDENTIFYING BASIC RELATIONSHIPS BETWEEN WORDS

Purpose. As you will have noticed while we were making the PEQR analysis, two words may be linked by means of the same R at the surface level, but their actual relationship may be very different. In this drill we want:

(a) to become aware of the almost unlimited kinds of relationships a single R can express, if not in actual fact hide, especially for the nonnative speaker of the language. For example, in the first sentence of the Gospel of Mark the RSV says "the beginning of the gospel of Jesus Christ." Now, what does of mean in the expression "the gospel of Jesus Christ"? Is Jesus Christ the owner of the gospel? Is Jesus Christ the writer or source of the gospel? Is this the gospel Jesus Christ preached during his ministry? Is Jesus Christ the content or the subject matter of the gospel? Too often we glibly say: "Why, it's all of these." But is it really?

(b) to learn to specify which of the many possible relationships is indicated in a given context. In the case of the phrase "the gospel of Jesus Christ," a careful study of the total context will convince most people that Jesus Christ is the subject matter of the good news; compare TEV "the Good News about Jesus Christ."

(c) to learn to express the actual relationship between two words as unambiguously as necessary in the receptor language. For example, most Bantu languages in one region of Africa have an equivalent of the English preposition of (resembling the Greek genitive case, or the Hebrew possessive construction). These languages can readily reproduce the form of the original, but usually the expected meaning then is "Jesus Christ is the owner of the gospel." However, most of these same languages can also unambiguously express that Jesus Christ is the subject matter of this good news.

Method. As we did in the beginning of the previous section of PEQR analysis, we here also want to concentrate first on of-phrases and then proceed to their close relatives, the possessive constructions, in which the R is always part of the word expressing the possessor. Compare the following:

$$
\begin{array}{ccccccc}
\text{P} & \text{R} & \text{P} & & \text{P-R} & \text{P} & & \text{P-R} & \text{P} \\
& & & \text{equals} & & & \text{equals} \\
\text{Son} & \text{of} & \text{God} & & \text{God's} & \text{Son} & & \text{his} & \text{Son}
\end{array}
$$

Basic Relationships Between Words in Of-Phrases

As part of the exegesis of every passage to be translated, we want to identify the actual relationship between all the words. To help us do this more efficiently, we are providing an inventory of examples of some of the more common types of of-phrases. This list is not exhaustive, but it can (1) make us more aware of the many, many kinds of relationships that can be expressed by of, and (2) serve as a handy reference source with which we can compare any other of-phrases we want to analyze.

To make it easier to refer to specific parts of the of-phrase, we will call the word which precedes the of "1" and the word that follows it "2." In order to be able to state a complete idea, it will sometimes be necessary to express the implicit participants explicitly. Wherever this will be required we will call the first participant "P^1," the second "P^2," etc.

Formulas with Examples	Clear Restatement of Relationship

1 does 2

God of our salvation (1 Chr 16.35) — God saves us
God of knowledge (1 Sam 2.3) — God knows
   [In other contexts this construction can mean "gives knowledge," as in the "tree of knowledge" (Gen 2.9).]
God of judgment (Mal 2.17 KJV) — God judges, or God judges justly
   [In this context it probably carries the added component of justly: God judges justly. God judges can also be expressed in a 2-does-1 formula; see next section.]
men of little faith (Luke 12.28) — men believe/trust little

2 does 1

snorting of...horses (Jer 8.16) — the horses snort
sin of Judah (Jer 17.1) — Judah sins
judgment of God (Rom 2.3) — God judges
word of God (Rev 1.2) — God speaks
teaching of Balaam (Rev 2.14) — Balaam teaches
rising of the sun (Rev 7.2) — the sun rises
faith of the saints (Rev 13.10) — the saints believe

1 does 1 to 2

commander of the army (2 Kgs 9.5) — he commands the army
maker of idols (Isa 45.16) — he makes idols
repairer of the breach (Isa 58.12) — he repairs the breach
destroyer of nations (Jer 4.7) — he destroys nations

P^1 does 1 to 2

salvation of Israel (Jer 3.23) — P^1 saves Israel
siege of Jerusalem (Ezek 4.7) — P^1 besieges Jerusalem
help of the woman (Rev 12.16) — P^1 helps the woman
   [In other contexts this could be: 2 does 1 to P^1, as in "vain is the help of man" (Psa 60.11).]
foundation of the world (Rev 13.8) — P^1 creates the world
   [In other contexts this could be: 1 is part of 2, as in "the foundations of the earth are shaken" (Psa 82.5).]
judgment of the great harlot (Rev 17.1) — P^1 judges the great harlot
   [In other contexts this phrase could mean 2 does 1, as in "the judgment of God" (Rom 2.3).]

P^1 does 1 by means of/with 2

washing of water (Eph 5.26) — P^1 washes P^2 with water
shield of faith (Eph 6.16) — P^1 shields himself by means of faith
punishment of...fire (Jude 7) — P^1 punishes P^2 by means of fire

P^1 does 2 by means of/with/in 1

pit of destruction (Psa 55.23 KJV) — P^1 destroys P^2 in a pit
furnace of affliction (Isa 48.10) — P^1 afflicts P^2 by means of a furnace

P^1 does 1 for 2

judgment of the LORD (2 Chr 19.8)
P^1 judges on the LORD's behalf

work of the Lord (1 Cor 15.58)
P^1 works on behalf of the Lord

2 is the content of 1

book of the law (Deut 29.21) — the book contains the law
bottle of wine (1 Sam 1.24 KJV) — the bottle contains wine
jar of meal (1 Kgs 17.14) — the jar contains meal
book of Psalms (Acts 1.20) — the book contains the Psalms

1 is the content of 2

water of the river (Exo 4.9 KJV) — the river consists of water
prophecy of this book (Rev 22.7) — the book contains prophecy
words of this book (Rev 22.9) — the book contains words (a message)

1 is a quality of 2

anger of the LORD (Jer 4.8) — the LORD is angry
pride of Judah (Jer 13.8) — Judah is proud
confidence of yours (Isa 36.4) — you are confident
wealth of her wantonness (Rev 18.3) — she is very wanton [this can be transformed as: her wantonness is great]

confidence of boasting (2 Cor 11.17) — P^1 boasts confidently

1 is a part of 2

foreheads of the men (Ezek 9.4) — the forehead is a part of man
pinnacle of the temple (Luke 4.9) — the pinnacle is a part of the temple

rocks of the mountains (Rev 6.15) — the rocks are a part of the mountainside

sand of the sea (Rev 12.17) — sand is a part of the seashore
leaves of the tree (Rev 22.2) — leaves are a part of the tree

1 marks a quantity of 2

band of survivors (2 Kgs 19.31) — so many survivors
a thousand talents of silver (1 Chr 19.6) — so much silver
loaf of bread (Jer 37.21) — such a quantity of bread
crowd of disciples (Luke 6.17) — so many disciples

1 is located in or near 2

court of the garden of the king's palace (Est 1.5) — the court was located in the garden and the garden was by the king's palace

cities of Judah (Jer 1.15) — the cities were located in the territory of Judah

streets of Jerusalem (Jer 7.34) — the streets were in the city of Jerusalem

mountains of Samaria (Jer 31.5) — the mountains were in the province of Samaria; or: located near the city of Samaria

2 is the usual habitat of 1

birds of the air (Jer 9.10)	birds live, move in the air
beasts of the field (Jer 28.14)	beasts live in the field
inhabitants of the coastlands (Ezek 27.35)	they inhabit the coast

1 originates or resides in 2

men of the place (Gen 26.7)	the men who lived in that place
Jecoliah of Jerusalem (2 Kgs 15.2)	Jecoliah, a resident/citizen of Jerusalem
Syrians of Damascus (1 Chr 18.5)	the Syrians originate from Damascus
the gold of Ophir (Isa 13.12)	the gold comes from Ophir
Joseph of Arimathea (Mark 15.43)	Joseph was born/lived in Arimathea

1 gives, produces, causes, leads to 2

land of grain (2 Kgs 18.32)	the land produces grain
rock of stumbling (Isa 8.14)	the rock causes stumbling
spring of water (Isa 58.11)	the spring brings forth water
way of peace (Isa 59.8)	the way leads to peace
man of strife (Jer 15.10)	the man creates strife
transgression of desolation (Dan 8.13 KJV)	the transgression leads to desolation
spirit of infirmity (Luke 13.11)	the spirit causes illness
tree of life (Rev 2.7)	the tree gives life
light of Israel (Isa 10.17)	P^1 produces light for Israel

[Note that the last example needs P^1 and the preposition for in the restatement.]

2 brings, produces or causes 1

encouragement of the scriptures (Rom 15.4)	the scriptures encourage/produce encouragement
plagues of the seven angels (Rev 15.8)	the seven angels bring the plagues
blood of war (1 Kgs 2.5)	killing, death caused by war

1 is made/composed of 2

pillar of fire (Exo 13.22)	the pillar was composed of fire
wall of precious stones (Isa 54.12)	the wall was made of precious stones
image of gold (Dan 3.1)	the image was made of gold
rod of iron (Rev 2.27)	the rod was made of iron
river of water (Rev 22.1)	the river was composed of water

2 is the name of 1

country of Moab (Ruth 1.1)	country called Moab
city of Susa (Est 8.15)	city called Susa
valley of Jezreel (Hos 1.5)	valley called Jezreel

1 is 2

[surname himself by] the name of Israel (Isa 44.5)	called himself Israel
[cursed] the name of God (Rev 16.9)	[cursed] God

1 is dedicated to 2

sacrifices of the LORD (Lev 10.13 KJV)	sacrifices dedicated to the LORD
vessels of the sanctuary (Num 3.31)	vessels dedicated to the service in the sanctuary
house of the LORD (Jer 52.13)	house dedicated to the LORD
synagogue of Satan (Rev 3.9)	synagogue dedicated to Satan

1 is about 2

chronicles of the kings (2 Kgs 8.23) — the chronicles are about the kings
[This could also be interpreted as chronicles compiled or ordered to be written by the king.]

tidings of Jacob (Gen 29.13)	the news is about Jacob
good news of the kingdom (Luke 4.42)	the good news is about the kingdom
doctrine of baptisms (Heb 6.2 KJV)	the teaching about baptisms
song of the Lamb (Rev 15.3)	the song is about the Lamb

[Note the contrast with "song of Moses" which occurs in the same verse and which refers to the song Moses and the people of Israel sang at the Red Sea after their salvation from the Egyptian pursuers.]

1 gives the time/occasion of 2

days of Josiah (Jer 1.2)	the time when Josiah was king
day of his death (Jer 52.11)	he died on that day
his time of service (Luke 1.23)	he served during that time
hour of his trial (Rev 3.10)	the hour when P^1 tries him

1 is the place where 2 is done

city of refuge (Josh 21.13)	city where one finds refuge
Hall of Judgment (1 Kgs 7.7)	hall where judgment is made
altar of incense (Luke 1.11)	altar where incense is burned
altar of burnt offering (1 Chr 22.1)	altar where sacrifices are burnt
house of prayer (Matt 21.13)	house where people pray

2 is the place where 1 is done

songs of the temple (Amos 8.3)	P^1 sings these songs in the temple
ministers of the altar (Joel 1.13)	1 does 1 at the altar
priest of the high places (1 Kgs 13.33)	1 does 1 on the high place

1 is for the purpose of 2

utensils of service (1 Chr 9.28)	the utensils are used in the ritual
wood of the burnt offering (Gen 22.6)	the wood is for making burnt offerings
weapons of war (Psa 76.3)	the weapons are used for war
instruments of righteousness (Rom 6.13)	instruments to do righteous deeds

1 is a symbolic representation of 2

arrow of victory (2 Kgs 13.17)	the arrow signifies victory
ark of the covenant (1 Chr 28.2)	the ark symbolizes the meaning of the covenant
mark of the beast (Rev 16.2)	the mark is the sign of the beast

1 gives rank of 2

the least of the apostles (1 Cor 15.9)	P^1 is the least important
the foremost of sinners (1 Tim 1.15)	P^1 is the foremost sinner
the smallest of all seeds (Matt 13.32)	P^1 is the smallest seed
greatest of all the people (Job 1.3)	P^1 is the most famous person

kinship 1[a]

granddaughter of Omri (2 Kgs 8.26)	or:	Omri is the grandfather of 1
descendants of Israel (2 Kgs 17.20)	or:	Israel is their ancestor
father of Gilead (1 Chr 2.21)	or:	Gilead is the son of 1
son of a woman (2 Chr 2.13)	or:	the woman is his mother
sons of Zebedee (Luke 5.10)	or:	Zebedee is the father of 1

marriage[a]

the wife of Shallum (2 Kgs 22.14)	or:	Shallum is the husband of 1
husband of Naomi (Ruth 1.3)	or:	Naomi is the wife of 1
widow of Mahlon (Ruth 4.10)	or:	Mahlon was her husband but he is dead

social or political[a]

servants of King Hezekiah (2 Kgs 19.5)	the king rules them, or they serve him
elders of Israel (1 Chr 11.3)	they lead Israel, or Israel obeys them
officers of the army (1 Chr 12.14)	they command the army, or the army obeys them
the servant of rulers (Isa 49.7)	they serve the ruler, or the ruler commands them

[a]Note that all relationships—biological, marriage, social, etc.—can usually be expressed in two directions; for example, Omri is the grandfather of 1, or 1 is the granddaughter of Omri.

1 owns 2

owner of the ox (Exo 21.28)	he owns the ox
owner of the hill (1 Kgs 16.24)	he owns the hill
possessors of lands (Acts 4.34)	they own the land

2 owns 1

sheep of Laban (Gen 29.10)	Laban owns the sheep
land of the rich man (Luke 12.16)	the rich man owns the land
house of the ruler (Luke 14.1)	the ruler owns the house

of replaces a verb

garden of the Lord (Gen 13.10)	the garden God established
city of David (2 Sam 5.9)	the city David conquered and built
book of the prophet Isaiah (Luke 4.17)	the book Isaiah wrote; or: which bears Isaiah's name
paradise of God (Rev 2.7)	the paradise God established

1 is a figure of 2

the thunder of his power (Job 26.14)	his power is like thunder
fire of my wrath (Ezek 22.21)	my wrath is like fire
wind of doctrine (Eph 4.14)	their teaching is as ephemeral as wind

1 gets name from association with 2

the Mount of Olives (Matt 26.30)	mountain associated with olives
the Field of Blood (Matt 27.8)	field associated with blood
place of a skull (Matt 27.33)	place associated with a skull
the law of Moses (1 Kgs 2.3)	law associated with Moses

Instructions

(a) Express by means of a simple formula the basic relationship which exists between the two words linked by "of" and marked 1 and 2 respectively. Write your formula on the line marked (a).

(b) On the line marked (b) restate "who does what to whom" as unambiguously as possible. Where it is necessary to introduce missing participants in order to make a complete statement, call the first participant P^1, the second one P^2, etc.

(c) Compare the other translations listed to see if and how they have expressed the actual relationship clearly. Write a simple statement of your findings in the space marked (c).

Examples
2 John 7

	1 2
RSV	coming of Jesus Christ

Compare:

TEV	Jesus Christ came
NIV/JB	Jesus Christ has come
LB/TNT	Jesus Christ came
NEB/NAS	Jesus Christ is coming
Mft	the coming of Jesus Christ
YL	

(a) 2 does 1
(b) Jesus Christ comes

(c) All translations except Mft more or less clearly express the actual relationship in a simple sentence.

Gal 3.7

	1 2
RSV	men of faith

Compare:

TEV	people who have faith
Phps/LB/NEB	men of faith
JB	those who rely on faith
TNT	those who have faith
NIV	those who believe
NAS	those who are of faith
YL	

(a) 1 does 2
(b) men believe/men trust

(c) NIV is the closest to a kernel statement. Phps/LB/NEB retain the form of RSV, and NAS actually becomes obscure.

Eph 5.26

	1 2
RSV	the washing of water

Compare:

TEV	by washing it in water
JB	by washing her in water
NEB	cleansing it by water
TNT	cleanse...her with water
NIV	the washing with water
NAS	the washing of water
YL	

(a) P^1 does 1 to P^2 with 2
(b) someone washes something with water

(c) All translations except NAS have tried to show water as the instrument. TEV/JB/NEB/TNT have all expressed P^2 in the text.

Acts 10.32

	1 2
RSV	the house of Simon

Compare:

TEV	the home of Simon
NEB	the house of Simon
JB	the house of Simon
LB	the home of Simon
YL	

(a) 2 owns or lives in 1
(b) the house which Simon owns or in which Simon lives

(c) All translations remain ambiguous as to the two possibilities.

Mark 3.17

	1	2
RSV	the brother of James	

Compare:

TEV	James and his brother
NEB	James and his brother
JB	the brother of James
YL	_____

(a) 1 and 2 are related as brothers

(b) P[1] is related to James as brother

(c) All translations just use variants of the same construction.

John 9.7

	1	2
RSV	the pool of Siloam	

Compare:

TEV	the Pool of Siloam
NEB	the pool of Siloam
JB	the Pool of Siloam
YL	_____

(a) 2 is the name of 1
(b) the pool is called Siloam

(c) TEV and JB make Pool part of the name. NEB and RSV leave it as a generic.

B-7 New Testament, Gr I: Of-Phrases

1. Matt 15.31

	1	2
RSV	the God of Israel	

Compare:

TEV	the God of Israel
NEB/JB	the God of Israel
Phps/TNT	the God of Israel
YL	_____

(a) _____

(b) _____

(c)

2. Matt 2.1

	1	2
RSV	Bethlehem of Judea	

Compare:

TEV	the town of Bethlehem in the land of Judea
NIV	Bethlehem in Judea
BE	Bethlehem of Judea
YL	_____

(a) _____

(b) _____

(c)

3. Acts 13.19

	1	2
RSV	land of Canaan	

Compare:

TEV	land of Canaan
NEB	Canaanite country
JB/LB	[seven nations in] Canaan ...their land
YL	_____

(a) _____

(b) _____

(c)

4. John 11.1

	1	2
RSV	Lazarus of Bethany	

Compare:

TEV	Lazarus, who lived in Bethany
NEB	Lazarus...his home was at Bethany
JB/LB	Lazarus who lived in the village of Bethany
Phps	Lazarus...he lived in Bethany
YL	_____

(a)_____
(b)_____
(c)

5. Luke 8.3

	1	2
RSV	wife of Chuza	

Compare:

TEV	wife of Chuza
Phps/NEB	wife of Chuza
LB	Chuza's wife
YL	_____

(a)_____
(b)_____
(c)

6. Matt 15.31

	1	2
RSV	the God of Israel	

Compare:

TEV	the God of Israel
NEB/JB	the God of Israel
Phps/TNT	the God of Israel
YL	_____

(a)_____
(b)_____
(c)

7. 2 Cor 3.3

	1	2
RSV	tablets of stone	

Compare:

TEV	stone tablets
JB/NEB	stone tablets
Phps/LB	on stone
YL	_____

(a)_____
(b)_____
(c)

8. John 4.14

	1	2
RSV	spring of water	

Compare:

TEV	spring which will provide ...water
NIV/TNT	spring of water
YL	_____

(a)_____
(b)_____
(c)

B-8 New Testament, Gr II: Of-Phrases (Instructions as for Drill B-7)

1. Mark 5.25

	1	2
RSV	a flow of blood	

Compare:

TEV	severe bleeding
NEB	haemorrhages
BE	a flow of blood
NIV	bleeding
YL	_____

(a)_____

(b)_____

(c)

2. 2 Tim 2.18

	1	2
RSV	the faith of some	

Compare:

TEV	the faith of some be-lievers
NEB	people's faith
JB	some people's faith
LB	the faith of some who believe
YL	_____

(a)_____

(b)_____

(c)

3. John 12.43

	1	2
RSV	the praise of men	

Compare:

TEV	the approval of men
NEB	their reputation with men
JB	honour from men
NIV	praise from men
AB	the approval and the praise and the glory that comes from men
YL	_____

(a)_____

(b)_____

(c)

4. Acts 16.13

	1	2
RSV	a place of prayer	

Compare:

TEV	a place where Jews gathered for prayer
JB	a customary place for prayer
Phps	a place for prayer
YL	_____

(a)_____

(b)_____

(c)

5. John 19.14

	1	2
RSV	the day of Preparation of the Passover	

Compare:

TEV	the day before the Pass-over
NEB	the eve of Passover
JB	Passover Preparation Day
Phps	the preparation day of the Passover
YL	_____

(a)_____

(b)_____

(c)

[53]

6. Mark 4.37

		1 2	(a) _____
RSV		a great storm of wind	(b) _____
	Compare:		(c)
TEV		a strong wind	
NEB		a heavy squall	
JB		to blow a gale	
Phps		a violent squall of wind	
NIV		a furious squall	
LB		a terrible storm	
YL		_____	

7. 2 Cor 10.1

```
                      1       1                (a)_____
RSV          the gentleness and meek-          (b)_____
                      2                        (c)
                ness of Christ
     Compare:
TEV          the gentleness and
                kindness of Christ
NEB          the gentleness and mag-
                nanimity of Christ
JB           the gentleness and pa-
                tience of Christ
LB           gently, as Christ himself
                would do
TNT          Christ's own meekness and
                gentleness
YL           _____
```

8. 2 Cor 8.2

```
                      1        2               (a)_____
RSV          a wealth of liberality            (b)_____
     Compare:                                  (c)
TEV          were extremely generous
NEB          lavishly open-handed
JB           a wealth of generosity
Beck         richly overflowing gen-
                erosity
YL           _____
```

B-9 Old Testament, Gr: Of-Phrases (Instructions as for Drill B-7)

1. Eccl 7.6

```
                      1        2               (a)_____
RSV          laughter of fools                 (b)_____
     Compare:                                  (c)
TEV          a fool laughs
NEB          laughter of a fool
JB           laughter of fools
YL           _____
```

2. Gen 21.16

	1	2
RSV	the death of the child	
Compare:		
TEV	my child die	
NEB/NAB	the child die	
LB	him die	
BE	the death of my child	
Mft	the child dying	
YL		

(a)_____

(b)_____

(c)

3. Isa 45.16

	1	2
RSV	makers of idols	
Compare:		
TEV	those who make idols	
NEB	those who make idols	
JB	makers of idols	
YL		

(a)_____

(b)_____

(c)

4. Gen 39.5

	1	2
RSV	the blessing of the LORD	
Compare:		
TEV	the LORD blessed	
NEB	the blessing of the LORD	
JB	Yahweh blessed	
BE	the blessing of the LORD	
YL		

(a)_____

(b)_____

(c)

5. 1 Sam 2.3

	1	2
RSV	God of knowledge	
Compare:		
TEV	a God who knows	
NEB	a god of all knowledge	
JB	an all-knowing God	
Mft	a God who knows it all	
YL		

(a)_____

(b)_____

(c)

6. Gen 2.9

	1	2
RSV	tree of the knowledge	
Compare:		
TEV	tree that gives knowledge	
NEB/JB	tree of the knowledge	
Mft	tree that yields know- ledge	
YL		

(a)_____

(b)_____

(c)

7. Ezek 40.5

	1	2
RSV	thickness of the wall	

  Compare:

TEV	the wall...[10 feet] thick
NEB	the thickness...of the wall
Mft	the wall [was ten and a half feet] thick
JB	the thickness of this construction
YL	_____

(a)_____
(b)_____

(c)

8. Ruth 2.1

	1	2
RSV	a man of wealth	

  Compare:

TEV	a rich...man
NEB	a well-to-do man
LB	a very wealthy man
JB	a kinsman...well-to-do
YL	_____

(a)_____
(b)_____

(c)

9. Gen 6.5

	1	2
RSV	the wickedness of man	

  Compare:

TEV	how wicked everyone...was
NEB	man had done much evil
LB	human wickedness
NAB	man's wickedness
JB	the wickedness of man
YL	_____

(a)_____
(b)_____

(c)

10. Psa 50.2

	1	2
RSV	the perfection of beauty	

  Compare:

TEV	perfect in its beauty
JB	perfection of beauty
BE	most beautiful
NEB	perfect in beauty
Mft	peerless in beauty
YL	_____

(a)_____
(b)_____

(c)

Basic Relationships Between Words in Possessive Constructions

Like the of-constructions we have just studied, the so-called possessive constructions exhibit a wide range of relationships between the two words of the construction. We are again providing a classified listing of examples to make the translator aware of the range of relationships and meanings that are involved. The listing will also serve as a check list against which to compare possessive constructions to be analyzed. The possessor will be labeled 1 and the possessed noun will be labeled 2 for easy reference.

Formulas with Examples

1 owns 2

his tent (Gen 13.18)	he owns or occupies the tent
your fields (1 Sam 8.14)	you own the fields
my sword (1 Sam 21.8)	I own the sword
their garments (Mark 11.7)	they own the garments

2 is a part of 1

his head (Rev 1.14)	the head is a part of the person
your feet (Rev 3.9)	the feet are a part of the person
his tail (Rev 12.4)	the tail is a part of the creature
its horns (Rev 13.1)	the horns are a part of the creature
their flesh (Rev 19.21)	the flesh is a part of the creatures

If the part is used figuratively to stand for the whole, then we have a synecdoche. (See pages 217-220.) In such cases the translator often has to treat the construction as: 1 is the same as 2; for example,

[I will say to] my soul (Luke 12.19)	I will say to myself
my tongue [will sing] (Psa 119.172)	I will sing

kinship[a]

your fathers (Jer 2.5)	they are your fathers/you are their sons
my cousin (Jer 32.8)	I am his cousin/he is my cousin
his sister (2 Sam 13.22)	he is her brother/she is his sister
her newborn calf (Jer 14.5)	she is the calf's mother/the calf is her child

marriage[a]

her husband (Jer 3.20)	he is her husband/she is his wife
my wife (Gen 20.12)	I married her/she married me
their widows (Psa 78.64)	they were husbands of the women, but the husbands are dead/the women were their wives, but the men are dead

[a]Since these relationships are between two sets of participants, they can usually be stated both ways.

<u>social or political</u>[a]

your master (Jer 3.14) | he controls you [inferred: you obey/serve him]

your lovers (Jer 4.30) | they love you [inferred: you love them]
her neighbor (Exo 3.22) | she lives next to you [inferred: you live next to her]

your...friends (Jer 38.22) | they are your friends [inferred: you are their friends]

my servants (Rev 2.20) | they serve me [inferred: I control them]
thy adversaries (Psa 74.23) | they are against you [inferred: you are against them]

their enemies (Jer 15.9) | they hate them [inferred: they hate each other]

their foes (Rev 11.12) | they fight them [inferred: they fight each other]

[a]Since these relationships are between two sets of participants we can infer that the relationship is reciprocal, but the restatements differ in focus, for example, <u>your master</u> "he controls you" versus "you obey him."

<u>2 is a quality of 1</u>

his beauty (Isa 33.17) | he is beautiful
thy faithfulness (Isa 38.18) | you are faithful
his might (Isa 40.26) | he is mighty
your youth (Jer 2.2) | you are young [usually involves: when]

[In other contexts this could refer to the young people of a social group, for example, <u>your youths</u> "young men" (Amos 4.10).]

your nakedness (Nahum 3.5) | you are naked

<u>1 does 2</u>

[sun] its setting (Psa 50.1) | it sets
my words (Jer 1.9) | I speak
my plans (Job 17.11) | I plan
her sins (Rev 8.4) | she sins

<u>2 does 2 to 1</u>

my guide (Psa 55.13 KJV) | the guide guides me
its owner (Isa 1.3) | the owner owns it
our judge (Isa 33.22) | the judge judges us
his counselor (Isa 40.13) | the counselor counsels him
my persecutors (Jer 15.15) | the persecutors persecute me

<u>2 does 2 for or on behalf of 1</u>

your prophets (Jer 29.8) | the prophets prophesy for you, or to you
your rowers (Ezek 27.8) | the rowers row for you

<u>P[1] does 2 to 1</u>

my punishment (Gen 4.13) | P[1] punishes me
your bonds (Jer 2.20) | P[1] binds you
our salvation (Jude 3) | P[1] saves us
your persecution (1 Thes 1.4) | P[1] persecutes you

1 gives/causes/produces 2

thy thunder (Psa 77.18)	you cause thunder
his signs (Psa 78.43)	he produces signs
my peace (Jer 16.5)	I give peace

1 experiences/suffers/has 2

your tumors (1 Sam 6.5)	you suffer/have tumors
his birth (Job 3.1)	he underwent birth
my grief (Jer 8.18)	I experience grief
their pain (Rev 16.11)	they experience pain

2 is the result of what P^1 did to 1

your wounds (Jer 30.17)	P^1 wounded you so you have wounds
his death (Acts 8.1)	[P^1 stoned him so] he is dead

[In other contexts <u>her death</u> could be analyzed as "she experienced death" (1 Sam 4.20).]

the possessive relationship replaces an E

my refuge (Jer 16.19)	I find/take refuge
your idols (Ezek 33.25)	you fear/worship/serve idols
your food (Dan 1.10)	you eat food
my country (Jonah 4.2)	I live/originate in the country
his garment (Matt 9.21)	he wears the garment
my God (Rev. 3.12)	I worship/serve God

2 is used figuratively

his mighty hand (Deut 11.2)	his great strength
his blood (Matt 27.25)	his death

Instructions

(a) On the line marked (a) express the specific relationship between the possessor numbered 1 and the noun labeled as 2. Where it is necessary to introduce missing participants in order to complete the thought, use P^1 for the first participant and P^2 for the second. Write out a simple statement that clearly expresses the relationship.

(b) Compare the various translations listed and see if and how they express the specific relationship between the possessor and the possessed noun. Write your evaluation in the space marked (b).

Examples

Luke 1.5

	1 2
KJV	his wife
Compare:	
TEV	his wife
JB/RSV/NAS	he had a wife
NEB/NIV	his wife
Knox	[Zachary] who had married a wife
YL	_____

(a) <u>1 is married to 2</u>

(b) JB/RSV/NAS are really unambiguous, but Knox is the most explicit.

[59]

```
1 John 1.9
                    1   2                      (a)  1 does 2
RSV                 our sin
    Compare:                                   (b)  Only the GeCL and TEV indicate that
TEV                 our wrongdoing                  1 has been doing 2. GeCL, however,
BE                  evil                            shifts from sin to guilt. GeCL also
NIV/NEB/TNT         our sins                        has a different exegesis.
GeCL                guilt...which we have
                       loaded upon ourselves
YL                  _____

1 Peter 2.24
                    1   2                      (a)  P¹ causes 2 in 1
RSV                 his wounds
    Compare:                                   (b)  Not one translation makes it explic-
TEV                 his wounds                      it that P¹ wounded 1, though Phps
TNT/NEB/NIV         his wounds                      comes closest.
Phps                the suffering that he
                       bore
YL                  _____
```

B-10 New Testament, Gr: Possessive Constructions

1. Rom 5.8

```
                    1   2                      (a) _____
RSV                 his love
    Compare:                                   (b)
TEV                 he loves us
NEB                 his love
JB                  God loves us
NIV                 his own love
YL                  _____
```

2. Matt 9.4

```
                    1     2                    (a) _____
RSV                 their thoughts
    Compare:                                   (b)
TEV                 what they were thinking
Phps/NEB            what they were thinking
NIV                 their thoughts
YL                  _____
```

3. Matt 7.28

```
                    1   2                      (a) _____
RSV                 his teaching
    Compare:                                   (b)
TEV                 the way he taught
Phps/NEB            his teaching
YL                  _____
```

4. 2 Cor 2.8

```
                  1      2              (a)_____
   RSV         your love for him
       Compare:                        (b)
   TEV         you really do love him
   JB/NEB      your love for him
   Phps        you love him
   LB          you still do love him
                  very much
   YL           _____
```

5. Luke 4.21

```
                  1      2              (a)_____
   RSV         your hearing
       Compare:                        (b)
   TEV         you heard it
   NEB         your very hearing
   JB          [even as] you listen
   NIV         your hearing
   Phps        you have been listening
                  to it
   YL           _____
```

6. 1 Cor 9.3

```
                  1      2              (a)_____
   RSV         my defense
       Compare:                        (b)
   TEV         how I defend myself
   Phps        my real ground of defense
   NEB         my answer
   YL           _____
```

7. Matt 5.25

```
                  1      2              (a)_____
   RSV         your accuser
       Compare:                        (b)
   TEV         someone brings a lawsuit
                  against you
   Phps        your opponent
   NEB         someone sues you
   YL           _____
```

8. Jude 25

```
                  1      2              (a)_____
   RSV         our Savior
       Compare:                        (b)
   TEV         our Savior
   LB/JB       who saves us
   NEB         our Saviour
   YL           _____
```

9. Matt 23.5

```
                  1      2              (a)_____
   RSV         their deeds
       Compare                         (b)
   TEV         they do everything
   NEB         whatever they do
   YL           _____
```

10. Rom 16.25

	1 2	(a) _____
RSV	my gospel	(b)

    Compare:
    TEV   the Good News I preach
    Phps   my Gospel
    NEB   the Gospel I brought you
    JB   the Good News I preach
    YL   _____

11. Matt 11.30

	1 2	(a) _____
RSV	my yoke	(b)

    Compare:
    TEV   the yoke I will give you
    Phps/NEB   my yoke
    YL   _____

B-11 Old Testament, Gr: Possessive Constructions (Instructions as for Drill B-10)

1. 1 Chr 12.18

	1 2	(a) _____
RSV	your helpers	(b)

    Compare:
    TEV   those who help you
    LB   who aid you
    BE   your helpers
    JB   him that helps you
    YL   _____

2. Psa 30.10

	1 2	(a) _____
RSV	[be thou] my helper	(b)

    Compare:
    TEV   help me!
    NEB   my helper
    LB/JB   help me!
    Mft   be my help!
    YL   _____

3. Psa 35.28

	1 2	(a) _____
RSV	thy praise	(b)

    Compare:
    TEV   I will praise you
    NEB   thy praise
    LB   I will praise you
    JB   your praises
    YL   _____

4. Jer 17.14

	1 2	(a) _____
RSV	[thou art] my praise	(b)

    Compare:
    TEV   you are the one I praise
    NEB/LB   my praise
    Beck   You are the One I praise
    Mft   I render praise
    YL   _____

5. Psa 145.13

	1	2
RSV	thy dominion	

Compare:

TEV	you are king
NEB	thy dominion
LB	you rule
JB	your sovereignty
YL	_____

(a)_____

(b)

6. Hos 5.13

	1	2
RSV	his sickness	

Compare:

TEV	how sick she was
NEB	he was sick
LB	how sick they are
JB	how sick he is
YL	_____

(a)_____

(b)

7. Psa 129.2

	1	2
RSV	my youth	

Compare:

TEV	I was young
JB/NEB	I was young
LB	my...youth (verse 1)
NAS	my youth
YL	_____

(a)_____

(b)

8. Deut 7.7

	1	2
RSV	his love [upon you]	

Compare:

TEV	the LORD did...love you
NEB	the LORD cared for you
LB	pour out his love upon you
YL	_____

(a)_____

(b)

9. Isa 43.3

	1	2
RSV	your Savior	

Compare:

TEV	who saves you
NEB	your deliverer
LB	your Savior
JB	your saviour
YL	_____

(a)_____

(b)

10. Job 2.13

	1	2
RSV	his suffering	

Compare:

TEV	he was suffering
LB/NEB	his suffering
BE	his pain
YL	_____

(a)_____

(b)

3. ANALYSIS III: IMPLICIT INFORMATION

Purpose. In this drill section we want to learn to recognize some of the many kinds of information which can be implicit, that is, not expressed in the surface structure of the text but still clearly implicit in the message. For example, in the previous section in which we were learning to identify the real relationship between two words from biblical surface structure, we often found it necessary to express implicit participants whom we called P^1 and P^2. The reason for this is the fact that all languages allow speakers to "bury" or leave implicit certain parts of the information, that is, the source does not need to make it visible in the surface structure because the receptors in that specific setting will be able to supply it from their background knowledge. When both the source and the receptor share certain historical and cultural information, it often will be unnecessary to express such shared information explicitly. In fact, the more experience the source and the receptor have in common, the more information they will be able to leave implicit. This is why a conversation between two close friends is often almost completely unintelligible to a stranger. He understands all the words they say, but since he does not share their experience, he cannot supply the implicit information which holds the key to the interpretation of the conversation. Translators need to be aware of the fact that, just as leaving information implicit can be a sign of closeness and intimacy, so making too much information explicit can be a way of expressing social distance.

Now let's get back to the implicit participants we mentioned earlier. For example, when English uses a noun derived from a verb, some of the participants are often hidden. For example, "his imprisonment," stated as a simple kernel sentence, forces us to make explicit that somebody imprisoned him. That implicit somebody is usually clearly spelled out by the larger context in which the expression occurs. But when the Sadducees claim "there is no resurrection," both God, the doer of the resurrection, and the dead people to be resurrected are left implicit; compare "the Sadducees claim 'God does not resurrect dead people.'"

Since languages differ in what they can leave implicit, it is important that the translator be aware of what is implicit in the Greek or Hebrew text. He can then decide whether his language can also leave it implicit or whether his language requires that it be made explicit. For example, the Greek in the New Testament uses many nouns derived from verbs and as a result leaves implicit many of the participants. However, many Bantu languages in Africa put a lot of emphasis on expressing all the participants explicitly, especially in unfamiliar contexts. These languages can make nouns from verbs in a way that is very similar to the Greek, but it is not natural to use them in as many contexts as the Greek does.

Making the implicit information explicit is a very important step in the exegesis of the text. The nature of our translation will then determine how near to the kernel structures our translation must remain. A translation for new literates will remain very close to kernel sentences in order to provide the redundancy which helps the new reader; but a literary-level translation will probably make a lot of the information implicit, using the full range of the resources of the language.

To help us in our exegesis of the text we want to learn to identify the following kinds of implicit information:

(a) Participants: for example, "his imprisonment" leaves out the participant(s) who did the imprisoning.

(b) Events: for example, in "Jesus of Nazareth" the of in a sense stands for lived in or came from, but in "Saul of Tarsus" the of stands for was born in, or his parents were citizens of Tarsus, etc.

(c) Qualities: for example, "John wore a garment of camel's hair" does not express the quality of rough, poor; thus "John wore a garment of rough camel's hair."

[64]

The rough, poor quality of the garment was culturally understood by all the Jews who heard the statement, but to a North American a camel's hair coat means a coat of very fine quality; and many Africans, who have never seen a camel, have no idea at all about the nature of John's clothes. This type of implicit information often comes from our general knowledge of the situation, but it is essential information for a receptor in a different cultural setting. Without such information he will not merely be unable to understand the full significance of the message, but he will probably misinterpret the situation according to the usage of his culture.

The implicit qualities are especially important in figurative language. For example, when Jesus speaks about Herod, saying "Go tell that fox," there is a hidden quality in the word fox. Most Europeans will hear clever or cunning. South American Indians might hear sex fiend, because foxes are felt to be highly sexual creatures. However, the people who heard Jesus would have heard the quality of being destructive; for example, Song of Solomon 2.15 speaks about "the foxes that destroy the vineyard." (Commentaries vary in their understanding of why Herod was called a fox. Some feel that the quality referred to is worthless or deceptive. This is the interpretation followed by many commentaries and is based on nonbiblical usage, because there are no other parallels in the Scriptures.)

(d) Next, we also want to become aware of implicit cultural information, such as when "Pilate washed his hands" to show his innocence. One group of South American Indians thought he was washing off anything by which Jesus could have bewitched him.

(e) Then we also need to be aware of certain kinds of implicit historical information; for example, Pharaoh is not the name of a person, but it is a title, King of Egypt. Most readers of the Bible have not understood it as a title but as a proper name, and thus they have concluded that it was the personal name of the king.

(f) Similarly there can be geographical information that was considered common knowledge in biblical times but which we today need to have expressed explicitly; for example, Mark 1.5 "went out to him all the country of Judea, and all the people of Jerusalem" (RSV) is rendered as "Many people from the province of Judea and the city of Jerusalem" (TEV, underscoring added). There are also many names in the Bible that carry meaning; for example, Matthew 4.25 "Galilee and the Decapolis" (RSV) is rendered "Galilee and the Ten Towns" (TEV) because Decapolis is the Greek word for "ten towns."

(g) Finally there are implicit transitions between sentences. Since these do not involve the recognition of parts of kernel sentences we treat them elsewhere.

Implicit Participants
Instructions
(a) Identify and make explicit any implicit (hidden) participants involved in the action in the phrases given below, and write them on the line marked (a).

(b) Compare the various translations listed to see if they have expressed the implicit participants explicitly. Give your evaluation in the space marked (b).

(c) Check whether the participants have been expressed in the translation in your language. If they have not been expressed but should be, restate the expression with all the participants expressed clearly on the line marked YL.

Examples

Mark 1.4
RSV   baptism of repentance   (a) John baptizes people and people
    Compare: repent
TEV   John...baptizing people and
          preaching...turn away from   (b) TEV makes explicit all three of the
          your sins   implicit participants and LB and
JB   a baptism of repentance   TNT make explicit one each. In all
NEB   a baptism in token of repent-   others the implicit participants
          ance   remain hidden.
LB   [taught that] all should be
          baptized as a public an-
          nouncement of their deci-
          sion to turn their backs
          on sin
NIV   repentance and baptism
TNT   people should repent and be
          baptized
YL   _____

1 John 4.17
RSV   day of judgment   (a) the day when God judges all people
    Compare:
Phps   the day when he [God] shall   (b) Only Phps makes both of the partici-
          judge all men   pants explicit.
NEB   day of judgement
TEV   Judgment Day
JB   day of Judgement
YL   _____

B-12 New Testament, Gr: Implicit Participants

1. Phil 1.16
   RSV   do it out of love   (a)_____
      Compare:
   TEV   do so from love   (b)
   Phps   out of their love for me
   NEB   moved by love for me
   LB   because they love me
   YL   _____

2. 2 Cor 6.2
   RSV   the day of salvation   (a)_____
      Compare:
   TEV   today is the day to be   (b)
                 saved
   NEB   the day of deliverance
   JB/NIV   the day of salvation
   LB   today he is ready to save you
   YL   _____

3. Rom 8.35
   RSV   [who shall separate us...]   (a)_____
             persecution
      Compare: (b)
   TEV   persecution
   JB   being persecuted
   Phps/NEB persecution
   LB   when we are hunted down
   YL   _____

4. Gal 3.2
   RSV   [receive Spirit] by hear-   (a)_____
             ing with faith
      Compare: (b)
   TEV   by hearing and believing
             the gospel
   NEB   by believing the gospel
             message
   JB   because you believed what
             was preached to you
   LB   you heard about Christ and
             trusted him to save
             you
   NIV   by believing what you heard
   GeCL   *because you heard the Good*
             News and trust in Jesus
             Christ
   YL   _____

5. 2 Cor 5.19
   RSV   message of reconciliation   (a)_____
      Compare: (b)
   TEV   the message of how he makes
             them his friends
   NEB/Phps the message of reconcilia-
             tion
   JB   the news that they are
             reconciled
   YL   _____

6. Luke 2.38
   RSV   looking for the redemption (a)_____
             of Jerusalem
      Compare: (b)
   TEV   waiting for God to redeem
             Jerusalem
   NEB   looking for the liberation
             of Jerusalem
   NIV   looking forward to the re-
             demption of Jerusalem
   YL   _____

7. 1 Tim 4.3
   RSV   who forbid marriage   (a)_____
      Compare:
   TEV   men teach that it is wrong   (b)
                to marry
   NEB   they forbid marriage
   JB   they will say marriage is
                forbidden
   Phps   these men forbid marriage
   Beck   order people not to marry
   NIV   they forbid people to
                marry
   YL   _____

8. 1 Thes 2.2
   RSV   in the face of great op-   (a)_____
                position
      Compare:
   TEV   there was much opposition   (b)
   NEB   a hard struggle it was
   NIV   in spite of strong oppo-
                sition
   TNT   many opposed us
   YL   _____

9. Matt 15.19
   RSV   out of the heart come...   (a)_____
                murder
      Compare:
   TEV   from his heart come...which (b)
                lead him to kill
   NEB   murder...proceed from the
                heart
   JB   from the heart come...mur-
                der
   NIV   out of the heart come...
                murder
   YL   _____

10. Acts 22.24
    RSV   to be examined by scourging (a)_____
       Compare:
    TEV   told them to whip him to   (b)
                find out why
    NEB   to examine him by flogging
    JB   to be examined under the
                lash
    NIV   that he be flogged and
                questioned
    YL   _____

[68]

1. Jer 2.2
   RSV   your love   (a)_____
       Compare:
   TEV   how you loved me   (b)
   JB/NEB   the love of your [bridal
                days]
   BE   your love
   Mft   the love of you
   Beck   how you loved
   LB   how you loved me
   YL   _____

2. 1 Sam 2.1
   RSV   thy salvation   (a)_____
       Compare:
   TEV   God has helped me   (b)
   NEB   thou hast saved me
   JB   your power of saving
   BE   your salvation
   Mft   thy deliverance
   Beck   You are the One who can
                save
   YL   _____

3. Psa 130.4
   RSV   there is forgiveness   (a)_____
       Compare:
   TEV   you forgive us   (b)
   NEB   in thee is forgiveness
   JB   you do forgive us
   BE   there is forgiveness
   Beck   You forgive us
   YL   _____

4. Isa 10.25
   RSV   their destruction   (a)_____
       Compare:
   TEV   I will destroy them   (b)
   NEB   [my wrath] will be all
                spent
   JB   [my anger] will destroy
                them
   BE   their destruction
   Mft   [my wrath] shall come to
                an end
   Beck   [My fury] will be used up
                on the Assyrians
   LB   [my anger]...destroy them
   YL   _____

5. Psa 76.6
   RSV   thy rebuke   (a)_____
      Compare:
   TEV   you threatened them   (b)
   NEB   thy rebuke
   JB   your reproof
   Beck   Your rebuke
   LB   when you rebuked them
   YL   _____

6. Job 15.11
   RSV   consolations of God   (a)_____
      Compare:
   TEV   God offers you comfort   (b)
   NEB   consolation of God
   JB   comfort that God gives
   LB   God's comfort
   BE   comforts of God
   Beck   God's comforts
   YL   _____

7. Ezek 22.7
   RSV   sojourner suffers extortion   (a)_____
      Compare:
   TEV   you cheat foreigners   (b)
   NEB   they have oppressed the
               alien
   JB   they ill-treat the settler
   LB   immigrants and visitors
               are forced to pay you
               for your "protection"
   Beck   stranger is oppressed
   YL   _____

8. Jer 22.17
   RSV   for practicing oppression   (a)_____
      Compare:
   TEV   you...oppress your people   (b)
   JB   perpetrating...oppression
   LB   oppress the poor
   Beck   practicing oppression
   YL   _____

Implicit Events
   Instructions
      (a) in each of the following of-phrases and possessive constructions there
is an implicit event. Identify the event or state and write it on the line marked
(a).
      (b) Compare the various translations listed below to see how many of the im-
plicit events have been made explicit and which of the ambiguous statements have
been made clear. Write your findings in the space marked (b).
      (c) See what has been done in your own language. If it needs improvement,
try to make a better translation and write it on the line marked YL.

```
Examples

Acts 7.46                                  (a)  the God whom Jacob worships, trusts,
RSV            the God of Jacob                 is loyal to, etc.
    Compare:
TEV            the God of Jacob            (b)  All translations fail to make ex-
NEB/NAS/NIV    the God of Jacob                 plicit the event which clarifies
YL             _____                the relationship between the two
                                                P's.

Acts 27.6
RSV            a ship of Alexandria        (a)  a ship based in, registered in,
    Compare:                                    originating from Alexandria
TEV            a ship from Alexandria
NEB            an Alexandrian vessel       (b)  None of the translations make explic-
NIV/JB         an Alexandrian ship              it the real relationship. LB indi-
LB             an Egyptian ship from            cates the country where Alexandria
               Alexandria                       is located.
YL             _____

Deut 29.17
RSV            idols of wood               (a)  idols made from wood
    Compare:
TEV            idols made of wood          (b)  Only TEV, Mft, and LB make the event
JB             their idols, the wood            explicit. All the others leave it
NEB            idols and false gods             implicit. In JB the idols and wood
                 they had, the gods             are not related at all.
                 of wood
LB             idols made of wood
Beck           idols of wood
BE             images of wood
Mft            idols, made of wood
YL             _____
```

B-14 New Testament, Gr: Implicit Events

1. 2 Tim 2.20
     RSV   vessels of gold and silver   (a) _____
         Compare:
     TEV   dishes and bowls...made of   (b)
                      silver and gold
     NIV   articles of gold and silver
     NEB   utensils of gold and silver
     JB   dishes...made of gold and
                      silver
     Phps   gold and silver vessels
     LB   dishes made of gold and
                      silver
     YL   _____

2. Luke 2,4
   RSV   city of David   (a)_____
      Compare:
   TEV   town...where King David   (b)
                 was born
   NEB   city of David
   NIV/JB   town of David
   TNT/Phps   David's town
   LB   King David's ancient home
   YL   _____

3. Acts 11.20
   RSV   men of Cyprus   (a)_____
      Compare:
   TEV   men from Cyprus   (b)
   Phps/NEB   natives of Cyprus
   JB   some...who came from Cyprus
   TNT   men of Cyprus
   YL   _____

4. John 19.38
   RSV   Joseph of Arimathea   (a)_____
      Compare:
   TEV   Joseph, who was from the   (b)
                 town of Arimathea
   JB/NEB   Joseph of Arimathaea
   Phps   Joseph (who came from Ari-
                 mathaea...)
   TNT   Joseph from Arimathaea
   YL   _____

5. Rev 6.15
   RSV   among the rocks of the   (a)_____
                 mountains
      Compare: (b)
   TEV   under rocks on the moun-
                 tains
   NEB   in...mountain crags
   NIV   among the rocks of the
                 mountains
   JB   mountains...among the rocks
   TNT/Phps   among mountain rocks
   YL   _____

6. Heb 11.2
   RSV   men of old   (a)_____
      Compare:
   TEV   men of ancient times   (b)
   NEB   men of old
   TNT/JB   our ancestors
   NIV   the ancients
   Phps   saints of old
   LB   men of God in days of old
   Beck   men of long ago
   YL   _____

7. Matt 6.26
   RSV   the birds of the air   (a)_____
       Compare:
   TEV   birds flying around   (b)
   TNT/NEB   birds of the air
   Phps/JB   birds in the sky
   BE   birds of heaven
   YL   _____

8. Acts 3.13
   RSV   God of Abraham   (a)_____
       Compare:
   TEV   God of Abraham   (b)
   JB/NEB   God of Abraham
   LB/NIV   God of Abraham
   YL   _____

B-15 Old Testament, Gr: Implicit Events (Instructions as for Drill B-14)

1. Lev 13.59
   RSV   anything of skin   (a)_____
       Compare:
   TEV   anything made of leather   (b)
   NEB   anything made of skin
   LB   anything made of skin or
                  leather
   Beck   any leather article
   Mft   or in leather
   BE   anything of skin
   YL   _____

2. 1 Kgs 1.39
   RSV   the horn of oil   (a)_____
       Compare:
   TEV   the container of olive oil   (b)
   JB/NEB   the horn of oil
   LB   flask of sacred oil
   Beck   the horn of oil
   BE   vessel of oil
   Mft   vial of oil
   YL   _____

3. Deut 4.28
   RSV   gods of wood and stone   (a)_____
       Compare:
   TEV   gods of wood and stone   (b)
   NEB   gods made...out of wood
                  and stone
   JB   gods...made, of wood and
                  of stone
   LB   idols made from wood and
                  stone
   Beck   gods that human hands
                  have made of wood and
                  stone
   Mft   gods of wood and stone
   BE   gods, made by men's hands,
                  of wood and stone
   YL   _____

4. 2 Kgs 18.32
   RSV   a land of grain and wine,   (a) _____
                 a land of bread and
                 vineyards   (b)
       Compare:
   TEV   a country...where there
                 are vineyards to give
                 wine and there is
                 grain for making bread
   NEB   a land of grain and new
                 wine, of corn and
                 vineyards
   JB   a land of corn and good
                 wine, a land of bread
                 and of vineyards
   LB   another land just like this
                 one—with plentiful
                 crops, grain, wine
   Beck   a land with grain and wine,
                 a land with bread and
                 vineyards
   BE   a land of grain and wine,
                 a land of bread and
                 vine-gardens
   Mft   a land of corn and wine, a
                 land of bread and vine-
                 yards
   YL   _____

5. Deut 2.14
   RSV   men of war   (a) _____
       Compare:
   TEV   fighting men   (b)
   NEB   fighting men
   JB   men fit for war
   LB   men...old enough to bear
                 arms
   Beck   men able to fight
   BE   men of war
   Mft   the warriors
   YL   _____

6. Judges 2.3
   RSV   their gods   (a) _____
       Compare:
   TEV   the worship of their gods   (b)
   JB/NEB   their gods
   LB   their gods
   Beck   their gods
   BE   their gods
   Mft   their gods
   YL   _____

Implicit Qualities, Quantities, Etc.

Instructions

(a) Study the RSV carefully and see if you can discover an implicit quality related to the underlined words. Write the quality on the line marked (a). If you find yourself unable to identify the implicit information from your own knowledge, consult a commentary.

(b) Compare the translations listed below to see if they have made the implicit quality explicit. Write your findings in the space marked (b).

(c) Study the translation in your language. If the implicit quality has not been made explicit, prepare a new translation that makes it explicit and write it on the line marked YL. (Implicit qualities in figurative language will be studied in more detail in Section E.)

Examples

Matt 7.15

RSV	come to you in sheep's clothing	(a)	harmless

Compare:

TEV   they come to you looking like sheep on the outside

JB/TNT   come to you disguised as sheep

NAS/NIV   come to you in sheep's clothing

LB   come disguised as harmless sheep

Phps/NEB   who come dressed up as sheep

GeCL   *they look like harmless sheep*

YL   _____

(b) Only LB and GeCL make the implicit quality explicit.

Matt 5.40

RSV	your coat...your cloak	(a)	cheaper shirt and more costly coat

Compare:

TEV   your shirt...your coat

NEB   your shirt...your coat

NIV/JB   your tunic...your cloak

Phps   your coat...your overcoat

LB   your shirt...your coat

YL   _____

(b) TEV, NEB, Phps, and LB by use of shirt and coat imply a value difference but do not make it explicit. All the others are obscure on this point.

---

[75]

1. Mark 15.46
   RSV   rolled a <u>stone</u> against the   (a)_____
             door
        Compare: (b)
   TEV   rolled a large stone across
             the entrance
   NEB/JB   rolled a stone against the
             entrance
   NIV   rolled a stone against the
             entrance
   Phps   rolling a stone over the
             entrance
   LB   rolled a stone in front of
             the entrance
   YL   _____

2. Matt 9.10
   RSV   many <u>tax collectors and</u>   (a)_____
             <u>sinners</u>
        Compare: (b)
   TEV   many tax collectors and
             other outcasts
   NEB   many bad characters—tax-
             gatherers and others
   JB   a number of tax collectors
             and sinners (footnote:
             "socially outcast")
   Phps   many tax-collectors and
             other disreputable peo-
             ple
   NIV   many tax collectors and
             "sinners"
   LB   many notorious swindlers
   YL   _____

3. Matt 18.6
   KJV   a <u>millstone</u>   (a)_____
        Compare:
   TEV   a large millstone   (b)
   JB/RSV   a great millstone
   NEB   a millstone
   NIV   a large millstone
   LB   a rock
   YL   _____

4. Matt 17.20
   RSV   faith as a grain of
            mustard seed
       Compare:
   TEV   faith as big as a mustard
            seed
   NEB   faith no bigger even than
            a mustard-seed
   JB   your faith were the size of
            a mustard seed
   NIV   faith as small as a mus-
            tard seed
   Phps   as much faith as a grain of
            mustard seed
   LB   faith even as small as a
            tiny mustard seed
   YL   _____

   (a)_____

   (b)

5. Matt 6.29
   RSV   was...arrayed like one of
            these
       Compare:
   TEV   had clothes as beautiful as
            one of these flowers
   JB   was robed like one of these
   NEB   was...attired like one of
            these
   NIV   was dressed like one of
            these
   Phps   arrayed like one of these
   LB   clothed as beautifully as
            they
   YL   _____

   (a)_____

   (b)

6. Matt 18.3
   RSV   become like children
       Compare:
   TEV   become like children
   NIV   become like little children
   NEB   become like children
   JB/Phps become like little children
   LB   become as little children
   YL   _____

   (a)_____

   (b)

7. Luke 16.22
RSV   carried...to <u>Abraham's
               bosom</u>
     Compare:
TEV   carried...to Abraham's side
LB   carried...to be with Abra-
               ham
JB   carried...to the bosom of
               Abraham
NEB   carried away...to be with
               Abraham
Phps   was carried...into Abraham's
               bosom
NIV   carried him to Abraham's
               side
Beck   carried him to Abraham's
               bosom
BE   took him to Abraham's breast
YL   _____

(a)_____

(b)

B-17 <u>Old Testament, Gr: Implicit Qualities</u> (Instructions as for Drill B-16)

1. Psa 32.9
RSV   be not like a <u>horse or a
               mule</u>
     Compare:
TEV   don't be stupid like a horse
               or a mule
NEB   do not behave like horse or
               mule
JB   do not be like senseless
               horse or mule
LB   don't be like a senseless
               horse or mule
Beck   don't be like a horse or a
               mule without sense
BE   do not be like the horse or
               the ass, without sense
Mft   be not like mules and colts,
               that do not understand
               the bridle
YL   _____

(a)_____

(b)

2. Isa 63.13
RSV   like a <u>horse</u> in the desert
     Compare:
TEV   as surefooted as wild horses
NEB   surefooted as horses in the
               wilderness
JB   as easily as a horse through
               the desert
LB   like fine stallions racing
               through the desert
Beck   a horse going through the
               desert
BE   a horse in the waste land
Mft   like horses on a level plain
YL   _____

(a)_____

(b)

3. Jer 22.6
RSV   are as <u>Gilead</u> to me   (a)_____
      Compare:
TEV   as beautiful as the land of   (b)
            Gilead
NEB   are dear to me as Gilead
JB   like a Gilead to me
LB   are as beloved to me as
            fruitful Gilead
Beck   are to Me like Gilead
BE   you are Gilead to me
Mft   you were a flourishing Gilead
YL   _____

4. Amos 4.1
RSV   <u>cows of Bashan</u>   (a)_____
      Compare:
TEV   fat like well-fed cows of   (b)
            Bashan
NEB   cows of Bashan
JB   cows of Bashan
LB   "fat cows" of Bashan
Beck   cows of Bashan
BE   cows of Bashan
Mft   cows of Bashan
YL   _____

5. Micah 7.14
RSV   <u>feed in Bashan</u>   (a)_____
      Compare:
TEV   feed in the rich pastures of   (b)
            Bashan
NEB   graze in Bashan
JB   pasture in Bashan
LB   enjoy the fertile pasture of
            Bashan
Beck   feed in Bashan
BE   get their food in Bashan
Mft   let Bashan...be their pas-
            ture
YL   _____

6. Hos 2.12
RSV   <u>beasts of the field</u>   (a)_____
      Compare:
TEV   the wild animals   (b)
JB/NEB   wild beasts
LB   wild animals
Beck   wild animals
BE   the beasts of the field
Mft   wild beasts
YL   _____

[79]

7. Isa 2.13
   RSV   <u>cedars of Lebanon</u>   (a) _____
        Compare:
   TEV   tall cedars of Lebanon   (b)
   NEB   cedars of Lebanon
   BE   high trees of Lebanon
   LB/JB   cedars of Lebanon
   Beck   lofty cedars of Lebanon
   Mft   cedars of Lebanon
   YL   _____

Implicit Cultural Information

Introduction. Implicit cultural information comes from at least three sources: (1) the cultural function of certain objects, for example, <u>sickle</u> is a curved knife used for cutting grass or harvesting grain; (2) the meaning of an event, for example, <u>kissing</u> as a normal cultural form of greeting; and (3) the general knowledge of the original setting including geographical reference, history, and cultural practices, for example, <u>half-sheckel tax</u> refers to the temple tax all male Jews were required to pay.

The first kind of implicit information we have already dealt with in Drills A-7 through A-10 dealing with cultural objects.

In this set of drills we want to focus on the latter two kinds of implicit information, namely the cultural meaning of events, and the general cultural information implicit in many biblical statements.

In the case of events with implicit symbolic meaning we need to remember that they are historical, people did as it says. Therefore we have to translate the event, but we also have to make its implicit meaning known to the receptor. If this can be done with a few words, the meaning can be put into the text. If a longer explanation is necessary, it can be given in a footnote or, if the expression occurs several times, in the glossary. (Symbolic acts and gestures will be treated once more in connection with figurative language in Drills F-40 through F-43.)

Instructions

(a) Consult a Bible dictionary, Handbook, or commentary; try to discover the cultural information implicit in the underlined words; and write it on the line marked (a).

(b) Compare the translations listed to see if they have made the implicit cultural information explicit. Write your findings in the space marked (b).

(c) Check the translation in your own language. If the implicit cultural information has not been expressed, write a new translation that expresses it clearly on the line marked YL.

Examples

2 Kgs 15.19

RSV	a thousand <u>talents</u> of silver	(a)	<u>A talent of silver weighed 76 pounds.</u>
	Compare:		
TEV	thirty-eight tons of silver		
NEB/JB	a thousand talents of silver	(b)	Only LB and TEV make an attempt to explain the amount. LB, by using an exchange rate, is not timeless like TEV.
BE	a thousand talents of silver		
Beck	1,000 talents of silver		
LB	$2,000.000		
YL	_____		

Luke 7.45

RSV	you gave me no <u>kiss</u>	(a)	<u>The kiss was a cultural way of greeting.</u>
	Compare		
TEV	you did not welcome me with a kiss		
NIV	you did not give me a kiss	(b)	Only TEV and LB make the greeting function of a kiss explicit. Phps leaves out the form and expresses only the meaning. All others merely express the form of the action, leaving the reader with either no meaning or a wrong meaning.
NAS	you gave Me no kiss		
Phps	there was no warmth in your greeting		
JB/NEB	you gave me no kiss		
TNT	you gave me no kiss		
LB	you refused...me the customary kiss of greeting		
YL	_____		

Matt 20.2

RSV	a <u>denarius</u> a day	(a)	<u>A denarius was a coin and was considered a normal day's wage.</u>
	Compare:		
TEV	the regular wage, a silver coin a day		
NEB	the usual day's wage	(b)	Only TEV and NEB make the function of the denarius explicit. LB uses an exchange rate that is highly questionable. Note that the value of the coin is not as important as its cultural function.
NIV	a denarius for the day		
JB	one denarius a day		
Phps	a silver coin a day		
LB	$20 a day		
YL	_____		

1. Matt 1.19

    RSV   resolved to <u>divorce</u>[a] her
          quietly

         Compare:

    TEV   to break the engagement pri-
          vately

    NEB   to have the marriage contract
          set aside quietly

    JB   to divorce her informally

    LB   to break the engagement but
          to do it quietly

    Phps to break off the engagement
          quietly

    YL   _____

          _____

(a)_____

   _____

(b)

[a]The translation problem in this verse arises from: (1) the fact that the Greek uses *apoluō* "to put away" both for breaking an engagement and for dissolving a marriage; (2) the RSV practice of using one English word <u>divorce</u> in both contexts.

2. Matt 10.10

    RSV   no <u>bag</u> for your journey

         Compare:

    TEV   do not carry a beggar's bag
          for the trip

    NEB   no pack for the road

    NIV   no bag for the journey

    JB   no haversack for the journey

    Phps nor a knapsack for the journey

    LB   don't even carry a duffel bag

    YL   _____

          _____

(a)_____

   _____

(b)

3. Matt 11.17

    RSV   we <u>wailed</u>

         Compare:

    TEV   we sang funeral songs

    NEB   we wept and wailed

    JB   we sang dirges

    Phps we played at funerals

    NIV   we sang a dirge

    LB   we played funeral

    YL   _____

(a)_____

   _____

(b)

4. Matt 21.33

    RSV   a <u>tower</u>

         Compare:

    TEV   a watchtower

    NEB   a watch-tower

    NIV/JB a tower

    LB   a platform for the watchman

    YL   _____

          _____

(a)_____

   _____

(b)

1. 1 Kgs 9.14
   RSV   one hundred twenty <u>talents</u>
           of gold

   (a) _____

       Compare:
         _____

   TEV   almost five tons of gold

   NEB   a hundred and twenty talents
           of gold

   (b)

   JB   one hundred and twenty tal-
           ents of gold

   Beck   120 talents of gold

   LB   gold...valued at $3,500,000

   YL   _____

            _____

2. Dan 11.6
   RSV   make an alliance...the <u>king</u>
           of the south shall <u>come</u> to
           <u>the king of the north</u>

   (a) _____

       Compare:
         _____

   TEV   the king of Egypt will make an
           alliance with the king of
           Syria

   (b)

   Mft   they shall join forces...king
           of the South...king of the
           North

   NEB   the two will enter into a
           friendly alliance...king of
           the south...king of the
           north

   BE   they will be joined togeth-
           er...king of the south...
           king of the north

   Beck   they will join one another...
           southern king...northern
           king

   JB   these will form an alliance...
           the king of the South will
           go to the king of the North

   LB   an alliance will be formed be-
           tween the king of Syria and
           the king of Egypt

   YL   _____

            _____

3. Ezra 9.3
   RSV   rent my garments   (a) _____
       Compare: _____
   TEV   tore my clothes in despair
   JB   tore my garment   (b)
   Beck   tore my tunic
   BE   with signs of grief
   Mft   tore my tunic
   LB   tore my clothing
   NEB   rent my robe
   YL   _____

           _____

4. Dan 10.21
   RSV   Michael, your prince   (a) _____
       Compare: _____
   TEV   Michael, Israel's guardian
               angel   (b)
   JB/NEB Michael your prince
   Mft   Michael, your own guardian
               angel
   LB   Michael, the angel who guards
               your people Israel
   YL   _____

           _____

Implicit Historical, Geographical, or Lexical Information
       Instructions
       (a) Consult a good Bible dictionary or commentary, try to ascertain what
historical, geographical, or lexical information is necessary or helpful to understand the RSV passages cited below, and write it on the line marked (a).
       (b) Compare the translations listed below to see if and how they have made
the implicit information explicit. Write your findings in the space marked (b).
       (c) On the line marked (c), classify the implicit information as historical,
geographical, or lexical.
       (d) Write the translation in your own language in the lines marked YL. If it
does not explicitly give the implicit historical, geographical, or lexical information, prepare a new translation that does.

Examples
Acts 8.27-28

RSV	the Candace, queen of the Ethiopians	(a)	Candace is the Ethiopian word for queen
Compare:			
TEV (third edition)	the Queen, or Candace, of Ethiopia	(b)	TEV, NEB, and JB make the meaning clear. LB, NIV, and BE make it sound as if Candace is her personal name.
NEB	the Kandake, or Queen, of Ethiopia		
LB	Candace the queen [of Ethiopia]	(c)	lexical
JB	the Kandake, or queen, of Ethiopia		
NIV/BE	Candace, queen of the Ethiopians		
YL	_____		

Matt 22.17

RSV	pay taxes to Caesar	(a)	Caesar is the name of the ruler of the Roman Empire
Compare:			
TEV	pay taxes to the Roman Emperor	(b)	TEV, NEB & LB all make this fact explicit. JB and NIV leave it implicit.
NEB	pay taxes to the Roman Emperor		
JB/NIV	pay taxes to Caesar	(c)	historical and lexical
LB	pay taxes to the Roman government		
YL	_____		

Dan 11.5

RSV	king of the south	(a)	south refers to Egypt
Compare:			
TEV	king of Egypt	(b)	Only TEV and LB make the identification of Egypt explicit.
NEB	king of the south		
JB	king of the South		
LB	king of Egypt	(c)	geographical
Beck	southern king		
BE	king of the south		
YL	_____		

B-20 New Testament, Gr: Implicit Historical, Geographical, or Lexical Information

1. Matt 27.11

RSV	before the governor	(a)	_____
Compare:			
TEV	the Roman governor		
NEB	the Governor		
JB/NIV	the governor	(b)	
LB	the Roman governor		
YL	_____		
		(c)	_____

[85]

2. Matt 6.29
   RSV   Solomon   (a) _____
        Compare:
   TEV   King Solomon   _____
   NEB/JB   Solomon
   LB   King Solomon   (b)
   YL   _____

             _____   (c) _____

3. Matt 2.1
   RSV   wise men from the East   (a) _____
        Compare:
   TEV   men who studied the stars   _____
             came from the east
   NEB   astrologers arrived from   (b)
             the east
   JB   wise men...from the east
   NIV   Magi...from the east   (c) _____
   Phps   from the east...a party of
             astrologers
   LB   some astrologers from east-
             ern lands
   YL   _____

             _____

4. Matt 5.41
   RSV   if any one forces you to go   (a) _____
             one mile
        Compare: _____
   TEV   if one of the occupation
             troops forces you to   (b)
             carry his pack one mile
   NEB   if a man in authority makes
             you go one mile   (c) _____
   JB   if anyone orders you to go
             one mile
   Phps   if anybody forces you to go
             a mile with him
   LB   if the military demand that
             you carry their gear for
             a mile
   YL   _____

             _____

5. Heb 11.24 (see Acts 7.10)
   RSV   son of Pharaoh's daughter   (a) _____
        Compare:
   TEV   son of Pharaoh's daughter   _____
   NEB   son of Pharaoh's daughter
   TNT   son of Pharaoh's daughter   (b)
   LB   the grandson of the king
   GeCL   *son of the Egyptian king's*
             daughter   (c) _____
   Br   *to be an Egyptian prince*
   YL   _____

             _____

(Instructions as for Drill B-20)

1. Isa 1.9
   RSV we should have been like Sodom
       and become like Gomorrah   (a) _____
     Compare: _____
   TEV Jerusalem would have been total-
       ly destroyed, just as Sodom   (b)
       and Gomorrah were
   NEB we should soon have been like
       Sodom, no better than Gomor-   (c) _____
       rah
   LB we would have been wiped out as
       Sodom and Gomorrah were
   NAS we would be like Sodom, we would
       be like Gomorrah
   Br *what happened to Sodom would
       have happened to us, we would
       have experienced the same
       fate as Gomorrah*
   YL _____

       _____

2. Jer 23.14
   RSV all of them have become like   (a) _____
       Sodom to me, and its inhabit-
       ants like Gomorrah   _____
     Compare:
   TEV to me, they are all as bad as   (b)
       the people of Sodom and Go-
       morrah
   JB to me they are all like Sodom   (c) _____
       and its inhabitants all like
       Gomorrah
   NEB to me all her inhabitants are
       like Sodom and Gomorrah
   LB as thoroughly depraved as the
       men of Sodom and Gomorrah were
   NAS all of them have become to Me
       like Sodom, and her inhabit-
       ants like Gomorrah
   YL _____

       _____

4. ANALYSIS IV: KERNEL SENTENCES

Purpose. The purpose of breaking down the surface structure of the text into its underlying kernels is:
   (a) to make sure the translator adequately understands difficult portions
of the text. Usually a translator does not have to break the text down all the way
to kernels, because he can usually readily understand the text and make the transfer
into the receptor language at well above kernel level. However, kernel analysis will
help him to make a proper exegesis when a passage is difficult to understand and
translate.
   (b) to be able to check whether all the truths and fragments of truth have
been translated. For example, Matthew 7.1, LB reads "Don't criticize, and then you

won't be criticized." Because the implicit actor God has not been made explicit, a wrong interpretation by the reader is almost inevitable.

Again, Matthew 7.2, LB reads "For others will treat you as you treat them." This translates only one truth of the text and there are two: God will judge you in the same way you judge others and he will apply to you the same rules or yardstick you apply to others. If the translator had counted the kernels of the truth in the text, he would have realized he was leaving something untranslated.

Or in Matthew 7.21, LB "Not all who sound religious are really godly people. They may refer to me as 'Lord,' but still won't get to heaven." The first kernel has been translated twice. Working only from surface structure a translator will sometimes translate one kernel twice and another not at all. If he checks the number of kernels, however, he can avoid such errors.

(c) to realize that a very complicated surface structure does not have to be translated word for word into a similar complicated surface structure in another language, but it can be broken into the simple kernel sentences which can then be built up into a new and, where necessary, simpler structure. For example, "the baptism of repentance for the remission of sins" (Mark 1.4 KJV) appears in the TEV as "Turn away from your sins and be baptized," he told the people, "and God will forgive your sins."

The number of kernel sentences in each language seems to be small. English, for example, has only seven basic types of kernel sentences:

1. John ran (quickly) [a participant and an intransitive verb with or without a modifying Q].
2. John hit Bill (hard) [a participant and a transitive verb with a second participant as direct object, with or without a modifying Q].
3. John gave Bill the ball [a participant and a transitive verb with two more participants, one direct and the other as the indirect object].
4. John is in the house [a participant linked to a prepositional phrase by the verb to be].
5. John is (very) sick [a participant linked to a Q which can be modified by another Q].
6. John is a boy [a participant linked to a class noun].
7. John is the president (TAPOT uses "John is my father") [two interchangeable participants linked by the verb to be. We can also say "the president is John" (while John F. Kennedy was president of the U.S.A.). This is different from type 6 because not all boys are John. The difference is signaled by the use of the article a or the]. (For more information on kernels, see TAPOT page 40.)

Identifying kernel sentences forces the translator to make the relationship between words clearly explicit. However, the translator needs to be aware that in actual translation many expressions will not occur as full kernels. For example, his son in kernel form could either be "he sired a son" or "he adopted a son." But even where we are dealing with biological descent there is a difference between his son and her son in that she gave birth to a son. Usually, however, his son and her son refer to biological descent. In such cases they are not ambiguous and need not occur as full kernel sentences.

Reducing Of-Phrases to Kernel Sentences
Instructions
(a) Using the previous steps (1) of the PEQR analysis, (2) of clearly stating the relationship between words, and (3) of making implicit information explicit, restate the following of-phrases and possessive constructions as simple kernel sentences. Write the kernel sentence in the space provided and classify each as types 1-7. Many of the examples in the graded drills have been repeated from the earlier drills in the section. This serves as a kind of review.

(b) Compare the translations listed to see whether the expression in question appears in kernel or near kernel form in them.

(c) Write in the translation from your language. If it should be restated closer to a kernel level for easier understanding, make a new translation restating the expression at the simpler level.

Examples

	Rom 15.33	Phil 4.7	Kernel	Type
RSV	God of peace	peace of God	God gives peace	3
Compare:				
TEV	God, our source of peace	God's peace	In Rom 15.33 TEV, TNT, LB, and GeCL	
TNT	God, the giver of peace	God's peace	are in near kernel form, but none ex-	
Phps/NIV/ NAS/NEB	God of peace	peace of God	press the kernel in Phil 4.7; in	
LB	God, who gives peace	God's peace...his peace	fact TEV, TNT sound like "the peace God	
GeCL	*God grant all of you his peace*	*the peace of God*	owns."	
YL	_____			

	Eph 1.18		Kernel	Type
KJV	his calling		he calls [you]	2
Compare:				
TEV	he has called you		All translations ex-	
NEB/TNT	he calls you		cept NAS are in near	
NAS	His calling		kernel form.	
LB/NIV	he has called you			
Phps	he is calling you			
YL	_____			

B-22 New Testament, Gr I: Of-Phrases

1. Acts 17.18

		Kernel	Type
RSV	preacher of foreign divinities	_____	___
Compare:			
TEV	talking about foreign gods		
NEB	propagandist for foreign deities		
LB	he's pushing some foreign religion		
AB	announcer of foreign deities		
YL	_____		

2. John 9.31

		Kernel	Type
RSV	worshiper of God	_____	___
Compare:			
TEV	people who respect him		
NEB	anyone who is devout		
JB	men who are devout		
Phps	the man who has a proper respect for God		
YL	_____		

3. Acts 4.34   Kernel   Type
   RSV   possessors of lands   _____   _____
      Compare:
   TEV   those who owned fields
   NEB   all who had property in land
   JB   all those who owned land
   YL   _____

4. Acts 1.19
   RSV   inhabitants of Jerusalem   _____   _____
      Compare:
   TEV   people living in Jerusalem
   NIV/NEB   everyone in Jerusalem
   NAS/TNT   [all] who were living in Jerusalem
   LB   people of Jerusalem
   Phps   residents of Jerusalem
   YL   _____

5. Phil 1.3
   RSV   my remembrance of you   _____   _____
      Compare:
   TEV   I think of you
   NEB/TNT   I think of you
   NAS   my remembrance of you
   BE   memory of you
   Phps/NIV   I think of you
   YL   _____

6. Matt 2.15
   RSV   death of Herod   _____   _____
      Compare:
   TEV   Herod died
   Phps/NEB   Herod's death
   JB   Herod was dead
   YL   _____

B-23 New Testament, Gr II: Of-Phrases (Instructions as for Drill B-22)

1. Rev 18.12   Kernel   Type
   RSV   articles of ivory   _____   _____
      Compare:
   TEV   objects made of ivory
   NIV   articles...made of ivory
   JB   every piece in ivory
   LB   ivory goods
   TNT   articles of ivory
   YL   _____

2. 2 Tim 1.8
   RSV   power of God   _____   _____
      Compare:
   TEV   God gives you the strength
   NEB   strength that comes from God
   JB   power of God
   Phps   strength that God gives you
   YL   _____

3. Acts 21.35   Kernel _____ Type ____

    RSV   the violence of the crowd

       Compare:

    TEV   the mob was wild

    Phps/NEB the violence of the mob

    JB   the crowd became so violent

    YL   _____

4. John 6.48   Kernel _____ Type ____

    RSV   bread of life

       Compare:

    TEV   bread of life

    Phps/NEB bread of life

    AB   Bread of life—that gives life,

                 the living bread

    SpCL   *the bread that gives life*

    YL

5. 1 Thes 5.23   Kernel _____ Type ____

    RSV   God of peace

       Compare:

    TEV   God who gives us peace

    JB/NEB   God of peace

    Brc   God...who gave you peace

    YL   _____

6. Rom 2.4   Kernel _____ Type ____

    KJV   goodness of God

       Compare:

    TEV   God is kind

    RSV   God's kindness

    Phps/NEB God's kindness

    YL   _____

B-24 Old Testament, Gr: Of-Phrases (Instructions as for Drill B-22)

1. Prov 22.2   Kernel _____ Type ____

    RSV   the maker of them

       Compare:

    TEV   the LORD made them

    JB   Yahweh has made them

    NEB   the LORD made them

    BE   the maker of them

    Mft   the Eternal who made them

    YL   _____

2. Isa 45.16   Kernel _____ Type ____

    RSV   makers of idols

       Compare:

    TEV   those who make idols

    NEB   those who make idols

    JB   makers of idols

    BE   makers of images

    YL   _____

3. Gen 14.19
   RSV   maker of heaven and earth
        Compare:
   TEV   who made heaven and earth
   JB/NEB   creator of heaven and earth
   YL

4. Eccl 7.6
   RSV   laughter of the fools
        Compare:
   TEV   a fool laughs
   NEB   laughter of a fool
   JB   laughter of fools
   YL

5. Psa 51.14
   RSV   God of my salvation
        Compare:
   TEV   God...save me
   JB   God my saviour
   NEB   God, my deliverer
   LB   God, you alone can rescue me
   YL

6. Psa 9.1
   RSV   thy wonderful deeds
        Compare:
   TEV   the wonderful things you have done
   JB   your marvels
   NIV   thy marvellous acts
   NAS   Thy wonders
   YL

7. Gen 21.14
   RSV   a skin of water
        Compare:
   TEV   a leather bag full of water
   NEB   a waterskin full of water
   LB   a canteen of water
   YL

8. Exo 5.3
   RSV   God of the Hebrews
        Compare:
   TEV   God of the Hebrews
   NEB/LB   God of the Hebrews
   YL

9. Gen 21.16
   RSV   [see] the death of the child
        Compare:
   TEV   my child die
   NEB/JB   the child die
   LB   him die
   BE   the death of my child
   Mft   the child dying
   YL

Kernel   Type

		Kernel	Type
10.	Eccl 5.19		
	RSV gift of God	_____	____
	Compare:		
	TEV/JB gift from God		
	BE given by God		
	NEB gift of God		
	YL	_____	

		Kernel	Type
11.	Hos 3.1		
	KJV love of the LORD	_____	____
	Compare:		
	TEV I [the LORD] still love		
	RSV the LORD loves		
	JB Yahweh gives his love		
	YL	_____	

		Kernel	Type
12.	1 Sam 2.3		
	RSV God of knowledge	_____	____
	Compare:		
	TEV God who knows		
	NEB God of all knowledge		
	JB an all-knowing God		
	LB the Lord knows		
	YL	_____	

Reducing Possessive Phrases to Kernel Sentences

B-25 New Testament, Gr: Possessive Phrases (Instructions as for Drill B-22)

		Kernel	Type
1.	Rom 1.9		
	RSV my prayers	_____	____
	Compare:		
	TEV I pray		
	JB/NEB my prayers		
	LB I pray		
	Phps my prayers		
	YL	_____	

		Kernel	Type
2.	Matt 11.5		
	RSV their sight	_____	____
	Compare:		
	TEV [the blind] can see		
	NEB/Phps their sight		
	BE [the blind] see		
	JB [the blind] see again		
	YL	_____	

		Kernel	Type
3.	Matt 12.18		
	RSV my beloved	_____	____
	Compare:		
	TEV the one I love		
	NEB my beloved		
	GeCL *I love him*		
	YL	_____	

4. Rom 11.34

    RSV   his counselor

      Compare:

    TEV   able to give him advice

    TNT   his adviser

    JB/LB   his counselor

    NEB/Phps his counsellor

    YL

Kernel   **Type**

5. Matt 13.44

    RSV   his joy

      Compare:

    TEV   he is so happy

    NEB   the man...for sheer joy

    Phps   a man...overjoyed

    TNT/NIV his joy

    JB   he...goes off happy

    YL

6. Matt 20.15

    RSV   my generosity

      Compare:

    TEV   I am generous

    NEB   I am kind

    JB/Phps I am generous

    TNT   I am generous

    YL

B-26 Old Testament, Gr: Possessive Phrases (Instructions as for Drill B-22)

1. Prov 14.31

    RSV   his Maker

      Compare:

    TEV   God who made them

    BE/NEB   his Maker

    LB   God who made them

    JB   his creator

    YL

Kernel   **Type**

2. Isa 1.3

    RSV   its owner

      Compare:

    TEV   who owns them

    JB/NEB   its owner

    LB   their owner

    YL

3. Psa 7.1

    RSV   my pursuers

      Compare:

    TEV   who pursue me

    NEB   my pursuers

    JB   who hound me

    LB   my persecutors

    YL

4. Psa 106.13
   RSV   his works
      Compare:
   TEV   what he had done
   NEB   all he had done
   JB   his achievements
   YL

5. 1 Chr 12.18
   RSV   your helpers
      Compare:
   TEV   those who help you
   LB   all who aid you
   BE   your helpers
   JB   him that helps you
   YL

6. Psa 51.15
   RSV   thy praise
      Compare:
   TEV   I will praise you
   NEB   thy praise
   JB   your praise
   LB   I will praise you
   YL

7. Jer 17.14
   RSV   [thou art] my praise
      Compare:
   TEV   [you are] the one I praise
   NEB   [thou art] my praise
   Mft   I render praise
   YL

8. Psa 30.10
   RSV   my helper
      Compare:
   TEV   help me
   NEB   my helper
   JB   help me
   YL

9. Psa 38.20
   RSV   my adversaries
      Compare:
   TEV   those who...are against me
   NEB   those who...oppose me
   LB   they...hate me
   YL

10. Hos 5.13
    RSV   his sickness
       Compare:
    TEV   how sick she was
    NEB   he was sick
    LB   how sick they are
    JB   how sick he is
    YL

		Kernel	Type

11. Gen 49.6
```
RSV        their anger
   Compare:
TEV        they...in anger
NEB        their anger
JB         their rage
YL         _____
```

12. Psa 89.8
```
RSV        thy faithfulness
   Compare:
TEV        you are faithful
NEB        thy...faithfulness
LB         faithfulness is your very character
YL         _____
```

13. Job 2.13
```
RSV        his suffering
   Compare:
TEV        he was suffering
LB/NEB     his suffering
BE         his pain
YL         _____
```

Passages Reduced to Kernel Sentences

Introduction. Up to this point we have been analyzing only short phrases and we have been doing our analysis only one step at a time. We now want to practice doing all the steps more or less at once and we want to apply them to whole passages of scripture.

Instructions

(a) Mark all the word pairs that function as single units by means of a hyphen, for example, "the-man."

(b) Make a PEQR analysis marking each word of the text in the space marked (b).

(c) Mark all the implicit PEQR's putting them in ( ).

(d) Whenever this is necessary, try to define the true relationship between words that occur next to each other and write it in the space marked (d).

(e) Now note any pertinent implicit cultural, historical, geographical, or contextual information and write it in the space marked (d).

(f) List the kernel sentences or near kernel sentences in their chronological order under the heading marked Kernels. Identify and write out the R's that link the kernel sentences under the heading Linking R's.

Example
Luke 5.27

(b) R   P(PEP)   P   E   R   (P) E   P   E-P
   After this   he went-out and   saw a-tax collector,
(d)   (context: Jesus healed a man)   (historical/cultural: for Roman government)

- -

(b) E   P   E   R   P-R   P(E)
   named Levi, sitting at his   tax
(d)   (he collected taxes at this office)

- -

(b) P   R   P   E   R   P   (P)   E   P   R   P   E   P
   office; and he said to him,   "Follow me." And he left everything,
(d)(Levi had an office)

- -

(b) R (P)   E   R (P)   E   P
   and   rose and   followed him.
(d)

- -

Linking R's	Kernels
After	(Jesus healed a man)
	Jesus went out
	Jesus saw a man
	the man was called Levi
	he collected taxes (for the Roman government)
	Levi had an office
	Levi sat there
	Levi collected taxes there
and	Jesus said to Levi
	you follow me
and	Levi rose
and	Levi left everything
and	Levi followed Jesus

[97]

Matt 26.6-7

(b)
Now   when   Jesus   was   at   Bethany   in   the   house   of   Simon   the   leper,
(d)

- -

(b)
a   woman   came   up   to   him   with   an   alabaster   jar   of   very   expensive
(d)

- -

(b)
ointment,   and   she   poured   it   on   his   head,   as   he   sat   at   table.
(d)

- -

Linking R's   Kernels

Gen 1.27

(b)
So   God   created   man   in   his   own   image,   in   the   image   of   God
(d)

- -

(b)
he   created   him;   male   and   female   he   created   them.
(d)

- -

Linking R's   Kernels

17552

Intertwined Kernels

Instructions. Frequently two or more kernel sentences are intertwined or doubled up, as it were, into a single phrase of surface structure. Sometimes they overlap totally, sometimes only partially. The overlap can either be in the participants or in space.

(a) Separate or untangle the kernel sentences contained in the following phrases or surface structure, and write the kernels contained in the space provided.

(b) Write in the translation from your language on the line marked YL and see if it retains the intertwining. If it would be better to separate the kernels, make a new translation that does this.

Example

our beloved ruler contains the kernels: (1) "we love him." (2) "he rules us," which overlap completely; our unbelieving ruler contains the kernels: (1) "he rules us," (2) "he believes not," which overlap only in part. See the kernels of the first expression separated in Spanish: *we have a ruler whom we love*

YL _____

B-29 New Testament: Intertwined Kernels

Note: "See" with references indicates that the meaning or idea is present even though the RSV may use a different construction.

1. our loving savior (see Titus 3.4)   _____

   YL _____   _____

2. our beloved fellow worker (Philemon 1)   _____

   YL _____   _____

3. our faithful creator (see Heb 4.19)   _____

   YL _____   _____

B-30 Old Testament: Intertwined Kernels (Instructions as for Drill B-29)

1. his trusted servant (see Gen 24.2)   _____

   YL _____   _____

2. my master's brethren (Gen 24.27 KJV)   _____

   YL _____   _____

B-31 Multiple Transforms of a Single Kernel

Instructions

(a) Study the following list of biblical and quasi-biblical expressions and write the kernel or kernels contained in them in the blank provided.

(b) Discuss any difference in emphasis, focus, or function that different transforms of the same kernel may have. The discussion can often be usefully begun by discussing a set of simple transforms such as:

[this] sin of ours   she sings beautifully
we and our sin   the beauty of her singing
our habit of sinning   her singing is beautiful
sin-prone as we are   her beautiful singing
the sin of all of us
the sin of us all

1. our sin _____   9. we, sinners _____

2. our sins _____   10. our own sinfulness _____

3. we sinful men _____   11. we continue in sin _____

4. we have sinned _____   12. our continual sinning _____

5. we have been sinful _____   13 [die] in our sin _____

6. we have done sinfully _____   14. sin committed by us _____

7. we have [no] sin _____   15. [forgive] sin _____

8. we are sinners _____   16. [saved us] from sin _____

B-32 New Testament: Kernels and Transforms

Instructions. In the blank area between the passages, write out as many transforms as possible of the biblical expressions listed below. Note the differences in focus, emphasis, or added components that can result from the transform. Consult B-31 as an example of a large number of transforms of a single kernel sentence.

1. Jesus taught his disciples (Mark 9.31 KJV)

2. my imprisonment (Phil 1.14)

B-33 Old Testament: Kernels and Transforms (Instructions as for Drill B-32)

1. Sarah denied (Gen 18.15)

2. Joseph was governor (Gen 42.6)

C. ANALYSIS OF MEANING

1. HIERARCHICAL RELATIONSHIPS BETWEEN MEANINGS OF WORDS

<u>Purpose</u>. In this section we want to become aware of how meanings of words can be related to each other in a hierarchical fashion. This is an important fact for the translator, because whenever a specific meaning gives him trouble in translation, he can then use a hierarchically related but more generic word; for example, if the word <u>wheat</u> is not known in a language but <u>millet</u>, <u>maize</u>, and <u>barley</u> are, the translator may be tempted to choose one of the known words instead. However, if he does use <u>millet</u>, he disregards the historical fact that it was <u>wheat</u>, not <u>millet</u>, in the biblical context. Furthermore, if a language has names for several specific grains or cereals, it usually will also have a way of referring to the group as a whole. In English, <u>grain</u> and <u>cereal</u> are two such generic words. If we used either one of them in a translation, we would be using a word that includes <u>wheat</u>. We applied this principle when we classified geographical names in Drills A-18 and A-19 and again when we adjusted the biblical form to the receptor language in Drills A-3 to A-16. In the latter we also learned that we can focus the meaning of the generic word by qualifying it; for example, when using the generic word <u>grain</u> for wheat, we might be able to refer to it as the <u>bread grain</u>, that is, the grain from which bread is made.

<u>Instructions</u>

(a) Arrange the following English words according to the hierarchical order of their meaning in the blank space provided on the right side of the paper. Remember that some words can function at more than one level in the hierarchy.

(b) Write the equivalent words from your language into the blank provided and see whether they form their pattern in the same hierarchical arrangement.

<u>Example</u>

dog, animal, mammal, canine, alsatian, Snoopy (name of a specific alsatian)

```
          \                    /
animal
    \                  /
     mammal (reptile, etc.)
        \            /
         canine (feline, bovine)
            \      /
             dog (wolf, fox, etc.)
               \  /
                alsatian (terrier, beagle, etc.)
                  \ /
                   Snoopy -/
```

YL _____

Evaluation:
   This series can be arranged in the above hierarchy. The expanding "V" over the words is merely an illustration of the broadening of the meaning as you go higher in the hierarchy. In the parentheses we have suggested other words at the same level.

C-1 Hierarchical Relationships Between Meanings of Words in General Vocabulary

1. whisper, speak, murmur, mutter

   YL_____

2. red, pink, color, scarlet, crimson

   YL_____

3. roast, cook, broil, boil, prepare

   YL_____

4. cat, kitten, mammal, tiger, animal

   YL_____

5. swim, crawl, move, walk, run, march,
   dance, stroll, sprint

   YL_____

6. worship, prayer, intercession, holy
   communion

   YL_____

C-2 Hierarchical Relationships Between More Generic and More Specific Meanings

   Instructions. In the blanks provided write in a more generic word (upper blank) and a more specific word (lower blank).

Example		
school	building	(generic)
	synagogue	(specific: a school for the Jews)

1. apostle   _____

2. ointment   _____

3. bread   _____

4. law of Moses   _____

5. cattle   _____

6. religious feast   _____

7. fish   _____

8. pray   _____

9. bird of prey   _____

10. sacrifice   _____

11. wolf   _____

12. centurion   _____

2. COMPONENTS OF MEANING

Purpose. In this drill section we want to learn to identify four kinds of components of meaning:

(a) Generic components give us the meaning domain to which the word belongs. They are the answer to the question: To what tribe or family of things does this word or series of words belong? We have already been doing this when we classified geographical names as cities, rivers, etc.

(b) Shared components help us recognize which words are more closely related to each other, because the more components of meaning two words share, the closer their meaning is to each other. Shared components answer the question: What makes these two to be close relatives?

(c) Distinctive components are those components that are unique to the meaning of a word. They help us to define or recognize a specific word. They answer the question: What characteristics help us to distinguish this one from all the others that are similar?

(d) Supplementary components are of two kinds. The first kind (d-1) are components that are not required for distinguishing one word from another; for example, when chair and bench are compared the chair may have an armrest, but that would be a supplementary component. If a group of chairs was being compared, however, the armrest, if it occurred only on one chair, could then be a distinctive component. The second kind of supplementary components (d-2) are special features of meaning which are added to a word in a given culture and which become the basis for figurative extensions; for example, when the fox in European stories always is a cunning cheater, people in that culture will understand the statement he is a fox to mean "he is a cunning cheater." Supplementary components of the second kind will be largely disregarded at this stage. They will be studied when we analyze figurative language. Not all words have the second kind of supplementary components attached to their meaning.

Instructions

(a) Study the following word series and list the four kinds of components we have described. If your language attaches a different supplementary component to any of the words, fill it in on line d-3.

(b) Where space is provided, select four words from your language in the same domain and make a similar componential analysis.

Example

	chair	bench	stool
a.	man-made articles, used for sitting		
b.	for one person only	for several people (distinguishes it from chair/stool)	for one person only
c.	with a back (distinguishes chair from stool)		
d-1	has armrests		has 3 or 4 legs
d-2	to lead a meeting	to be a judge	
d-3	_____	_____	_____

Components of Meaning in Words with Related Meanings

C-3 Components of Meaning in General Vocabulary

1. [Frame: With a bicycle one can travel on a...]

	path	street	road	highway
a.				
b.				
c.				
d-1				
d-2				
d-3				

2. [Frame: In every home there should be...]

	axe	hoe	machete	pick
a.				
b.				
c.				
d-1				
d-2				
d-3				

3. [Frame: Some sinners experience...]

	repentance	remorse	conversion	penance
a.				
b.				
c.				
d-1				
d-2				

Select words from your language which cover approximately the same area of meaning as the above words.

YL				
a.				
b.				
c.				
d-3				

Restating the Meanings of Words on the Basis of Their Essential Components

Purpose. Many words, especially those whose cultural meaning is unknown to us, are hard to translate. In this drill we want to practice restating the meaning of words on the basis of their essential components. This may involve a generic component and one or more distinctive components, or merely some of the distinctive ones.

Instructions

(a) Restate the meaning of the following biblical words on the basis of their essential components in English (on the line marked E) and in your own language (on the line marked YL).

(b) Compare the translations listed below and see whether they have made the essential components readily understandable for the reader. Write your evaluation in the space marked (c).

Example
Gen 8.20

RSV	altar	E.	place of sacrifice, usually built of stone
	Compare:		
TEV	altar		
NEB	altar	YL	
*	a sacrificing place built of stone		
YL	_____	(c)	The special translation gives us the generic component and says of what it is built.

C-4 New Testament: Restating Meanings of Words by Components

1. Matt 18.6

KJV	millstone	E.	_____
	Compare:		
TEV	large millstone	YL	_____
BE	great stone		
LB	rock	(c)	
YL	_____		

2. Matt 19.12

RSV	eunuch	E.	_____
	Compare:		
TEV	[reasons why] men cannot marry	YL	_____
BE	men...without sex	(c)	
LB	some...without the ability to marry		
NEB	some are incapable of marriage		
YL	_____		

3. Matt 21.23

RSV	[by what] authority	E.	_____
	Compare:		
TEV	[what] right do you have	YL	_____
GeCL	*who gave you the right*		
YL	_____	(c)	

4. Matt 26.71
   RSV   porch   E. _____
         Compare:
   TEV   entrance of the courtyard   YL _____
   BE   doorway
   LB   gate   (c)
   NEB   gateway
   YL   _____

5. Mark 1.5
   RSV   baptized   E. _____
         Compare:
   TEV   baptized   YL _____
   Em   *head-poured*
   YL   _____   (c)

6. Mark 1.13
   RSV   angels   E. _____
         Compare:
   TEV   angels   YL _____
   GeCL   *God's angels*
   ZT   *messenger from heaven*   (c)
   YL
           _____

7. Luke 1.11
   RSV   altar of incense   E. _____
         Compare:
   TEV   altar where the incense was   YL _____
                   burned
   *   incense burning place   (c)
   YL   _____

8. Luke 2.7
   RSV   manger   E. _____
         Compare:
   TEV   manger   YL _____
   BE   the place where the cattle
                   had their food   (c)
   GeCL   *crib for animal feed*
   YL   _____

C-5 Old Testament: Restating Meanings of Words by Components (Instructions as for
    Drill C-4)

1. Gen 3.24
   RSV   cherubim   E. _____
         Compare:
   TEV   living creatures   YL _____
   LB   mighty angels
   JB   cherubs   (c)
   Ch   *heavenly guards*
   YL   _____

2. Gen 4.3
   RSV   offering   E. _____
        Compare:
   TEV   offering   YL _____
   NEB/LB   gift
   Em   *given to God freely*   (c)
   YL   _____

3. Gen 35.17
   RSV   midwife   E. _____
        Compare:
   TEV   midwife   YL _____
   LB/JB/NEB   midwife
   Em   *birth helper*   (c)
   YL   _____

4. Gen 38.18
   RSV   signet   E. _____
        Compare:
   TEV   seal   YL _____
   LB   identification seal
   YL   _____   (c)

5. Gen 40.1
   RSV   butler
        Compare:
   TEV   wine steward
   LB   wine-taster
   JB   cup-bearer
   YL   _____

6. 2 Kgs 16.3
   KJV   heathen   E. _____
        Compare:
   TEV   people   YL _____
   JB/NEB   nations
   LB   nations around Judah   (c)
   ZT   *not knowing God*
   YL   _____

<u>Components of Meaning in Single Words with Multiple Meanings</u>
   <u>Purpose.</u> In this drill section we want to learn to recognize:
   (a) that the meaning of a word usually does not represent a point of meaning
but rather covers an area of meaning.
   (b) that the area of meaning, covered by one word in Greek, need not be
covered by the one word in other languages; in fact, languages seldom match completely in the areas of meaning covered by individual words.
   (c) that in a given context not the entire area of meaning of the word is
indicated but rather a specific part of it, namely, the part that fits into this
context.
   (d) that a careful analysis of the different components in focus in different contexts can help us make a more faithful translation.
   (e) that very often the context, over and beyond the general contextual in-
dicators, contains markers that point out the specific meaning intended. We will
try and learn the above by using several approaches to studying words with many
meanings.

C-6 Componential Analysis of Some Meanings of the Word "Coat"

Instructions

(a) Study the following sentences using the English word "coat" and make a componential analysis of the various meanings.

(b) Define the specific components that are essential to each context and see whether they are expressed explicitly by means of a marker.

1. I have a warm coat for winter.
2. The coat of my suit has a torn elbow.
3. In winter some dogs have a very shaggy coat.
4. Coat all the metal parts with grease.
5. One coat of paint will be enough.
6. The coat of this seed is very tough.

(a) generic component(s) _____

(b) shared components _____

_____

(c) essential components _____

indicated by the general context	indicated by a special marker
1. _____	_____
2. _____	_____
3. _____	_____
4. _____	_____
5. _____	_____
6. _____	_____

C-7 Componential Analysis of Greek *oikos* "House"

Instructions

(a) Analyze the meanings of the Greek word *oikos* "house" in the contexts provided, following the instructions for C-6 (a). Be sure to consult a good commentary to understand the exegesis of the passage.

(b) Fill in the translation from your language and compare it with the RSV and TEV renderings provided. If the meaning is not clearly expressed, make a new translation that expresses it clearly.

1. Matt 2.11
   RSV going into the <u>house</u>
       Compare:
   TEV went into the house
   YL _____

2. Luke 1.27
   RSV Joseph, of the <u>house</u> of David
       Compare:
   TEV Joseph, who was a descendant of King David
   YL _____

3. Acts 16.31
   KJV thou shalt be saved and thy <u>house</u>
        Compare:
   TEV you will be saved—you and your family
   YL   _____

   generic component(s) _____

   _____

   shared components _____

   _____

   distinctive components (1) _____

   _____

                       (2) _____

   _____

                       (3) _____

   _____

C-8 Componential Analysis of Hebrew *Etsba* "Finger" (Instructions as for Drill C-7)

1. Exo 8.19
   RSV this is the <u>finger</u> of God
        Compare:
   TEV God has done this
   NEB it is the finger of God
   YL   _____

2. Jer 52.21
   RSV its thickness was four <u>fingers</u>
        Compare:
   TEV was 3 inches thick
   JB   it was four fingers thick
   LB   with three-inch walls
   YL   _____

3. Lev 4.6
   RSV shall dip his <u>finger</u>
        Compare:
   TEV shall dip his finger
   NEB shall dip his finger
   YL   _____

4. Psa 8.3
   RSV thy heavens, the work of thy <u>fingers</u>
        Compare:
   TEV the sky, which you have made
   JB   your heavens, made by your fingers
   YL   _____

5. Psa 144.1
   RSV trains...my <u>fingers</u> for battle
        Compare:
   TEV he trains me for battle
   LB   he gives me...skill in battle
   YL   _____

generic component(s) _____   _____

shared components   _____   _____

distinctive components (1) _____   _____

                       (2) _____   _____

                       (3) _____   _____

                       (4) _____   _____

                       (5) _____   _____

Components of Meaning and Contextually Faithful Translation
     Purpose. In this section of drills on words with many meanings, we want to learn to identify the specific components of meaning that must be made explicit in a given context. This is to help the translator achieve contextual accuracy and consistency rather than verbal consistency which often takes away the meaning from the modern reader.
     Instructions
     (a) Study the different translations and underline the word or expression equivalent to the underlined word in the ASV/KJV/RSV. Now compare the expressions and see which components of the total range of meaning of the word have been made explicit in the various contexts. Write a clear statement of the meaning of the word in this context on the line marked (a).
     (b) Write in the translation from your own language on the line marked YL and underline the equivalent expression.
     (c) Now fill in the summary sheet provided and answer the following questions: What kind of consistency does the ASV/KJV/RSV demonstrate? How many different renderings does English require to express the meaning clearly in all the contexts given? Which translations are contextually consistent? What kind of consistency does your language show? How many different renderings do you need in your language to express the meaning clearly?

C-9 New Testament: Contextually Faithful Translation of Greek *Sarcs* "Flesh"

1. Matt 16.17   (a) _____
   ASV <u>flesh</u> and blood hath not revealed it unto thee
   TEV <u>this</u> truth did not come to you from any human being
   NEB you did not learn that from mortal man
   JB   it was not flesh and blood that revealed this to you
   NIV this was not revealed to you by man
   YL   _____

2. Matt 19.5   (a)_____
ASV   the twain shall become one <u>flesh</u>
TEV   the two will become one
NEB   the two shall become one flesh
NIV   the two will become one flesh
JB   the two become one body
YL   _____

3. Matt 26.41   (a)_____
ASV   the spirit indeed is willing, but the <u>flesh</u> is weak
TEV   the spirit is willing, but the flesh is weak
GeCL *you have good intentions, but you are only weak human beings*
NEB   the spirit is willing, but the flesh is weak
JB   the spirit is willing, but the flesh is weak
NIV   the spirit is willing, but the body is weak
YL   _____

4. Luke 24.39   (a)_____
ASV   a spirit hath not <u>flesh</u> and bones
TEV   a ghost doesn't have flesh and bones
NEB   no ghost has flesh and bones
JB   a ghost has no flesh and bones
NIV   a ghost does not have flesh and bones
YL   _____

5. John 1.14   (a)_____
ASV   the Word became <u>flesh</u>
TEV   the Word became a human being
GeCL *he, whose name is "the Word," became a human being*
NEB   the Word became flesh
JB   the Word was made flesh
NIV   the Word became flesh
YL   _____

6. John 8.15   (a)_____
ASV   ye judge after the <u>flesh</u>
TEV   you make judgments in a purely human way
NEB   you judge by worldly standards
JB   you judge by human standards
NIV   you judge by human standards
YL   _____

7. Acts 2.17   (a)_____
ASV   pour out my Spirit upon all <u>flesh</u>
TEV   pour out my Spirit upon all men
NEB   pour out upon everyone a portion of my spirit
JB   pour out my spirit on all mankind
NIV   pour out my Spirit on all people
YL   _____

8. Rom 2.28   (a)_____
ASV   circumcision, which is outward in the <u>flesh</u>
TEV   whose circumcision is a physical thing
NEB   neither is the true circumcision the external mark in the flesh
JB   circumcision is more than a physical operation
NIV   nor is circumcision merely outward and physical
YL   _____

9. Rom 8.3a   (a)_____

    ASV   what the law could not do, in that it was weak through the flesh

    TEV   what the Law could not do, because human nature was weak

    NEB   what the law could never do, because our lower nature robbed it of all
           potency

    JB   what the Law, because of our unspiritual nature, was unable to do

    NIV   what the law was powerless to do in that it was weakened by our sinful
           nature

    YL   _____

10. Rom 8.3b   (a)_____

    ASV   in the likeness of sinful flesh

    TEV   a nature like man's sinful nature

    NEB   in a form like that of our own sinful nature

    JB   in a body as physical as any sinful body

    NIV   in the likeness of sinful man

    YL

11. Rom 11.14   (a)_____

    ASV   provoke to jealousy them that are my flesh

    TEV   make the people of my own race jealous

    NEB   to stir emulation in the men of my own race

    JB   make my own people envious of you

    NIV   arouse my own people to envy

    YL   _____

12. 1 Cor 1.26   (a)_____

    ASV   not many wise after the flesh

    TEV   few of you were wise...from the human point of view

    NEB   few of you are men of wisdom, by any human standard

    JB   how many of you were wise in the ordinary sense of the word

    NIV   not many of you were wise by human standards

    YL   _____

13. 2 Cor 7.5   (a)_____

    ASV   our flesh had no relief

    TEV   we did not have any rest

    NEB   there was still no relief for this poor body of ours

    JB   there was no rest for this body of ours

    NIV   this body of ours had no rest

    YL   _____

14. 2 Cor 10.3   (a)_____

    ASV   for though we walk in the flesh, we do not war according to the flesh

    TEV   it is true that we live in the world; but we do not fight from worldly
           motives

    NEB   weak men we may be, but it is not as such that we fight our battles

    JB   we live in the flesh...but the muscles that we fight with are not flesh

    NIV   we live in the world, we do not wage war as the world does

    YL   _____

15. Gal 2.20   (a)_____
    ASV   that life which I now live in the flesh
    TEV   this life that I live now
    NEB   the life I now live
    JB   the life I now live in this body
    NIV   the life I live in the body
    YL   _____

    Summary Sheet on *Sarcs*

Reference	ASV	TEV	NEB	JB	NIV	YL
Matt 16.17	flesh					
Matt 19.5	flesh					
Matt 26.41	flesh					
Luke 24.39	flesh					
John 1.14	flesh					
John 8.15	flesh					
Acts 2.17	flesh					
Rom 2.28	flesh					
Rom 8.3a	flesh					
Rom 8.3b	flesh					
Rom 11.14	flesh					
1 Cor 1.26	flesh					
2 Cor 7.5	flesh					
2 Cor 10.3	flesh					
Gal 2.20	flesh					

C-10 Old Testament: Contextually Faithful Translation of Hebrew *Basar* "Flesh" (Instructions as for Drill C-9)

1. Gen 2.21   (a)_____
    KJV   he took one of his ribs, and closed up the flesh
    TEV   he took out one of the man's ribs and closed up the flesh
    JB   he took one of his ribs and enclosed it in flesh
    NAS   He took one of his ribs, and closed up the flesh
    LB   took one of his ribs and closed up the place
    YL   _____

2. Gen 2.23   (a)_____
   KJV   bone of my bones and flesh of my flesh
   TEV   bone taken from my bone and flesh from my flesh
   JB   bone from my bones, and flesh from my flesh
   NAS   bone of my bones, and flesh of my flesh
   LB   part of my own bone and flesh
   YL   _____

3. Gen 2.24   (a)_____
   KJV   cleave unto his wife: and they shall be one flesh
   TEV   united with his wife, and they become one
   JB   joins himself to his wife, and they become one body
   NAS   cleave to his wife; and they shall become one flesh
   LB   joined to his wife in such a way that the two became one person
   YL   _____

4. Gen 6.3   (a)_____
   KJV   my spirit shall not always strive with man, for that he also is flesh
   TEV   I will not allow people to live forever; they are mortal
   JB   my spirit must not for ever be disgraced in man, for he is but flesh
   NAS   My Spirit shall not strive with man forever, because he also is flesh
   LB   my Spirit must not forever be disgraced in man, wholly evil as he is
   YL   _____

5. Gen 6.12   (a)_____
   KJV   all flesh had corrupted his way
   TEV   the people were all living evil lives
   JB   corrupt were the ways of all flesh
   NAS   all flesh had corrupted their way
   LB   all mankind was vicious and depraved
   YL   _____

6. Gen 6.19   (a)_____
   KJV   of every living thing of all flesh
   TEV   of every kind of animal and of every kind of bird
   JB   from all living creatures, from all flesh
   NAS   of every living thing of all flesh
   LB   of every animal
   YL   _____

7. Gen 17.11   (a)_____
   KJV   ye shall circumcise the flesh of your foreskin
   TEV   you must circumcise every baby boy
   JB   you shall circumcise your foreskin
   NAS   you shall be circumcised in the flesh of your foreskin
   LB   be circumcised; the foreskin of his penis shall be cut off
   YL   _____

8. Gen 17.13   (a)_____
   KJV   my covenant shall be in your flesh for an everlasting covenant
   TEV   this will be a physical sign to show that my covenant with you is everlast-
         ing
   JB   my Covenant shall be marked on your bodies as a Covenant in perpetuity
   NAS   shall My covenant be in your flesh for an everlasting covenant
   LB   your bodies will thus be marked as participants in my everlasting covenant
   YL   _____

9. Exo 16.3   (a)_____
   KJV   in the land of Egypt when we sat by the flesh pots
   TEV   there [in Egypt] we could at least sit down and eat meat
   JB   in the land of Egypt, when we were able to sit down to pans of meat
   NAS   in the land of Egypt, when we sat by the pots of meat
   LB   in Egypt...we had plenty to eat
   YL   _____

10. Num 18.15   (a)_____
   KJV   every thing that openeth the matrix in all flesh
   TEV   every first-born child or animal
   JB   every first-born...of all living creatures, whether man or beast
   NAS   every first issue of the womb of all flesh
   LB   the firstborn sons of the people of Israel, and the firstborn of their
             animals
   YL   _____

11. Deut 32.42   (a)_____
   KJV   my sword shall devour flesh
   TEV   my sword will kill all
   JB   my sword shall feed on flesh
   NAS   My sword shall devour flesh
   LB   my sword devours the flesh and the blood
   YL   _____

12. 2 Kgs 5.10   (a)_____
   KJV   thy flesh shall come again to thee and thou shalt be clean
   TEV   he would be completely cured of his disease
   JB   your flesh will become clean once more
   NAS   your flesh shall be restored to you and you shall be clean
   LB   he would be healed of every trace of his leprosy
   YL   _____

13. 2 Chr 32.8   (a)_____
   KJV   with him is an arm of flesh
   TEV   he has human power
   JB   he has only an arm of flesh
   NAS   with him is only an arm of flesh
   LB   he has a great army, but they are all mere men
   YL   _____

14. Job 7.5   (a)_____
   KJV   my flesh is clothed with worms
   TEV   my body is full of worms
   JB   vermin cover my flesh
   NAS   my flesh is clothed with worms
   LB   my skin is filled with worms
   YL   _____

15. Job 10.4   (a)_____
   KJV   hast thou eyes of flesh?
   TEV   do you see things as we do?
   JB   have you got human eyes?
   NAS   hast Thou eyes of flesh?
   LB   are you unjust like men?
   YL   _____

16. Ezek 16.26　　　　　　　　　　　　　　(a)_____
　　　KJV　the Egyptians thy neighbors, great of <u>flesh</u>
　　　TEV　your lustful neighbors, the Egyptians
　　　JB　　those big-membered neighbours, the Egyptians
　　　NAS　the Egyptians, your lustful neighbors
　　　LB　　lustful Egypt
　　　YL　　_____

17. Hag 2.12　　　　　　　　　　　　　　　(a)_____
　　　KJV　if one bear holy <u>flesh</u> in the skirt of his garment
　　　TEV　suppose someone takes a piece of consecrated meat from a sacrifice and
　　　　　　carries it in a fold of his robe
　　　JB　　if a man carries consecrated meat in the fold of his gown
　　　NAS　if a man carries holy meat in the fold of his garment
　　　LB　　if one of you is carrying a holy sacrifice in his robes
　　　YL　　_____

Summary Sheet on *Basar*

Reference	KJV	TEV	NAS	JB	LB	YL
Gen 2.21	flesh					
Gen 2.23	flesh					
Gen 2.24	flesh					
Gen 6.3	flesh					
Gen 6.12	flesh					
Gen 6.19	flesh					
Gen 17.11	flesh					
Gen 17.13	flesh					
Exo 16.3	flesh					
Num 18.15	flesh					
Deut 32.42	flesh					
2 Kgs 5.10	flesh					
2 Chr 32.8	flesh					
Job 7.5	flesh					
Job 10.4	flesh					
Ezek 16.26	flesh					
Hag 2.12	flesh					

3. MARKING SPECIFIC MEANINGS IN WORDS WITH MULTIPLE MEANINGS

Purpose. As we have seen in the previous section, a word can have a wide range of meanings. As a result, if the intended meaning is not marked specifically in the context, the statement may be ambiguous. We therefore want to learn to recognize those contexts in which words with multiple meanings already carry a marker, as well as those contexts where the specific meanings are not marked, thereby leaving the meaning ambiguous.

C-11 Marking Specific Meanings of "Father"

Instructions. In the blanks provided, add the necessary markers to the English word father so as to specify the various specific meanings. List as many alternatives as possible. How do we distinguish 1-3 in direct address?

1. as biological progenitor _____
_____
_____
_____

2. referring to God _____
_____
_____
_____

3. referring to a priest _____
_____
_____
_____

4. referring to the originator _____
_____
_____
_____

Passages with Marked Meanings
    Instructions
    (a) Study the RSV passages and identify the word or words which mark the specific meaning of the underlined expression and write them on the line marked (a).
    (b) Compare the various translations presented to see whether they contain adequate marking, and write your findings in the space marked (b). If the translation into your language is not clearly marked, make one with the necessary marker(s).

Example
Ezra 1.7   (a) of the LORD [see (a continued) below
RSV   vessels of the house of the LORD   for more explanation]
    Compare:
TEV   bowls and cups...from the Temple
        in Jerusalem
NEB   vessels of the house of the LORD
JB   vessels of the Temple of Yahweh
LB   gold bowls and other valuable
        items...from the Temple at
        Jerusalem
NAS   articles of the house of the LORD
YL   _____

    (a continued) The word house is here marked with the expression of the LORD to show that we are referring to the Temple and not just an ordinary house.

    (b) All translations have clearly indicated the Temple, either by using the word Temple instead of house, or by retaining a marking similar to RSV. TEV and LB add "at Jerusalem" to further specify which Temple.

C-12 Old Testament: Words with Marked Meanings

1. Gen 16.12   (a)_____
    RSV   he shall be a wild ass of a man
        Compare:
    TEV   your son will live like a wild donkey
    NEB   he shall be a man like the wild ass
    JB   a wild-ass of a man he will be
    LB   son of yours...will be a wild one—
            free and untamed as a wild ass
    NAS   he will be a wild donkey of a man
    YL   _____

    (b)

2. Gen 24.16   (a)_____
   RSV   a virgin, whom <u>no man had known</u>
              Compare:
   TEV   a...young girl and still a
              virgin
   NEB   a virgin, who had had no inter-
              course with a man
   JB   a virgin, no man had touched her
   LB   a...young girl
   NAS   a virgin, and no man had had
              relations with her

   YL   _____

   (b)

3. Gen 30.2   (a)_____
   RSV   who withheld from you the <u>fruit</u>
              of the womb
              Compare:
   TEV   the one who keeps you from
              having children
   JB   who has refused you motherhood
   NEB   who has denied you children
   LB   the one who is responsible for
              your barrenness
   NAS   who has withheld from you the
              fruit of the womb

   YL   _____

   (b)

4. Gen 40.1   (a)_____
   RSV   offended their <u>lord</u> the king
              of Egypt
              Compare:
   TEV   the king of Egypt...offended
              the king
   NEB/JB offended their master the king
              of Egypt
   LB   the king of Egypt became angry
   NAS   offended their lord, the king
              of Egypt

   YL   _____

   (b)

5. Gen 41.46   (a) _____
   RSV   he entered the service of
           Pharaoh king of Egypt
       Compare:
   TEV   he began to serve the king of
           Egypt
   NEB   he entered the service of
           Pharaoh king of Egypt
   JB   he appeared before Pharaoh
           king of Egypt
   LB   he entered the service of the
           king [of Egypt]
   NAS   he stood before Pharaoh, king
           of Egypt

   YL   _____

   (b)

Passages with Specific Meanings Unmarked
     Instructions
     (a) The underlined word has several meanings, but the context here does not
mark the specific meaning intended. Provide the necessary marker on the line marked
(a).

     (b) Study the other translations provided, including the one from your lan-
guage, to see whether they have cleared up the ambiguity and how they have done it,
and write your findings in the space marked (b). If the translation in your language
is ambiguous, make a new translation that clearly specifies the intended meaning.

Example
Ezra 3.12   (a) of the LORD [see (a continued) be-
RSV when they saw the foundation of   low for more explanation]
        this house being laid
     Compare:
TEV as they watched the foundation of
        this Temple being laid
NEB when they saw the foundation of
        this house laid
JB   since the foundations of the Temple
        of Yahweh had now been laid
LB   because the foundation of the Temple
        had been laid [verse 11]
NAS when the foundation of this house
        was laid before their eyes
YL   _____

     (a continued) House here refers to the Temple at Jerusalem. The ambiguity
can be removed by adding of the LORD or by calling it by the specific name Temple
rather than using the generic word house.

     (b) NEB and NAS retain the nonspecific expression, while TEV, LB and JB use
Temple. JB adds of Yahweh.

---

1. Gen 7.2   (a)_____
   RSV   take with you seven pairs
                     of all <u>clean</u> animals
         Compare:
   TEV   take with you seven pairs
                     of each kind of ritually
                     clean animal
   NEB   take with you seven pairs,
                     male and female, of all
                     beasts that are ritually
                     clean
   JB   of all the clean animals you
                     must take seven of each
                     kind
   LB   a pair of each, except those
                     kinds I have chosen for
                     eating and for sacrifice:
                     take seven pairs of each
                     of them
   NAS   you shall take with you of
                     every clean animal seven
                     pairs
   YL   _____

   (b)

2. Gen 21.14   (a)_____
   RSV   took...a <u>skin</u> of water
         Compare:
   TEV   gave...a leather bag full
                     of water
   NEB   took...a waterskin full of
                     water
   JB   took...a skin of water
   LB   strapped a canteen of water
   NAS   took...a skin of water
   YL   _____

   (b)

3. Gen 29.11   (a)_____
   RSV   Jacob <u>kissed</u> Rachel
         Compare:
   TEV   he kissed her
   NEB   he kissed Rachel
   NAS/LB/JB   Jacob kissed Rachel
   *   Jacob greeted Rachel with
                     a kiss
   YL   _____

   (b)

4. Gen 29.11   (a)_____
   RSV   and wept aloud
        Compare:
   TEV   and began to cry for joy
   NEB   and was moved to tears
   JB   and burst into tears
   LB   and started crying
   NAS   and lifted his voice and
                    wept

   YL   _____

   (b)

5. Exo 4.27   (a)_____
   RSV   [Aaron met Moses] and kissed
                    him
        Compare:
   TEV   when he met him, he kissed
                    him
   NAS/JB/NEB Aaron met him and he kissed
                    him
   LB   [Aaron] met Moses there, and
                    they greeted each other
                    warmly
   YL   _____

   (b)

Marked and Unmarked Meanings
     Instructions
     (a) Some of the passages quoted contain expressions that require marking.
Identify them and write the necessary marker on the line marked (a). Other passages
contain words with markers. Identify the clarifying marker and write it on the line
marked (a).
     (b) Compare the translations listed, including your language, and see how
they have treated the context. Write your findings in the space marked (b). If there
are ambiguities left in your translation, remove them by providing the necessary
specific markers.

1. Matt 1.6   (a)_____

   RSV   by the <u>wife</u> of Uriah

        Compare:

   TEV   his mother had been Uriah's
                    wife

   NEB   his mother had been the wife
                    of Uriah

   JB   whose mother had been Uriah's
                    wife

   LB   his mother was the ex-wife of
                    Uriah [40th printing]

   TNT   by the widow of Uriah

   Phps/NIV   whose mother had been Uriah's
                    wife

   NAS   by her who had been the wife
                    of Uriah

   YL   _____

   (b)

2. Matt 8.16   (a)_____

   RSV   and he cast out the <u>spirits</u>
                    with a word

        Compare:

   TEV   Jesus drove out the evil
                    spirits with a word

   NEB   he drove the spirits out with
                    a word

   JB   he cast out the spirits with
                    a word

   LB   when he spoke a single word,
                    all the demons fled

   TNT   he drove out the spirits with
                    a word

   Phps   evil spirits, which he ex-
                    pelled with a word

   NIV   he drove out the spirits with
                    a word

   NAS   He cast out the spirits with
                    a word

   YL   _____

   (b)

1. Gen 33.4   (a)_____
   RSV   kissed him, and they <u>wept</u>
         Compare:
   TEV   kissed him. They were both
                   crying
   NAS/NEB   kissed him, and they wept
   JB   held him close and wept
   LB   kissed him; and both of them
                   were in tears
   *   kissed him and both wept tears
                   of reconciliation
   YL   _____

   (b)

2. Gen 35.18   (a)_____
   RSV   her <u>soul was departing</u> (for
                   <u>she died)</u>
         Compare:
   TEV   she was dying, and as she
                   breathed her last
   NEB   with her last breath, as she
                   was dying
   JB   she breathed her last, for she
                   was dying
   LB   with Rachel's last breath (for
                   she died)
   NAS   her soul was departing (for
                   she died)
   YL   _____

   (b)

3. Gen 46.29   (a)_____
   RSV   Joseph...fell on his neck, and
                   <u>wept</u>
         Compare:
   TEV   threw his arms around his fa-
                   ther's neck and cried for a
                   long time
   NEB   Joseph...threw his arms round
                   him and wept
   JB   he threw his arms round his
                   neck and...wept
   LB   they fell into each other's
                   arms and wept
   NAS   he fell on his neck and wept
   YL   _____

   (b)

4. Gen 50.1   (a) _____

    RSV   Joseph fell on his father's
             face and wept
          Compare:
    TEV   Joseph threw himself on his
             father, crying
    NEB   Joseph threw himself upon his
             father, weeping
    JB   Joseph threw himself on his
             father, covering his face
             with tears
    LB   Joseph threw himself upon his
             father's body and wept
    NAS   Joseph fell on his father's
             face, and wept
    YL   _____

  (b)

4. CONNOTATIONAL MEANING

C-16 Connotational Meaning in General Vocabulary

    Purpose. In this drill section we want to sharpen our awareness of the fact
that words have connotations over and above their referential meanings. Since languages differ in the connotations they attach to words, the translator must exercise
great care to avoid words with the wrong connotation.
    Instructions
    (a) Analyze the connotative value of the following words as "G" good, "N"
neutral, or "B" bad in both English and in your language. If there are any differences discuss them.

    (b) Classify them according to language level: "T" technical, "F" formal, or
"I" informal.

| | Connotational value | | Language level |
	Your language	English	English
1. communist	_____	_____	_____
2. preacher	_____	_____	_____
3. blood	_____	_____	_____
4. native	_____	_____	_____
5. woman	_____	_____	_____
6. pope	_____	_____	_____
7. son	_____	_____	_____
8. propitiation	_____	_____	_____
9. Portuguese	_____	_____	_____
10. call girl	_____	_____	_____

C-17 Connotational Meaning in Biblical Vocabulary

 Instructions. Identify the connotational overtones in the biblical setting and in your culture. Discuss any differences.

> Example
> John 2.4
> KJV   woman, what have I to do with thee?
>
> In common language English, to address one's own mother as woman would be very impolite.

	Biblical context	Your culture
1. bethrothed (Matt 1.18)	_____	_____
2. dream (Matt 2.22)	_____	_____
3. salt (Matt 5.13)	_____	_____
4. heathen (Matt 6.7; 18.17 KJV)	_____	_____
5. leper (Matt 8.2)	_____	_____
6. tax collectors (Matt 9.11; 11.19)	_____	_____
7. pig/swine (Mark 5.11)	_____	_____
8. poor (Luke 4.18)	_____	_____
9. spirit (Mark 1.12)	_____	_____
10. lightning (Luke 10.18)	_____	_____

C-18 Contradictory Connotations

 Instructions. Sometimes the connotation of a word may weaken, rather than reinforce, the intended meaning in a context. Study the following biblical passages (from unidentified translations). Pay special attention to the connotations of the underlined words, and identify those that do not fit connotationally. Why don't they fit? Write your evaluation in the space provided.

> Example
> Matt 5.3
> "Humble men are very fortunate," he told them, "for the Kingdom of Heaven is given to them."
>   Evaluation:
> Fortunate usually means lucky by chance; this certainly is not the intended meaning.

1. The sight of the star filled them with delight (Matt 2.10).

    Evaluation:

2. One day as he was walking along the beach beside the Lake of Galilee, he saw two brothers—Simon, also called Peter, and Andrew—out in a boat fishing with a net, for they were commercial fishermen (Matt 4.18).

    Evaluation:

3. You are the world's seasoning, to make it <u>tolerable</u>. If you lose your flavor, what will happen to the world? And you yourselves <u>will be</u> thrown out and <u>trampled</u> underfoot as worthless (Matt 5.13).

   Evaluation:

4. You are the earth's salt. But if the salt should become tasteless, what can make it salt again? It is completely useless and can only be thrown out of doors and <u>stamped under foot</u> (Matt 5.13).

   Evaluation:

5. But I warn you—unless your <u>goodness</u> is greater than that of the Pharisees and other Jewish leaders, you <u>can't get</u> into the Kingdom of Heaven at all (Matt 5.20).

   Evaluation:

6. So if your eye—even if it is your <u>best</u> eye!—causes you to lust, <u>gouge it out</u> and throw it away (Matt 5.29).

   Evaluation:

7. If your right eye is <u>your undoing</u>, <u>tear</u> it out and <u>fling</u> it away; it is better for you to lose one part of your body than for the <u>whole</u> of it to be thrown into hell (Matt 5.29).

   Evaluation:

5. EMOTIVE MEANING

Emotively Higher or Lower

   Purpose. In this drill we want to become aware of the fact that the translator's responsibility includes not only accuracy in information, but also emotive accuracy. The translation should not become "jazzed up" emotionally where this emotion is not present in the original, nor should it become blander than the original. The translation should be a faithful reflection of the original, not only in the content of the message, but in the warmth with which this message is communicated. However, since the RSV is already a translation that emphasizes form more than meaning, our translation should probably be at least 30 percent more emotive than the RSV text in order to faithfully reflect the emotive force of the original.

   Instructions

   (a) Study the RSV passage, paying special attention to the underlined words and expressions preceded by a number in parentheses.

   (b) Now compare the equivalent expression in each of the translations listed below with the one underlined in the RSV and try to rank it as the same (s), higher (h), or lower (1), by writing "s," "h," or "1" over the expression.

   (c) When you have marked all the translations, check whether some are consistently higher or lower than the RSV by entering your judgments on the summary lines below the translations.

   (d) Compare the translation in your language with the RSV and rate it "s," "h," or "1."

Example
Matt 15.8-9
RSV This people (1) honors me with their lips, but their (2) heart is far from
     me; (3) in vain do they (4) worship me, teaching (5) as doctrines the
     (6) precepts of men.
   Compare:
                                          s   h
TEV These people, says God, honor me with their words, but their heart is really

                     s   s
     far away from me. It is no use for them to worship me, because they teach

                  h   h
     man-made commandments as though they were God's rules!

                              h   s
NEB This people pays me lip-service, but their heart is far from me; their wor-

          s   s   s   l
     ship of me is in vain, for they teach as doctrines the commandments of men.

YL   _____

   Summary:

TEV (1) s   (2) h   (3) s   (4) s   (5) h   (6) h
NEB   h   s   s   s   s   l
YL   —   —   —   —   —   —

[129]

Luke 7.37

RSV   And (1) behold, a (2) woman of the city, (3) who was a sinner, when she learned that he was (4) at table in the Pharisee's house, brought (5) an alabaster flask of (6) ointment,

    Compare:

TEV   There was a woman in that town who lived a sinful life. She heard that Jesus was eating in the Pharisee's house, so she brought an alabaster jar full of perfume

LB   A woman of the streets—a prostitute—heard he was there and brought an exquisite flask filled with expensive perfume

Phps   A woman, known in the town as a bad character, found out that Jesus was there and brought an alabaster flask of perfume

JB   A woman came in, who had a bad name in the town. She had heard he was dining with the Pharisee and had brought with her an alabaster jar of ointment

YL   _____

    Summary:

	(1)	(2)	(3)	(4)	(5)	(6)
TEV	__	__	__	__	__	__
LB	__	__	__	__	__	__
Phps	__	__	__	__	__	__
JB	__	__	__	__	__	__
YL	__	__	__	__	__	__

Gen 27.39-40

RSV   (1) Behold, away from (2) the fatness of the earth shall your dwelling be, and away from the (3) dew of heaven on high. (4) By your sword you shall live, and you shall (5) serve your brother; but when you (6) break loose you shall (7) break his yoke from your neck.

   Compare:

TEV   No dew from heaven for you, No fertile fields for you. You will live by your sword, But be your brother's slave. Yet when you rebel, You will break away from his control.

NEB   Your dwelling shall be far from the richness of the earth, far from the dew of heaven above. By your sword shall you live, and you shall serve your brother; but the time will come when you grow restive and break off his yoke from your neck

LB   Yours will be no life of ease and luxury, but you shall hew your way with your sword. For a time you will serve your brother, but you will finally shake loose from him and be free

JB   Far from the richness of the earth shall be your dwelling-place, far from the dew that falls from heaven. You shall live by your sword, and you shall serve your brother. But when you win your freedom, you shall shake his yoke from your neck

YL   _____

   Summary:

	(1)	(2)	(3)	(4)	(5)	(6)	(7)
TEV	__	__	__	__	__	__	__
NEB	__	__	__	__	__	__	__
LB	__	__	__	__	__	__	__
JB	__	__	__	__	__	__	__
YL	__	__	__	__	__	__	__

Rhetorical Questions Expressing Emotions

Purpose. Rhetorical questions not only express affirmation or negation, but often they also express distinct feelings of irony, reproof, doubt, indignation, humility, etc.

Instructions

(a) Read the following rhetorical questions and identify the emotion or attitude expressed. Write it on the line marked (a).

(b) Check the translation in your own language and see whether this attitude has been made explicit. If it hasn't, should it be made explicit? If yes, make a new translation that expresses the emotion or attitude clearly. You may consult the TEV when you make your translation.

Example

Matt 8.26

    Why are you afraid, O men of little faith?

YL _____

(a) rebuke

Matt 8.29

    What have you to do with us, O Son of God? Have you come here to torment us before the time?

YL _____

(a) fear

C-21 New Testament: Rhetorical Questions Expressing Emotions

1. Matt 17.17

    And Jesus answered, "O faithless and perverse generation, how long am I to be with you? How long am I to bear with you?"

YL _____

(a)_____

2. Matt 21.20

    When the disciples saw it they marveled, saying, "How did the fig tree wither at once?"

YL _____

(a)_____

3. Mark 4.38

    ...and they woke him and said to him, "Teacher, do you not care if we perish?"

YL _____

(a)_____

4. John 6.9

    There is a lad here who has five barley loaves and two fish; but what are they among so many?

YL _____

(a)_____

5. John 6.30
   So they said to him, "Then what
   sign do you do, that we may
   see, and believe you?"
   YL _____

   (a)_____

6. John 6.52
   The Jews then disputed among themselves, saying, "How can this
   man give us his flesh to eat?"
   YL _____

   (a)_____

7. John 6.70
   Jesus answered them, "Did I not
   choose you, the twelve, and one
   of you is a devil?"

   YL _____

   (a)_____

C-22 Old Testament: Rhetorical Questions Expressing Emotions (Instructions as for
      Drill C-21)

1. Gen 3.13
   The LORD God said to the woman,
   "What is this that you have
   done?"
   YL _____

   (a)_____

2. Gen 13.9
   Abraham said to Lot..."Is not the
   whole land before you?"
   YL _____

   (a)_____

3. Gen 18.12
   Sarah laughed to herself saying,
   "After I have grown old, and my
   husband is old, shall I have
   pleasure?"
   YL _____

   (a)_____

4. Gen 21.7
   [Sarah said] "Who would have said
   to Abraham that Sarah would
   suckle children?"
   YL _____

   (a)_____

5. Gen 25.22
   The children struggled together
   within her; and she said, "If
   this is thus, why do I live?"
   YL _____

   (a)_____

6. Gen 30.15   (a) _____

    [Leah said to Rachel] "Is it a
      small matter that you have taken
      away my husband? Would you take
      away my son's mandrakes also?"

  YL _____

7. Gen 31.36   (a) _____

    Jacob said to Laban, "What is my
      offense? What is my sin, that
      you have hotly pursued me?"

  YL _____

8. Gen 37.10   (a) _____

    [Jacob said to Joseph] "What is this
      dream that you have dreamed? Shall I
      and your mother and your brothers
      indeed come to bow ourselves to the
      ground before you?"

  YL _____

9. Gen 37.30   (a) _____

    [Reuben said] "The lad is gone, and
    I, where shall I go?"

  YL _____

D. TRANSFER AND ADJUSTMENT

Introduction. Languages differ markedly regarding the shape in which they prefer words and expressions to appear in the surface structure of a text. Some languages, like Greek, often change verbs into noun forms, and by so doing they make all the participants in the event implicit. In some languages it is more polite to use the passive instead of the active, especially in cases of aggression, etc. Others use the passive to convey deviousness. In some languages the choice of active over against passive depends on the focus. The item in focus becomes the subject; for example, if the focus is on Bill in a situation where John hits Bill, then the passive will be used as in Bill was hit by John. At other times it may be a matter of old or new information. In such cases the known information appears as the subject of the verb. For example, if John is the known character and Bill, a new character, is the aggressor, then the statement will come out as then John was attacked by Bill. For the Hebrews, for whom the pronouncing of the divine name was taboo, the passive voice is often used in order to avoid the use of God's name, as in you will be judged for "God will judge you." This means that the translator must be aware of the requirements of the receptor language so that he can adjust or change constructions from the original language into the shape required by the receptor language.

In this drill section we want to practice making a few of the many kinds of adjustments that may be required. If a text has been broken down into kernels, such adjustment would come naturally, but all too often the translator goes from the surface structure of the text directly into the surface structure of the receptor language. In the latter case, awareness of the need for adjustment is very important, otherwise foreign usages will be introduced into the translation. Wrong usages may not cause the reader to misunderstand, but they may subtly undermine his psychological confidence in the message without him really being aware of what is actually happening.

1. CHANGING PASSIVE INTO ACTIVE VOICE

Purpose. We want to learn to handle the passive voice so that our translation will reflect the natural usage of the receptor language. Many languages reserve the passive voice for special functions. The translator must not follow the text in its use of the passive, but must change all passives which do not fit the receptor language into their corresponding active or other forms.

Instructions

(a) Rewrite in English the passive constructions as active constructions on the line marked (a).

(b) Now write both the active and the passive, or similar constructions, in your language, and discuss the usage of the passive in this passage. Would the passive be natural here, or would the active or another construction be preferred in your language?

Example

your sins are forgiven (Mark 2.5)   (a) God has forgiven your sins

YL _____   _____

they shall be comforted (Matt 5.4)   (a) God will comfort them

YL _____   _____

he who loves me will be loved (John   (a) my Father will love him who loves me
14.21

YL _____   _____

D-1 New Testament: Changing Passive Into Active Voice

1. you will be hated by all nations (Matt 24.9)

   YL _____

   (a) _____

   _____

2. he who endures to the end will be saved (Matt 24.13)

   YL _____

   (a) _____

   _____

3. this gospel of the kingdom will be preached throughout the whole world (Matt 24.14)

   YL _____

   (a) _____

   _____

4. after two days...the Son of man will be delivered up to be crucified (Matt 26.2)

   YL _____

   (a) _____

   _____

5. this ointment might have been sold for a large sum and given to the poor (Matt 26.9)

   YL _____

   (a) _____

   _____

6. all authority...has been given to me (Matt 28.18)

   YL _____

   (a) _____

   _____

D-2 Old Testament: Changing Passive Into Active Voice (Instructions as for Drill D-1)

1. daughters were born to them (Gen 6.1)

   YL _____

   (a) _____

   _____

2. the windows of the heavens were closed (Gen 8.2)

   YL _____

   (a) _____

   _____

3. blessed by the LORD my God be Shem (Gen 9.26)

   YL _____

   (a) _____

   _____

4. let a little water be brought (Gen 18.4)

   YL _____

   (a) _____

   _____

5. so Isaac was comforted (Gen 24.67)

   YL _____

   (a) _____

   _____

6. Abraham was buried (Gen 25.10)

   YL _____

   (a) _____

   _____

2. CHANGING ACTIVE INTO PASSIVE VOICE

Instructions. Some languages prefer a wide use of the passive or similar forms. If this is the case, many biblical active expressions must be changed into passive or other constructions.

(a) Change the following active constructions into passive voice and write them on the lines marked (a).

(b) Write the passive or similar construction in your language and discuss whether the active or the passive, or another construction, would be more appropriate.

Example
he killed James (Acts 12.2)   (a) James was killed by him _____
YL _____

D-3 New Testament: Changing Active Into Passive Voice

1. so as to lead astray, if possible,   (a)_____
    even the elect (Matt 24.24)
    YL _____

2. when you see all these things, you   (a)_____
    know that he is near (Matt 24.33)
    YL _____

3. you welcomed me (Matt 25.35)   (a)_____
    YL _____

4. Herod feared John, knowing that he was (a)_____
    a righteous and holy man (Mark 6.20)
    YL _____

D-4 Old Testament: Changing Active Into Passive Voice (Instructions as for Drill D-3)

1. he built a city (Gen 4.17)   (a)_____
    YL _____

2. I have slain a man (Gen 4.23)   (a)_____
    YL _____

3. God remembered Noah (Gen 8.1)   (a)_____
    YL _____

4. [Noah] sent forth a raven (Gen 8.7)   (a)_____
    YL _____

5. God blessed Noah (Gen 9.1)   (a)_____
    YL _____

3. CHANGING NOUNS INTO VERBS

Instructions. The Greek uses very many nouns made from verbs. African languages often can make similar abstract nouns, but the resulting constructions are clumsy and unnatural.

(a) Change the underlined nouns to verbal expressions and write your construction on the line marked (a). All quotations are from KJV.

(b) Write the verbal construction in your language and try to decide whether the noun or the verbal expression would be more appropriate.

Examples

he is guilty of <u>death</u> (Matt 26.66)
YL _____

(a) he must die _____

if thou knewest the <u>gift of God</u> (John 4.10)
YL _____

(a) what God gives or God gives something _____

D-5 New Testament: Changing Nouns Into Verbs

1. blessed are they which are persecuted for <u>righteousness'</u> sake (Matt 5.10)
YL _____

(a) _____

2. shall be in danger of <u>judgment</u> (Matt 5.22)
YL _____

(a) _____

3. broad is the way, that leadeth to <u>destruction</u> (Matt 7.13)
YL _____

(a) _____

4. is brought to <u>desolation</u> (Matt 12.25)
YL _____

(a) _____

5. the <u>baptism</u> of John, whence was it? (Matt 21.25)
YL _____

(a) _____

6. let us seize on his <u>inheritance</u> (Matt 21.38)
YL _____

(a) _____

7. which say that there is no <u>resurrection</u> (Matt 22.23)
YL _____

(a) _____

D-6 Old Testament: Changing Nouns Into Verbs (Instructions as for Drill D-5)

1. write this for a <u>memorial</u> in a book   (a)_____
    (Exo 17.14)
    YL_____

2. for out of the abundance of my <u>com-
    plaint</u> (1 Sam 1.16)   (a)_____
    YL_____

3. his eyes shall see his <u>destruction</u>   (a)_____
    (Job 21.20)
    YL_____

4. I will fetch my <u>knowledge</u> from afar   (a)_____
    (Job 36.3)
    YL_____

4. CHANGING NOUNS INTO Q'S (QUALITIES OR QUANTITIES)

    <u>Instructions</u>. The surface structure of Greek (and also the RSV) often expresses quantities and qualities in the form of nouns. This can be misleading in a translation.

    (a) Change the underlined nouns to expressions of quantity or quality on the line marked (a).

    (b) On the line marked YL write an equivalent Q-expression in your language. Try to decide whether the noun or the Q-expression is more natural in your language.

Examples

in their <u>greed</u> (2 Peter 2.3)   (a) they are greedy_____
YL_____

walk in the <u>newness</u> of life (Rom 6.4)   (a) they live in a new different way____
YL_____

the <u>power</u> of the lions (Dan 6.27)   (a) the lions are strong, powerful_____
YL_____

the <u>riches</u> of his <u>kindness</u> (Rom 2.4)   (a) he is kind, he is very kind[a]_____
YL_____

    [a]The last example contains two nouns that express Q's. One Q qualifies the other Q.

D-7 New Testament: Changing Nouns Into Q's

1. they were astonished beyond measure
   (Mark 7.37)
   YL _____

   (a) _____

2. the...power of Elijah (Luke 1.17)
   YL _____

   (a) _____

3. the abundance of his possessions (Luke
   12.15)
   YL _____

   (a) _____

4. the brightness of that light (Acts
   22.11)
   YL _____

   (a) _____

5. overflowed in a wealth of liberality
   (2 Cor 8.2)
   YL _____

   (a) _____

6. by his poverty you might become rich
   (2 Cor 8.9)
   YL _____

   (a) _____

7. elated by the abundance of revelations
   (2 Cor 12.7)
   YL _____

   (a) _____

D-8 Old Testament: Changing Nouns Into Q's (Instructions as for Drill D-7)

1. my power and the might of my hand
   (Deut 8.17)
   YL _____

   (a) _____

2. out of the abundance of my complaint
   (1 Sam 1.16 KJV)
   YL _____

   (a) _____

3. you have an abundance of workmen (1 Chr
   22.15)
   YL _____

   (a) _____

4. the power of his wrath (Ezra 8.22)
   YL _____

   (a) _____

5. the splendor of his riches (Est 5.11)
   YL _____

   (a) _____

6. the greatness of his power (Job 23.6)
   YL _____

   (a) _____

7. the abundance of thy steadfast
   love (Psa 5.7)
   YL _____

   (a) _____

5. ADJUSTING DIFFICULT Q'S (QUALITIES OR QUANTITIES)

Purpose. As we have seen in the previous section, not all Q's appear as Q's in the surface form of biblical languages. Even when they do appear in Q form, they do not always correspond to the usage of the receptor language. This makes them hard to understand and to translate. If they are translated in the same form, they will often be misunderstood in the receptor language. The translator must therefore learn to rephrase them until the meaning is easily understood.

Instructions

(a) Study the meaning of the underlined Q-expressions and restate them into easily understood expressions. Write your restatement on the line marked (a). Do not hesitate to consult a commentary so that you will get the correct meaning.

(b) Check the translation in your language. If the expression is not easily understood, restate it on the line marked YL.

Examples

false Christs (Matt 24.24)

YL _____

(a) those who say they are Christ, but are not

false prophets (Matt 24.24)

YL _____

(a) prophets who are lying when they say they have a message from God; what they prophesy is false

you who are spiritual (Gal 6.1)

YL _____

(a) you who are led by the Spirit of God

D-9 New Testament: Adjusting Difficult Q's (Qualities or Quantities)

1. faithless and perverse generation (Matt 17.17)

   YL _____

   (a) _____

2. to proclaim the acceptable year of the Lord (Luke 4.19)

   YL _____

   (a) _____

3. fearful sights (Luke 21.11 KJV)

   YL _____

   (a) _____

4. I am the living bread (John 6.51)

   YL _____

   (a) _____

5. as the living Father sent me (John 6.57)

   YL _____

   (a) _____

6. Ananias, a devout man (Acts 22.12)

   YL _____

   (a) _____

[141]

7. the weak man eats only vegetables (Rom 14.2)

(a)_____

YL_____

8. but the natural man receiveth not the things of the Spirit (1 Cor 2.14 KJV)

(a)_____

YL_____

9. not by earthly wisdom (2 Cor 1.12)

(a)_____

YL_____

D-10 Old Testament: Adjusting Difficult Q's (Instructions as for Drill D-9)

1. God created great whales and every living creature (Gen 1.21)

(a)_____

YL_____

2. cattle and creeping things (Gen 1.24)

(a)_____

YL_____

3. a divorced woman (Lev 21.14 KJV)

(a)_____

YL_____

4. a betrothed damsel (Deut 22.25 KJV)

(a)_____

YL_____

5. the armed men went before the priests (Josh 6.9)

(a)_____

YL_____

6. a graven and a molten image (Judges 17.3)

(a)_____

YL_____

7. I am this day weak, though anointed king (2 Sam 3.39)

(a)_____

YL_____

8. had charge of the ministering vessels (1 Chr 9.28 KJV)

(a)_____

YL_____

9. all the days of my appointed time (Job 14.14 KJV)

(a)_____

YL_____

6. CHANGING INDIRECT SPEECH INTO DIRECT SPEECH

Instructions. Some languages have a strong preference for direct speech.

(a) Change the following expressions in clearly marked indirect speech to direct speech on the line marked (a).

(b) Write the expression in your language and discuss with your classmates whether your language would prefer direct or indirect speech in this case.

Example
tell my brethren to go to Galilee   (a)_ tell my brethren: "Go to Galilee."_
     (Matt 28.10)

YL_____

D-11 New Testament: Changing Indirect Speech Into Direct Speech

1. if you are the Son of God, command these stones to become loaves of bread (Matt 4.3)

     (a)_____

     YL_____

2. he went to Pilate and asked for the body of Jesus (Matt 27.58)

     (a)_____

     YL_____

3. [the king] gave orders to bring his head (Mark 6.27)

     (a)_____

     YL_____

4. he charged them to tell no one (Mark 9.9)

     (a)_____

     YL_____

D-12 Old Testament: Changing Clearly Marked Indirect Speech Into Direct Speech (Instructions as for Drill D-11)

Clearly marked indirect speech is not as frequent in the Old Testament as in the New Testament. When it does occur it is often within a direct speech that contains a second or third layer of direct speech which is presented as indirect speech.

1. who told you that you were naked? (Gen 3.11)

     (a)_____

     YL_____

2. why did you not tell me that she was your wife? (Gen 12.18)

     (a)_____

     YL_____

3. why did you treat me so ill as to tell the man that you had another brother (Gen 43.6)

     (a)_____

     YL_____

4. tell all the congregation of Israel
    that on the tenth day of this
    month they shall take every man a
    lamb (Exo 12.3)

    YL _____

(a) _____

7. WORDS THAT IMPLY DIRECT SPEECH

D-13 Direct Speech Following Words That Imply Speech

    Instructions. Many words like command, proclaim, beg, etc., imply direct speech. All quotations are from KJV.

    (a) Change into direct speech the expression following the word which implies direct speech and write it on the line marked (a).

    (b) Write it in your language and discuss which would be better—direct or indirect speech.

Example
he sent me...to proclaim liberty to
    the captives (Isa 61.1)

    YL _____

(a) he sent me to announce: "All cap-
    tives are free."

Command
1. he commanded the multitude to sit
    down (Matt 14.19)

    YL _____

(a) _____

2. [he] commanded the porter to watch
    (Mark 13.34)

    YL _____

(a) _____

Beseech
1. they beseech him to put his hand upon
    him (Mark 7.32)

    YL _____

(a) _____

2. they besought him that he would tarry
    with them (John 4.40)

    YL _____

(a) _____

Declare
1. [he] declared unto them how the Lord
    had brought him out of prison
    (Acts 12.17)

    YL _____

(a) _____

2. they declared all the things that God
    had done with them (Acts 15.4)

    YL _____

(a) _____

Desire
1. desired him that he would show them a   (a)_____
   sign from heaven (Matt 16.1)

   YL_____

2. [the multitude] began to desire him to   (a)_____
   do as he had ever done unto them
   (Mark 15.8)

   YL_____

8. ADJUSTING DOUBLE NEGATIVES

    Purpose. The double negative in English translations, carried over from biblical languages, functions as an emphatic positive; for example, nothing shall be impossible really means that "absolutely everything will be possible." Many languages, including Bantu languages of East-Central Africa, do not make a positive statement by means of two negatives. Some interpret two negatives as a strong negation, as did the African translator using the NEB, who translated do not stint soap as "never use soap." Others are just confused by the two negatives.

    Double negatives in English come in at least four varieties (see example box for details).

    In this drill we want to learn both to recognize and to translate properly the various kinds of double negative statements.

    Instructions

    (a) Restate the following expressions, which contain double negatives, as positives on the line marked (a).

    (b) Write the expression in your language on the line marked YL and decide whether you should use the double negative or a positive statement.

Examples
1. two obvious negatives:
   nothing is covered up that will not   (a) everything that is covered up will
       be revealed (Luke 12.2)   be revealed
     YL_____

2. a negative plus a negative prefix like im-, un-, non-, etc.:
   nothing will be impossible to you   (a) everything will be possible to you
       (Matt 17.20)
     YL_____

3. a negative plus without, outside of:
   a prophet is not without honor (Mark   (a) a prophet is honored
       6.4)
     YL_____

4. a negative plus a word with a negative component:
   we would not have you ignorant   (a) we want you to know
       (1 Thes 4.13)
     YL_____

   I will not deny (Mark 14.31)   (a) I will say "Yes"
     YL_____

D-14 New Testament: Adjusting Double Negatives

1. a prophet is not without honor except (a)_____
   in his own country (Matt 13.57)
   YL_____

2. nothing will be impossible to you (a)_____
   (Matt 17.20)
   YL_____

3. there is nothing hid, which shall not (a)_____
   be manifested (Mark 4.22 KJV)
   YL_____

4. there will not be left here one stone (a)_____
   upon another, that will not be
   thrown down (Mark 13.2)
   YL_____

5. with God nothing will be impossible (a)_____
   (Luke 1.37)
   YL_____

6. he confessed, he did not deny (John (a)_____
   1.20)
   YL_____

D-15 Old Testament: Adjusting Double Negatives (Instructions as for Drill D-14)

1. all that is in the house be not made (a)_____
   unclean (Lev 14.36 KJV)
   YL_____

2. you shall do no injustice in judgment (a)_____
   (Lev 19.15)
   YL_____

3. neither be discouraged (Deut 1.21 KJV) (a)_____
   YL_____

4. he left nothing undone of all that the (a)_____
   LORD had commanded (Josh 11.15)
   YL_____

5. eat nothing unclean (Judges 13.7) (a)_____
   YL_____

6. lacking nothing that is in the earth (a)_____
   (Judges 18.7)
   YL_____

7. nothing was missing (1 Sam 30.19) (a)_____
   YL_____

9. CHANGING NEGATIVES TO "ONLY"

Purpose. In some languages a negative plus an exception is expressed by only, only if, only when, etc., depending on the nature of the exception. The exceptions are marked in English by except, till, unless, until, but, etc.

Instructions

(a) Change the following negative expressions using only, only if, etc., as required by the context. Write your new expression on the line marked (a).

(b) On the line marked YL write the expression in your language using only, and see which of the two is preferred—the double negative or the expression using only.

Examples

which no man knows except him who receives it (Rev 2.17)
YL _____

(a) which only the one who receives it knows

I will not boast, except of my weakness (2 Cor 12.5)
YL _____

(a) I will boast only of my weakness

this cannot pass unless I drink it (Matt 26.42)
YL _____

(a) this can pass only if I drink it

you will never get out till you have paid the last penny (Matt 5.26)
YL _____

(a) you will get out only when you have paid the last penny

but he knew her not until she had borne (Matt 1.25)
YL _____

(a) he knew her only after she had given birth

D-16 New Testament: Changing Negatives to "Only"

1. no sign shall be given to it except the sign of the prophet Jonah (Matt 12.39)
   YL _____

   (a) _____

2. this kind never comes out except by prayer and fasting (Matt 17.21)
   YL _____

   (a) _____

3. unless you turn and become like little children, you will never enter the kingdom of heaven (Matt 18.3)
   YL _____

   (a) _____

[147]

4. did not know until the flood came
   (Matt 24.39)
   YL_____

(a)_____

5. I shall not drink again of this fruit
   of the vine until that day when I
   drink it new with you in my Father's kingdom (Matt 26.29)
   YL_____

(a)_____

6. except they wash they eat not (Mark
   7.4 KJV)
   YL_____

(a)_____

7. [they should] tell no one what they
   had seen, until the Son of man
   should have risen from the dead
   (Mark 9.9)
   YL_____

(a)_____

D-17 Old Testament: Changing Negatives to "Only" (Instructions as for Drill D-16)

1. I have not heard of it until today
   (Gen 21.26)
   YL_____

(a)_____

2. I will not let you go, unless you
   bless me (Gen 32.26)
   YL_____

(a)_____

3. you shall not see my face, unless
   your brother is with you (Gen 43.5)
   YL_____

(a)_____

4. shall not eat the holy things unless
   he has bathed (Lev 22.6)
   YL_____

(a)_____

5. if you had not ploughed with my heif-
   er, you would not have found out my
   riddle (Judges 14.18)
   YL_____

(a)_____

6. the people will not eat till he comes
   (1 Sam 9.13)
   YL_____

(a)_____

7. [I] did not turn back until they were
   consumed (2 Sam 22.38)
   YL_____

(a)_____

8. there was none that followed the
   house of David, but the tribe of
   Judah (1 Kgs 12.20)
   YL_____

(a)_____

[148]

10. RHETORICAL QUESTIONS

Purpose. In this drill we want:

(a) to learn to distinguish between questions asking for information and rhetorical questions which do not seek information but rather provide special effects.

(b) to learn to recognize the distinctive function of rhetorical questions. Unlike questions for information, rhetorical questions usually have a definite "yes" or "no" answer implicit in them. Rhetorical questions are used in many languages, but most of them do not use these questions as widely as the Bible does. In some languages, like Zapotec in Mexico, they are used in bereavement settings; in Trique, another Central American language, they are used largely for scolding. Other languages use the rhetorical questions for expressing certain emotions (see Drills C-21 and C-22).

(c) to become aware in what contexts rhetorical questions are normally used in the receptor language.

(d) to learn to translate rhetorical questions meaningfully. Even languages that make little use of rhetorical questions can permit them in translation if they are properly answered. This, of course, means we are treating them as questions for information.

Instructions

(a) Read the following questions and decide which are rhetorical questions and which are requests for information. Mark them with "R" for rhetorical and "I" for information in the blank preceding each question.

(b) If the question is rhetorical, mark the implicit "yes" or "no" answer in the blank following the question. If the question asks for information, answer it.

Example

__R__ teacher, do you not care if we perish? (Mark 4.38) __no__

__I__ what is your name? (Mark 5.9) __My name is Legion.__

__R__ are not all these who are speaking Galileans? (Acts 2.7) __yes__

(c) Assume that you cannot use the rhetorical question form in a translation. Rephrase the idea expressed in nonquestion form on the line marked (c). Be sure that your rendering agrees with the question both in content and in intent.

Example

how can a man be born when he is old? (John 3.4)
(c) __a man just cannot be born when he is old__

(d) Write your own language translation on the line marked YL and decide whether you can use it unanswered as in the Bible, or whether you can retain it with its answer, or whether you should rewrite it as a statement. If the existing translation should be changed, rewrite it on the line marked (d).

D-18 New Testament: Answering Rhetorical Questions

1. ___ where is he who has been born king of the Jews? (Matt 2.2) _____

   YL _____

   (c) _____

   (d) _____

2. ___ you brood of vipers! Who warned you to flee from the wrath to come? (Matt 3.7) _____

   YL _____

   (c) _____

   (d) _____

3. ___ if you salute only your brethren, what more are you doing than others? Do not even the Gentiles do the same? (Matt 5.47) _____

   YL _____

   (c) _____

   (d) _____

4. ___ is not life more than food, and the body more than clothing? (Matt 6.25) ___

   YL _____

   (c) _____

   (d) _____

D-19 Old Testament: Answering Rhetorical Questions (Instructions as for Drill D-18)

1. ___ where is Sarah your wife? (Gen 18.9) _____

   YL _____

   (c) _____

   (d) _____

2. ___ shall I indeed bear a child, now that I am old? (Gen 18.13) _____

   YL _____

   (c) _____

   (d) _____

3. ___ is anything too hard for the LORD? (Gen 18.14) _____

   YL _____

   (c) _____

   (d) _____

4. ___ shall I hide from Abraham what I am about to do? (Gen 18.17) _____

   YL _____

   (c) _____

   (d) _____

11. TRANSLATING DOUBLETS

Purpose

(a) to become aware of the function of parallelism or doublets in both the Old and the New Testaments. Doublets are a literary or poetic device which some languages use to make the statement more beautiful and/or more emphatic. The similarity in meaning of the doublets ranges from partial overlap to complete identity of meaning. In some languages, to say the same thing or nearly the same thing twice suggests that the speaker is not quite honest. In other languages it merely sounds very unnatural.

(b) to learn to translate the doublets properly according to the usage of the receptor language. The receptor language may not be able to employ synonymous doublets at all. In such cases one doublet must be made implicit or treated as an intensifier. Some languages permit doublets but restrict them to certain kinds of discourse, for example, praise songs in Africa. Whatever the usage, the translator must be aware of what the receptor language requires and make the necessary adjustments.

Instructions

(a) Assume that the receptor language does not permit synonymous or nearly synonymous doublets. On this basis translate only one member, and wherever possible, translate the other doublet as an intensifier of the one being translated. Write your version on the line marked (a).

(b) Compare the translations listed below, including your language, to see how they have treated the doublets in translation. Write your findings in the space marked "evaluation." If the doublets have not been treated as required by your language, make a correct translation on the line marked (c).

Examples

Note three degrees of overlap.

(1) Total: John 3.3
RSV   truly, truly   (a) __I solemnly affirm__

    Compare:
TEV   I tell you the truth
NEB   in truth, in very truth
LB   with all the earnestness I possess
JB   most solemnly
Phps believe me
YL   _____   (c)_____

    Evaluation:
NEB is the only translation that has retained the doublet, but it introduces degree in the repetition. All the others have reduced the doublet. LB and JB use one adverbial phrase for emphasis.

(2) Almost synonymous: Mark 4.39
RSV   Peace! Be still!   (a) __(storm) be quiet__
                                               __(waves) be calm__

    Compare:
TEV   Be quiet...Be still!
JB   Quiet now! Be calm!
NEB   Hush! Be still!
LB   Quiet down!
YL   _____   (c)_____

    Evaluation:
All except LB retain the doublet form. The reason lies in the two aspects of the storm—the noise and the waves.

(3) Could be two technical terms: Eph 2.19
RSV strangers and sojourners   (a) really aliens
     Compare:
TEV foreigners or strangers
NEB aliens in a foreign land
LB   strangers to God and foreigners
         to heaven
JB   aliens or foreign visitors
SpCL *aliens in a land not their own*
YL   _____   (c)_____

     Evaluation:
NEB and SpCL probably have the best translation for a language which cannot use
doublets. LB is overtranslated. TEV treats the doublet as containing two technical
terms.

D-20 New Testament I: Synonymous Doublets

1. Matt 2.18
   RSV wailing and loud lamentation   (a)_____
        Compare:
   TEV the sound of bitter weeping
            [fourth edition]
   JB   sobbing and loudly lamenting
   LB   weeping unrestrained
   Phps weeping and great mourning
   YL_____   (c)_____

        Evaluation:

2. Matt 4.23
   RSV every disease and every infir-   (a)_____
            mity
        Compare:
   TEV every kind of disease and sick-
            ness
   Phps every disease and disability
   BE   ill with any disease
   SpCL *every kind of sickness*
   Brc all kinds of illness and all
            kinds of sickness
   YL   _____   (c)_____

        Evaluation

3. Matt 5.12
   RSV   rejoice and be glad   (a)_____
      Compare:
   TEV   be glad and happy
   NEB   with gladness and exultation
   LB   be happy about it! Be very glad
   Phps   be glad then, yes, be tremen-
             dously glad
   YL   _____ (c)_____

      Evaluation:

4. Matt 7.21
   RSV   Lord, Lord   (a)_____
      Compare:
   TEV   Lord, Lord
   LB   [not all who] sound religious...
             they may refer to me as Lord
   GeCL   *who constantly uses my name*
   YL   _____ (c)_____

      Evaluation:

D-21 New Testament II: Synonymous or Nearly Synonymous Doublets

   Instructions. In this drill we want:
   (a) to study carefully the meaning of the doublets listed and to see how they
have been handled in the various translations including YL. If there is any doubt
about the meaning, be sure to consult a good commentary.
   (b) to learn to evaluate usage of the various translations and to identify
the best. Write your evaluation of the translations in the space provided. You may
use the examples for Drill D-20 as model.
   (c) to prepare a new translation for YL if the existing one is not satisfac-
tory. Write your new translation on the line marked (c).

1. Mark 1.45
   RSV   began to talk freely about it and to spread the news
      Compare:
   TEV   began to spread the news everywhere. Indeed, he talked so much that...
   NEB   made the story public; he spread it far and wide
   JB   started talking about it freely and spread the story everywhere
   LB   he began to shout the good news
   Phps   began to talk a great deal about it in public, spreading his story far and
             wide
   YL   _____ (c)_____

      Evaluation:

2. Mark 5.4
   RSV   bound with fetters and chains
      Compare:
   TEV   his feet and hands had been tied
   JB   secured with fetters and chains
   LB   put into handcuffs and shackles
   YL   _____ (c)_____

      Evaluation:

3. Mark 14.33
   RSV   greatly distressed and troubled
      Compare:
   TEV   distress and anguish came over him
   JB   a sudden fear came over him, and great distress
   NEB   horror and dismay came over him
   LB   filled with horror and deepest distress
   Phps   horror-stricken and desperately depressed
   YL   _____ (c)_____

      Evaluation:

D-22 New Testament III: Synonymous Doublets in Figurative Language (Instructions as
    for Drill D-21)

1. Matt 4.16
   RSV   the people who sat in darkness...those who sat in the region and shadow of
         death
      Compare:
   TEV   people who live in darkness...those who live in the dark land of death
   LB   people who sat in darkness...they sat in the land of death
   YL   _____ (c)_____

      Evaluation:

2. Matt 11.30
   RSV   my yoke is easy and my burden is light
      Compare:
   TEV   the yoke...is easy, and the load,..is light
   LB   my yoke...fits perfectly...I give you only light burdens
   YL   _____ (c)_____

      Evaluation:

3. Matt 24.31
   RSV   gather his elect from the four winds, from one end of heaven to the other
       Compare:
   TEV   send...angels to the four corners of the earth...gather his chosen people
         from one end of the world to the other
   NEB   will gather his chosen from the four winds, from the farthest bounds of
         heaven on every side
   LB   gather my chosen ones from the farthest ends of the earth and heaven
   YL   _____ (c)_____

   Evaluation:

D-23 New Testament IV: Synonymous Doublets—One Figurative and One Literal (Instructions as for Drill D-21)

1. Matt 2.11
   RSV   they fell down and worshiped him
       Compare:
   TEV   they knelt down and worshiped him
   JB   falling on their knees they did him homage
   NEB   bowed to the ground in homage to him
   LB   they threw themselves down before him, worshiping
   YL   _____ (c)_____

   Evaluation:

2. Matt 16.4
   RSV   an evil and adulterous generation
       Compare:
   TEV   how evil and godless are the people of this day
   JB   an evil and unfaithful generation
   NEB   a wicked generation
   LB   this evil, unbelieving nation
   AB   a wicked and morally unfaithful generation
   YL   _____ (c)_____

   Evaluation:

D-24 New Testament V: Synonymous Doublets—One Negative and One Positive (Instructions as for Drill D-21)

1. Matt 21.21
   RSV   have faith and never doubt
      Compare:
   TEV   if you believe and do not doubt
   JB   if you have faith and do not doubt at all
   Brc   have unquestioning faith
   YL   _____ (c)_____

   Evaluation:

2. Mark 10.14
   RSV   let the children come to me and do not hinder them
      Compare:
   TEV   let the children come to me, and do not stop them
   LB   let the children come to me...don't send them away
   AB   allow the children to come to Me—do not forbid, or prevent or hinder them
   YL   _____ (c)_____

   Evaluation:

D-25 Old Testament I: Synonymous or Nearly Synonymous Doublets (Instructions as for Drill D-21)

1. Job 26.6
   RSV   Sheol is naked before God and Abaddon has no covering
      Compare:
   TEV   the world of the dead lies open to God; no covering shields it from his sight
   NEB   Sheol is laid bare, and Abaddon uncovered before him
   JB   before his eyes, Sheol is bare, Perdition itself is uncovered
   LB   the dead stand naked, trembling before God in the place where they go
   YL   _____ (c)_____

   Evaluation:

2. Psa 5.1-2
   RSV   give ear to my words, O LORD; give heed to my groaning. Hearken to the
            sound of my cry, my King and my God
      Compare:
   TEV   listen to my words, O LORD, and hear my sighs. Listen to my cry for help,
            my God and king
   NEB   listen to my words, O LORD, consider my inmost thoughts; heed my cry for
            help, my king and my God
   JB   Yahweh, let my words come to your ears, spare a thought for my sighs. Lis-
            ten to my cry for help, my King and my God
   LB   O Lord, hear me praying; listen to my plea, O God my King
   YL   _____   (c)_____

      Evaluation:

D-26 Old Testament II: Synonymous Doublets in Figurative Language (Instructions as
      for Drill D-21)

1. 1 Sam 2.8
   RSV   he raises up the poor from the dust, he lifts the needy from the ash heap
      Compare:
   TEV   he lifts the poor from the dust and raises the needy from their misery
   NEB   he lifts the weak out of the dust and raises the poor from the dunghill
   JB   he raises the poor from the dust, he lifts the needy from the dunghill
   LB   he lifts the poor from the dust—yes, from a pile of ashes
   YL   _____   (c)_____

      Evaluation:

2. Job 16.13
   RSV   his archers surround me. He slashes open my kidneys, and does not spare;
            he pours out my gall on the ground
      Compare:
   TEV   shoots arrows at me from every side—arrows that pierce and wound me; and
            even then he shows no pity
   NEB   his arrows rained upon me from every side; pitiless, he cut deep into my
            vitals, he spilt my gall on the ground
   JB   shooting arrows at me from every side. Pitiless, through the loins he
            pierces me, and scatters my gall on the ground
   YL   _____   (c)_____

      Evaluation:

E. RECONSTRUCTION OF THE TEXT

1. LINKING KERNEL SENTENCES

Purpose. We have now arrived at step three of the translation process. In this section we now want to learn how to rebuild the meanings we have discovered into a new structure. The new structure may be required because the audience we aim at requires a different level of translation such as the new common-language translations that are being made in many languages, like the TEV, SpCL, and GeCL. The new structure may also be required by the receptor language, which uses surface patterns that are quite different from the Hebrew, Greek, or English original. In order to be able to rebuild a text broken into kernels, the translator must develop at least two skills:

(a) He must be able to shape the kernel sentence, or to speak figuratively, the language "bricks," so that they fit into the new "wall." We have been trying to develop the skill to shape the kernels by making transforms and by becoming aware of the differences in emphasis, focus, and function which the various transforms of a kernel sentence have.

(b) He must be able to link the kernels meaningfully. A series of unlinked statements cannot convey the message properly. Learning to link kernels involves at least two aspects. First, he must learn to use the full range of relationals the receptor language has. Secondly, he must learn to link the kernels in the relationship required by the biblical text. We will try to gain experience in the former by learning to link kernels in many ways, and in the latter, by practicing the reconstruction of a variety of passages of scripture.

E-1 Linking Kernel Sentences with Many Different Relationals

Instructions. Link the kernel sentences provided in as many ways as possible. Then read the reconstructions to the group and discuss the different shades of meaning that result.

Examples
(a) we confess   (b) we sin

These two kernels can be linked as follows (the list is not exhaustive):

we confess because we sin	gives reason for confession
we sin and confess	suggests an endless cycle
we confess our sin	the second kernel becomes object of confess
having confessed our sin	the whole is now part of a larger construction
we have sin to confess	focus is on confession
if we sin we have to confess	condition and response
the confession of our sin	the kernels linked as a noun phrase

---

1. (a) he forgives   (b) we sin

_____   _____

_____   _____

_____   _____

_____   _____

2. (a) I have a son   (b) he is sick

3. (a) Christ died   (b) he saves us   (c) we sin

4. (a) he commanded them   (b) they are holy

5. (a) you repent (as a command)   (b) John baptizes you

6. (a) she married him   (b) he does not believe

Linking Kernel Sentences in Biblical Passages

Instructions

(a) Review the kernels of the passage you prepared previously in Drills B-27 and B-28 and list them in the space provided.

(b) Study the original context to identify the proper links between the kernels and write the relationship in the space provided.

(c) Make a reconstruction (restatement) of the passage that has the proper linkage, but which leaves the kernels as visible as possible for a common-language reader.

(d) Compare your reconstruction with the translations provided. Are the kernels equally visible? Discuss any striking differences.

Example

Eph 1.7 (KJV)

```
R    P   P        E       R   P   PE        E    R   E      R
in whom we have redemption through his blood, the forgiveness of sins according

R      Q    R    P    E
to the riches of his grace
```

Kernels:
1. God redeems us (God sets us free)
2. Christ died (shed his blood)
3. God forgives
4. We sin
5. God "graces" (that is, is kind even though we don't deserve it) richly

Relationships between kernels:

2 is the means of achieving 1
3 and 1 are the same thing
4 is the object of the verb in 3
1-4 shows us 5

Restatement of linked kernels:

God forgave our sins and set us free when Christ died for us. By doing this God showed how great his kindness to us really is.

Compare:

TEV   for by the death of Christ we are set free, that is, our sins are forgiven. How great is the grace of God

NEB   for in Christ our release is secured and our sins are forgiven through the shedding of his blood. Therein lies the richness of God's free grace lavished upon us

GeCL *He let him (Christ) die for us in order to set us free from our sin (debt). In this act the wealth of God's kindness reveals itself*

E-2 New Testament: Linking Kernel Sentences (See Drill B-27 for kernels)

Now when Jesus was at Bethany in the house of Simon the leper, a woman came up to him with an alabaster flask of very expensive ointment, and she poured it on his head, as he sat at table (Matt 26.6-7).

List kernels: Relationship between kernels:

Restatement of linked kernels:

Compare:

TEV   While Jesus was at the house of Simon the leper, in Bethany, a woman came to him with an alabaster jar filled with an expensive perfume, which she poured on Jesus' head as he sat eating.

NEB   Jesus was at Bethany in the house of Simon the leper, when a woman came to him with a small bottle of fragrant oil, very costly; and as he sat at table she began to pour it over his head.

E-3 Old Testament: Linking Kernel Sentences (Instructions as for Drill E-2; see Drill B-28 for kernels)

So God created man in his own image, in the image of God he created him; male and female he created them (Gen 1.27).

List kernels: Relationship between kernels:

Restatement of linked kernels:

Compare:

TEV   So God created human beings, making them to be like himself. He created them male and female.

NEB   So God created man in his own image; in the image of God he created him; male and female he created them.

Ellipsis in Kernel Linkage

   Purpose. Ellipsis involves omitting or making implicit a part or parts of a kernel in the surface structure. Ellipsis takes place especially in those parts of the kernel that are redundant. We need to know how ellipsis functions because it is a very important part of proper reconstruction of the text. To become aware of how it works we will study a number of passages in which a part or parts of kernels have been omitted or left implicit.

   Instructions. Study the following passages carefully and supply parts of kernels that have been omitted or left implicit. Write the full kernel in the blank provided.

Examples. (Omitted parts have been underlined in the restatement)
1. Jesus left the temple and was going away. Part omitted: he/Jesus was going away (Matt 24.1)

2. Jesus took bread, and blessed, and broke it. Part omitted: he blessed it, and he broke it (Matt 26.26)

3. Have you come out as against a robber, with swords and clubs? Parts omitted: Have you come out with swords, have you come out with clubs (Matt 26.55)

E-4 New Testament: Ellipsis

1. every man serves the good wine first; and when men have drunk freely, then the poor wine (John 2.10)

   _____

2. Jesus himself did not baptize, but only his disciples (John 4.2)

   _____

3. [he] drank from it himself, and his sons and his cattle (John 4.12)

   _____

4. he himself believed, and all his household (John 4.53)

   _____

5. at once the man was healed, and he took up his pallet and walked (John 5.9)

   _____

6. there is a lad here who has five barley loaves and two fish (John 6.9)

   _____

7. he distributed them to those who were seated; so also the fish (John 6.11)

   _____

2. REORDERING KERNELS

E-5 Putting Kernels Into Chronological Order

Purpose. Many biblical passages contain flashbacks; that is, they refer to events that happened earlier in time. Some languages have a strong preference for actual chronological order. If this is so, the kernels need to be reordered according to the actual time sequence. In this drill we want to practice how to restructure a text by putting the kernels into chronological order. Learn to do this even if it is not required by your own language.

Instructions

(a) Read Mark 6.16-18 and check if the following list of kernel sentences is accurate.

(b) In the column marked "Number" write the actual order in time in which the events recorded in the kernels took place.

(c) Now rewrite the kernels in their proper order.

(d) Indicate the required links between the kernels (see Drill E-1 for instructions). Write the suggested link in the blank provided.

(e) Which kernels must be transformed in the reconstruction, and what transforms do you suggest? (See Drills B-32 and B-33 for instructions.)

	Number	Link	Reordered kernels
1. [Jesus preached]	___	___	_____
2. [Jesus healed]	___	___	_____
3. Herod heard of it	___	___	_____
4. Herod said	___	___	_____
5. I beheaded John	___	___	_____
6. John arose from the dead	___	___	_____
7. Herod sent [men]	___	___	_____
8. They seized John	___	___	_____
9. They bound him	___	___	_____
10. they put him in prison	___	___	_____
11. Herodias wanted it	___	___	_____
12. Philip was Herod's brother	___	___	_____
13. Herodias was Philip's wife	___	___	_____
14. Herod had married her	___	___	_____
15. John said to Herod	___	___	_____
16. it is not lawful	___	___	_____
17. you have your brother's wife	___	___	_____

3. IMPLICIT TRANSITIONAL KERNELS

Purpose. In narrative, usually only those aspects of the event that are pertinent to the narrator's purpose are expressed explicitly. In translation, however, some languages have special stylistic requirements, such as indicating the completion of an action initiated, the arrival at a destination, the occasion for a new action sequence, etc. Where this is the case, implicit intervening actions may sometimes have to be expressed explicitly.

Instructions

(a) Identify the missing transitional actions in the following passages.

(b) Compare the translations listed to see how they have handled these transitions.

(c) Look at the translation in your language. If it does not have a good transition and requires one, make a new translation with a transition.

Example

Mark 1.9

KJV   Jesus came from Nazareth of Galilee, and when he arrived where John was, (he) was baptized of John in Jordan. (The implicit transitional kernel which has been added is underlined.)

Compare:

TEV   Not long afterward Jesus came from Nazareth, in the region of Galilee, and John baptized him in the Jordan. [Third edition.]

NEB   It happened at this time that Jesus came from Nazareth in Galilee and was baptized in the Jordan by John.

JB   It was at this time that Jesus came from Nazareth in Galilee and was baptised in the Jordan by John.

Wn   *At that time Jesus left Nazareth town. That town was in Galilee. When Jesus arrived at the Jordan, John baptized him.*

LB   Then one day Jesus came from Nazareth in Galilee, and was baptized by John there in the Jordan River.

YL   _____

Evaluation:

None of the translations except Wn makes the transitional kernel explicit.

E-6 New Testament: Implicit Transitional Kernels

1. Mark 1.35-36
   RSV   he [Jesus] rose and went out to a lonely place, and there he prayed. And
         Simon and those who were with him pursued him
      Compare:
   TEV   Very early the next morning, long before daylight, Jesus got up and left
         the house. He went out of the town to a lonely place, where he prayed.
         But Simon and his companions went out searching for him
   YL   _____

      Evaluation:

2. Mark 2.4
   RSV   And when they could not get near him because of the crowd, they removed the
         roof above him
      Compare:
   TEV   Because of the crowd, however, they could not get the man to him. So they
         made a hole in the roof right above the place where Jesus was
   YL   _____

      Evaluation:

E-7 Old Testament: Implicit Transitional Kernels (Instructions as for Drill E-6)

1. Gen 9.20-21
   RSV   Noah was the first tiller of the soil. He planted a vineyard; and he drank of
         the wine, and became drunk
      Compare:
   TEV   Noah, who was a farmer, was the first man to plant a vineyard. After he
         drank some wine, he became drunk
   YL   _____

      Evaluation:

2. Gen 12.17-18
   RSV   But the LORD afflicted Pharaoh and his house with great plagues because of
         Sarai, Abram's wife. So Pharaoh called Abram, and said, "What is this
         you have done to me? Why did you not tell me that she was your wife?"
      Compare:
   TEV   But because the king had taken Sarai, the LORD sent terrible diseases on
         him and on the people of his palace. Then the king sent for Abram and
         asked him, "What have you done to me? Why didn't you tell me that she
         was your wife?"
   YL   _____

      Evaluation:

4. RECONSTRUCTING AT DIFFERENT LEVELS OF LANGUAGE

Purpose. In this series of exercises we want to become aware of and gain experience in reconstructing translated texts at different language levels. Languages with a long history of writing and education usually have developed a very wide range of levels in vocabulary and grammatical constructions that are characteristic of the different socioeconomic levels exhibited by the society using that language. We could illustrate the differences in language levels by means of the following diagram.

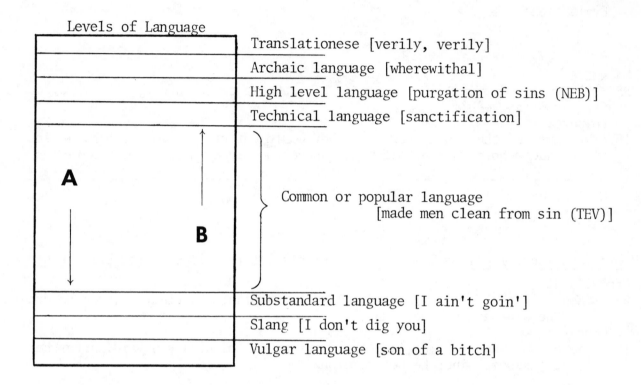

In his book Bible Translations for Popular Use, Dr. William L. Wonderly illustrates such differences of language level in translation by presenting several translations in a multidimensional matrix.

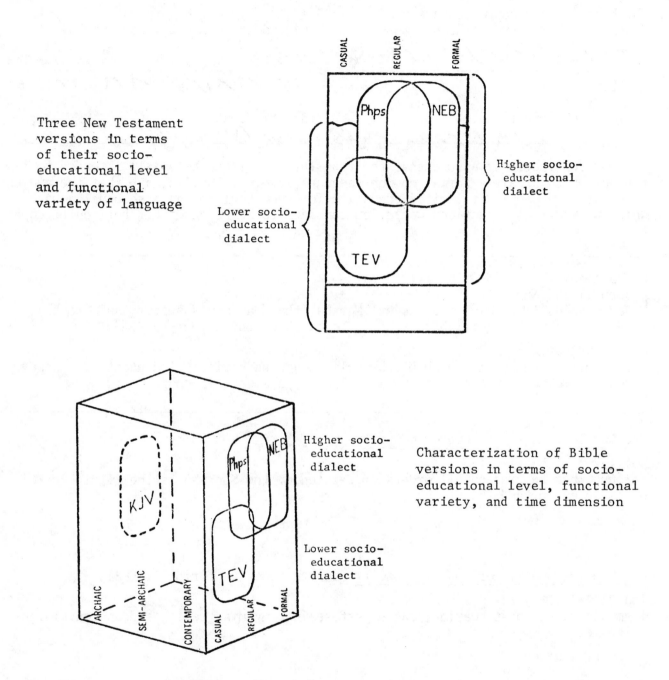

Three New Testament versions in terms of their socio-educational level and functional variety of language

Lower socio-educational dialect

Higher socio-educational dialect

Higher socio-educational dialect

Lower socio-educational dialect

Characterization of Bible versions in terms of socio-educational level, functional variety, and time dimension

We want to see now if on the basis of our own experience we can duplicate Dr. Wonderly's classification by studying a series of Bible translations comparatively.

Horizon of Capacity: English as a Second Language

Purpose. In this exercise we want to become aware of the concept "horizon of capacity." By "horizon of capacity" we mean that level of language (marked LL) which a person of a given socioeducational level can handle without difficulty. We could illustrate the horizon (marked H) as follows:

The horizon of receptor capacity:

(a) too far above horizon

LL:
H:
LL:

(b) too far below horizon

(c) about right

H & LL:

(d) some peaks too high

Instructions. Assume that the translations listed below all intended to limit themselves to a fairly formal common language level of English, and that the audience aimed at were people of limited education for whom English was a second language. Which words or constructions would you consider to be beyond their horizon of capacity?

Example
John 11.39 (NEB)
Jesus said, 'Take away the stone.' Martha, the dead man's sister, said to him, 'Sir, by now there will be a stench; he has been there four days.'

Evaluation:
The word "stench" will probably be well above the horizon of capacity for a person of limited education for whom English is a second language.

E-8 New Testament: Horizon of Capacity

Heb 1.2-3 (NEB)
through whom he created all orders of existence: the Son who is the effulgence of God's splendour and the stamp of God's very being...

Evaluation:

E-9 Old Testament: Horizon of Capacity (Instructions as for Drill E-8)

Isa 21.3-4 (NEB)
I am distraught past hearing, dazed past seeing, my mind reels, sudden convulsions seize me.

Evaluation:

Channel Capacity of a Person with Only Primary Education

Purpose. In this drill we want to sharpen our awareness of the fact that a translation should not only aim at the proper horizon, but that it should try and maintain a constant level without any sudden sharp rises or drops in level that will be beyond the capacity of the channel of the receptor. We could illustrate channel capacity with the following diagram:

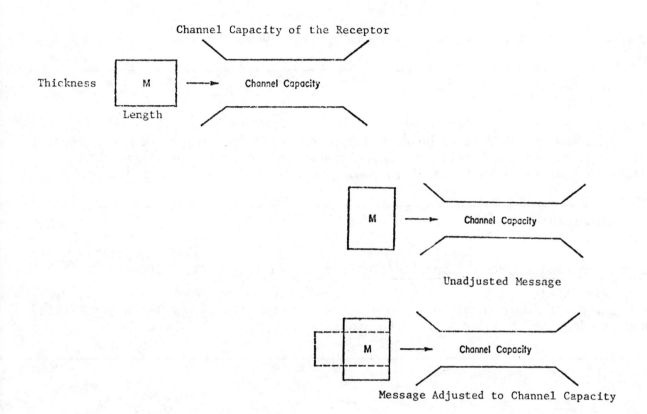

Channel Capacity of the Receptor

Thickness | M | Channel Capacity
Length

M → Channel Capacity

Unadjusted Message

M → Channel Capacity

Message Adjusted to Channel Capacity

Instructions

(a) In the passages listed below, mark by underlining any "lumps" in the message that will be "too big" for the channel of understanding of a person who has only had primary school education.

(b) How could you reduce the "thickness" of these "lumps"? Express the difficult item by means of a descriptive phrase that the receptor's channel can handle.

(c) On the line marked YL write in your language translation and see if it contains any "lumps." If so, try to simplify them.

Example
Isa 3.12 (NEB)
usurers lord it over them

YL _____

Evaluation:
The word usurers will not be understood. Likewise, the use of the word lord as a verb will be difficult. The "lumps" could be removed by the following restatement which "spreads out" the components of meaning: Moneylenders charging too much interest have become the masters of the people.

E-10 New Testament: Channel Capacity

1. Luke 15.13 (JB)
   A few days later, the younger son got together everything he had and left for a distant country where he squandered his money on a life of debauchery.

   YL _____

   Evaluation:

2. John 1.16 (NEB)
   Out of his full store we have all received grace upon grace...

   YL _____

   Evaluation:

3. John 15.2-3 (NEB)
   Every barren branch of mine he cuts away; and every fruiting branch he cleans, to make it more fruitful still. You have already been cleansed by the word that I spoke to you. Dwell in me, as I in you.

   YL _____

   Evaluation:

E-11 Old Testament: Channel Capacity (Instructions as for Drill E-10)

1. Eccl 1.8 (NEB)
   All things are wearisome; no man can speak of them all. Is not the eye surfeited with seeing, and the ear sated with hearing?

   YL _____

   Evaluation:

2. Isa 1.25 (NEB)
   I will act against you to refine away your base metal as with potash...

   YL _____

   Evaluation:

3. Isa 1.30-31 (NEB)
   You shall be like a terebinth whose leaves have withered, like a garden without water; the strongest tree shall become like tow and what is made of it shall go up in sparks...

   YL _____

   Evaluation:

4. Isa 3.14 (NEB)
   ...the spoils of the poor are in your houses.

   YL _____

   Evaluation:

5. LANGUAGE LEVELS IN TRANSLATION

<u>E-12 Comparing Translations</u>

Instructions

(a) Compare the following translations of Luke 8.22-25 and note any differences in level of vocabulary or grammatical constructions. What words or constructions do you consider too high for a person with only primary school education? Are there any words you consider old-fashioned? Do any of the translations use slang or vulgarisms which would offend the average person?

<u>RSV</u>	<u>TEV</u>	<u>NEB</u>
One day he got into a boat with his disciples, and he said to them, "Let us go across to the other side of the lake." So they set out, and as they sailed he fell asleep. And a storm of wind came down on the lake, and they were filling with water, and were in danger. And they went and woke him, saying, "Master, Master, we are perishing!" And he awoke and rebuked the wind and the raging waves; and they ceased, and there was a calm. He said to them, "Where is your faith?" And they were afraid, and they marveled, saying to one another, "Who then is this, that he commands even wind and water, and they obey him?"	One day Jesus got into a boat with his disciples and said to them, "Let us go across to the other side of the lake." So they started out. As they were sailing, Jesus went to sleep. A strong wind blew down on the lake, and the boat began to fill with water, putting them all in great danger. The disciples came to Jesus and woke him up, saying, "Master, Master! We are about to die!" Jesus got up and gave a command to the wind and to the stormy water; and they quieted down and there was a great calm. Then he said to the disciples, "Where is your faith?" But they were amazed and afraid, and said to one another, "Who is this man? He gives orders to the winds and waves, and they obey him!"	One day he got into a boat with his disciples and said to them, 'Let us cross over to the other side of the lake.' So they put out; and as they sailed along he went to sleep. Then a heavy squall struck the lake; they began to ship water and were in grave danger. They went to him, and roused him, crying, 'Master, Master, we are sinking!' He awoke, and rebuked the wind and the turbulent waters. The storm subsided and all was calm. 'Where is your faith?' he asked. In fear and astonishment they said to one another, 'Who can this be? He gives his orders to wind and waves, and they obey him.'

(b) In the space provided write out the same passage from the Bible in your own language. Which of the English translations is most similar in level and style to the one in your own language? Is the level of translation in your language right for a person who has only four years of primary education?

LB

One day about that time,
as he and his disciples
were out in a boat, he
suggested that they cross
to the other side of the
lake. On the way across
he lay down for a nap,
and while he was sleeping,
the wind began to rise.
A fierce storm developed
that threatened to swamp
them, and they were in
real danger. They rushed
over and woke him up.
"Master, Master, we are
sinking!" they screamed.
So he spoke to the storm:
"Quiet down," he said,
and the wind and waves
subsided, and all was
calm! Then he asked them,
"Where is your faith?"
And they were filled with
awe and fear of him and
said to one another, "Who
is this man, that even
the winds and waves obey
him?"

YL _____

NRT (Selection NLE 690P, 1973)

One day Jesus got into a boat
    with his followers.
  He said to them,
    "Let us go across
        to the other side of the lake."
  So they started out.
As they were going,
  Jesus went to sleep.
A strong wind blew down on the lake,
  and the boat began to fill with water.
    So they were all in great danger.
The men with Jesus
    woke him up.
  They said, "Master, Master!
    We are about to die!"
Jesus got up and told the wind
    and the stormy water to stop.
  They stopped right away,
    and there was a great calm.
Then Jesus said to his followers,
  "Where is your faith?"
But they were surprised and afraid.
  They said to one another,
"Who is this man?
He told the wind and waves to stop
  and they obey him!"

<u>Consistency of Language Level</u>

   <u>Purpose</u>. Since languages as a rule can express the same meaning at several different levels of language, we want:

   (a) to learn to distinguish different levels of English.

   (b) to become aware that a translation can be inconsistent in regard to language level, sometimes moving from one level to another even in the same sentence. As a background, review <u>The Bible Translator</u> (TBT) 21:126-137.

   <u>Instructions</u>

   (a) Study the passage in question considering both the RSV, which preserves much of the original form, and the TEV, which focuses more on the meaning.

   (b) Now study each of the translations listed below and try to determine whether it uses the same level of language as the TEV. If it does not, try to decide whether it is on a higher or lower language level. Discuss as a group and try to determine whether this difference in level is a result of simpler or more difficult words, or whether it grows out of simpler or more complicated grammatical or rhetorical structure, or out of a combination of these.

   (c) Study each of the translations presented to see whether it has maintained a consistent level of language, or whether it has changed from one level to another within the quoted passage. Write your findings for (b) and (c) in the space marked "Evaluation."

Example

Jer 4.30

RSV   you enlarge your eyes with paint

TEV   and paint your eyes

   Compare:

NEB   make your eyes big with antimony

LB   brighten your eyes with mascara

JB   enlarge your eyes with paint

YL   _____

Evaluation:

NEB avoids the higher level "enlarge" of RSV, but then goes on to use the very specialized high-level word "antimony." LB keeps to the TEV level, but introduces a new focus with the verb "brighten," and with the word "mascara" wrongly introduces modern Western cultural usage into the biblical setting. TEV uses a low-level idiom which suggests putting on eye make-up; thus only the TEV and LB make clear what is meant by "painting" or "enlarging the eyes." The other translations leave the reader with questions: Do the eyes themselves become bigger? Is the paint put into the eye?

E-13 New Testament: Consistency of Language Level

1. Matt 3.8
   RSV   bear fruit that befits repentance
   TEV   do the things that will show that you have turned from your sins
      Compare:
   NRT   do the things that will show you have turned away from your sins
   JB   but if you are repentant, produce the appropriate fruit
   NEB   then prove your repentance by the fruit it bears
   Knox come, then, yield the acceptable fruit of repentance
   BE   let your change of heart be seen in your works
   TNT   show by your conduct that you have truly repented

   YL   _____

      Evaluation:

2. Matt 3.15
   RSV   for thus it is fitting for us to fulfil all righteousness
   TEV   for in this way we shall do all that God requires
      Compare:
   NEB   we do well to conform in this way with all that God requires
   JB   it is fitting that we should, in this way, do all that righteousness demands
   Knox it is well that we should thus fulfill all due observance
   TNT   for in this way it is fitting for us to fulfill all that God requires

   YL   _____

      Evaluation:

E-14 Old Testament: Consistency of Language Level (Instructions as for Drill E-13)

1. Isa 1.20
   RSV   but if you refuse and rebel, you shall be devoured by the sword
   TEV   but if you defy me, you are doomed to die
      Compare:
   JB   but if you persist in rebellion, the sword shall eat you instead
   NAS   but if you refuse and rebel, you will be devoured by the sword
   LB   but if you keep on turning your backs and refusing to listen to me, you will
            be killed by your enemies

   YL   _____

      Evaluation:

2. Jer 2.5
   RSV   [your fathers] went after worthlessness, and became worthless
   TEV   [your ancestors] they worshiped worthless idols and became worthless them-
            selves
      Compare:
   NEB   pursuing empty phantoms, themselves becoming empty
   JB   vanity they pursued, and vanity they became
   NAS   walked after emptiness and became empty

   YL   _____

      Evaluation:

6. TRANSLATING FOR SPECIAL AUDIENCES

E-15 Translating for a Five-Year-Old Child

Purpose. We now want to practice keeping to a specific level of language in our translation. All too often translators just translate words without really thinking of the people for whom they are translating. In order to learn to maintain a specific level of language, it is important that the translator translate for a specific audience. If the audience aim is clear, then it is easier to know whether the level is right, and if one is in doubt, one can go and ask this specific type of person.

Instructions

(a) Study the list of kernels on the following page and compare them with the RSV original. Check whether the list of near-kernel expressions includes all the information in the text. If not, make the necessary adjustments.

(b) Reconstruct these kernels into a translation that could be easily understood by an English-speaking five-year-old child. In order to make sure your level is correct, think of a specific child and write on the top of your work: This translation is for (name of child). If convenient, read your version to the child you have selected and see whether the level is right or whether there still are some "lumps" left.

(c) Compare your English version with the version for new readers at the bottom of this page. Remember the NRT was prepared for adults who are just learning to read, not for children. Also note that for new readers and for children it is best to print the text with short lines.

(d) Now select a five-year-old child who speaks your language and prepare a similar translation; again check with the specific child of your choice to see if you need to make any further adjustments.

Luke 8.22-25 NRT (adapted)

One day Jesus got into a boat with his followers.
    He said to them,
        "Let us go across
            to the other side of the lake."
    So they started out.
As they were sailing,
    Jesus went to sleep.
A strong wind blew down on the lake,
    and the boat began to fill with water.
        So they were all in great danger.
The men with Jesus
        woke him up.
    They said, "Master, Master!
    We are about to die!"
Jesus got up and told the wind
        and the stormy water to stop.
    They stopped right away
    and there was a great calm.
Then Jesus said to the followers,
    "Where is your faith?"
But they were surprised and afraid.
    They said to one another,
        "Who is this man?
        He told the wind and waves to stop
            and they obey him!"

Luke 8.22-25 RSV

One day he got into a boat with his disciples, and he said to them, "Let us go across to the other side of the lake." So they set out, and as they sailed he fell asleep. And a storm of wind came down on the lake, and they were filling with water, and were in danger. And they went and woke him, saying, "Master, Master, we are perishing!" And he awoke and rebuked the wind and the raging waves; and they ceased, and there was a calm. He said to them, "Where is your faith?" And they were afraid, and they marveled, saying to one another, "Who then is this, that he commands even wind and water, and they obey him?"

List of near-kernel expressions	Your text for a five-year-old child
it happened one day	For_____
Jesus got into a boat	(name of child)
his disciples got into a boat	
Jesus said to them	
let us cross to the other side of the lake	
they set out	
they were sailing	
Jesus fell asleep	
a strong wind came (suddenly)	
it blew upon the lake	
the boat began to fill with water	
they were in danger (of going under)	
they went to Jesus	
they awoke him	
they said to him	
Master, Master	
we are perishing	
Jesus awoke	
he rebuked the wind	
he rebuked the raging waves	
the wind stopped	
the waves stopped	
it was very calm	
Jesus said to them	
where is your faith?	
they were afraid	
they marveled	
they said to one another	
who is this now?	
he commands the wind	
he commands the water	
the wind obeys him	
the water obeys him	

7. FEATURES OF STYLE

E-16 Features of Style in Luke 15.11-24

      Purpose. In this drill we want to learn how to distinguish between good and bad features of style by comparing different translations.

      Instructions. Study the different renderings of each of the items listed comparatively. Note and discuss both the good and the bad points you find.

Verse 11	ASV	RSV	NEB
1	and he said	and he said	again he said
2	a certain man	there was a man	there once was a man

Verse 12			
3	the younger of them	the younger of them	the younger
4	the portion of thy substance that falleth to me	the share of property that falls to me	my share of the property
5	and he divided	and he divided	so he divided
6	his living	his living	his estate

Verse 13			
7	and not many days after	not many days later	a few days later
8	gathered all together	gathered all he had	turned the whole of his share into cash
9	took his journey	took his journey	left home
10	a far country	a far country	a distant country
11	there	there	where
12	his substance	his property	it
13	riotous living	loose living	reckless living

Verse 14			
14	when he...spent...a mighty famine	when he...spent...a great famine	he...spent...when a severe famine
15	spent all	spent everything	spent it all
16	a mighty famine	a great famine	a severe famine
17	[famine] arose	famine arose	famine fell
18	to be in want	to be in want	to feel the pinch

Verse 15			
19	joined himself to	joined himself to	attached himself to
20	one of the citizens of that country	one of the citizens of that country	one of the local landowners
21	into his fields	into his fields	on to his farm
22	to feed swine	to feed swine	to mind the pigs

Verse 16			
23	fain would have been filled with the husks	have fed on the pods	to fill his belly with the pods
24	that the swine did eat	that the swine ate	that the pigs were eating

TNT	TEV	LB
he said	Jesus went on to say	to further illustrate the point
a man	there was a man	he told them this story: "A man
the younger of them	the younger one	when the younger
my due share of the property	now my share of the property	I want my share of your estate now instead of waiting until you die
and he divided	so the man divided	his father agreed to divide
his possessions	the property	his wealth
not many days later	after a few days	a few days later
gathered everything to-gether	sold his part of the property	packed all his belongings
went abroad	left home	took a trip
a distant country	a country far away	a distant land
there	where	there
all he had	his money	all his money
dissolute life	reckless living	on parties and prostitutes
when he...spent...a severe famine	he spent...then a severe famine	about the time his money was gone a great famine
spent everything	spent everything he had	his money was gone
a severe famine	severe famine	a great famine
famine occurred	famine spread over	famine swept over the land
to be in need	was left without a thing	and he began to starve
attached himself to	went to work for	he persuaded a local farmer to hire him
a citizen of that coun-try	one of the citizens of that country	a local farmer
to his field	out to his farm	(absent)
to feed pigs	to take care of the pigs	to feed his pigs
longed to satisfy his hunger with the pods	he wished he could fill himself with the bean pods	the boy became so hungry that even the pods...looked good to him
which the pigs were eat-ing	the pigs ate	he was feeding the swine

Verse 17	ASV	RSV	NEB
25	came to himself	came to himself	came to his senses
26	hired servants	hired servants	paid servants
27	have bread enough and to spare	have bread enough and to spare	have more food than they can eat
28	I perish here with hunger	I perish here with hunger	here I am starving to death
Verse 18			
29	I will arise and go	I will arise and go	I will set off and go
30	sinned against heaven and in thy sight	sinned against heaven and before you	sinned against God and against you
Verse 19			
31	I am no more worthy	I am no longer worthy	I am no longer fit
Verse 20			
32	and he arose	and he arose	so he set out
33	came to his father	came to his father	for his father's house
34	yet afar off	yet at a distance	still a long way off
35	was moved with compassion	had compassion	his heart went out to him
36	fell on his neck	embraced him	flung his arms round him
Verse 21			
37	and the son said	and the son said	the son said
Verse 22			
38	bring forth quickly the best robe	bring quickly the best robe	quick! fetch a robe, my best one
39	put a ring on his hand	put a ring on his hand	put a ring on his finger
Verse 23			
40	let us eat and make merry	let us eat and make merry	let us have a feast to celebrate the day
Verse 24			
41	this my son	this my son	this son of mine
42	is alive again	is alive again	has come back to life
43	they began to be merry	they began to make merry	the festivities began

TNT	TEV	LB
came to	came to his senses	came to his senses
hired men	hired workers	hired men
have more than enough food	have more than they can eat	have food enough and to spare
I am dying here of hunger	here I am, about to starve	and here I am, dying of hunger
I will get up and go	I will get up and go	I will go home
sinned against heaven and against you	sinned against God and against you	I have sinned against both heaven and you
I no longer deserve	I am no longer fit	and am no longer worthy
he got up and went	so he got up and started back	so he returned home
to his father	to his father	to his father
still a long way off	still a long way from home	and while...still a long distance away
was moved with pity	his heart was filled with pity	was filled with loving pity
embraced...him	threw his arms around his son	embraced him
the son said	the son said	the son said
quick! bring out the best garment	hurry!...bring the best robe	quick! bring the finest robe in the house
put a ring on his hand	put a ring on his finger	and a jeweled ring for his finger
let us eat and enjoy ourselves	let us celebrate with a feast	we must celebrate with a feast
this son of mine	this son of mine	this son of mine
has come to life again	now he is alive	has returned to life
they began to enjoy themselves	and so the feasting began	so the party began

Features of Style in Selected Passages

      Purpose. A good translation aims to achieve a uniform style and an even level of language. This is not always easy since languages exhibit different levels (higher to lower), varying degrees of formality (formal to slang), and differences in time (archaic to newly coined) as well as words transliterated from other languages.

Differences of Level:
He bought a house. (common language)
He purchased a house. (higher level)
He effected the purchase of a house. (unnecessarily high)

Differences in Degree of Formality:
Hi ya! (slang)   Hello! (informal)
Hi! (very casual)   How do you do? (formal)

Differences in Age of the Speaker:
Paxo! (as a newly coined greeting used by a teen-age gang meaning "peace." Probably a
      corruption of the old Latin greeting *Pax vobiscum*)
Hail! (archaic)

      Instructions. Read the following passages and underline those words or constructions that you consider out of place for a translation to be read in church services for people for whom English is a second language and who have had only primary education. What types of "misfit" do the underlined items represent?

> Example
> John 4.36 (LB)
> The reapers will be paid good wages and will be gathering eternal souls into the granaries of heaven. What joys await the sower and the reaper, both together!
>
>   Evaluation:
> The expression eternal souls is church jargon and granaries is not a common-language word.

E-17 New Testament: Features of Style

1. Believe me, you will never get out again till you have paid your last farthing (Matt 5.26 Phps)

    Evaluation:

2. The Old Testament laws said, 'If anyone wants to be rid of his wife, he can divorce her merely by giving her a letter of dismissal' (Matt 5.31 LB)

    Evaluation:

E-18 Old Testament: Features of Style (Instructions as for Drill E-17)

1. Hell is licking its chops in anticipation of this delicious morsel (Isa 5.14 LB)

    Evaluation:

2. thou art with me, thy staff and thy crook are my comfort (Psa 23.4 NEB)

    Evaluation:

F. UNDERSTANDING AND TRANSLATING FIGURATIVE LANGUAGE

1. LITERAL OR FIGURATIVE?

Purpose. In all languages some words have figurative meanings as well as literal meanings; therefore it is important that we learn to recognize when a meaning is literal and when it is nonliteral or figurative. The reasons for using figurative language are many: it can describe a new experience for which there is no specific word, or it can express something old in a new and striking way, or it can make the message more emotive. While all languages use figures of speech, they usually use different words as the basis of figures; and even when they do use the same word, the figurative meaning in two languages may be quite different, because figurative extensions of meaning are usually based on supplementary components which occur in specific languages only. In the drills in this section we want to learn: (a) to distinguish between literal and nonliteral meaning, (b) to identify some of the major types of figurative language found in the Bible, and (c) to gain some experience in handling nonliteral meaning in translation.

Instructions. Study the following quotations from the RSV (sometimes KJV) and try to decide whether the underlined word is used literally. Then, according to your decision, write L (literal) or F (figurative/nonliteral) in the blank preceding the number.

Examples
F 1. (Luke 23.28) daughters of Jerusalem, do not weep for me
L 2. (Acts 21.9) he had four unmarried daughters
    L 3. (John 13.5) he poured water into a basin
    F 4. (Rom 5.5) love has been poured into our hearts
L 5. (Luke 12.24) ravens: they neither sow nor reap
F 6. (Gal 6.8) from the Spirit reap eternal life
    F 7. (1 Tim 6.18) they are to do good, to be rich in good deeds
    L 8. (Mark 12.41) many rich people put in large sums
L 9. (Matt 6.6) shut the door and pray to your Father
F 10. (Luke 13.24) strive to enter by the narrow door
F 11. (John 10.9) [Jesus said] I am the door
L 12. (John 18.16) Peter stood outside at the door
F 13. (Acts 14.27) how he [God] had opened a door of faith to the Gentiles
F 14. (Rev 3.8) behold, I have set before you an open door

F-1 New Testament: Literal or Figurative?

____ 1. (Matt 12.39)   adulterous generation
____ 2. (John 8.3-4 KJV) adulterous woman
____ 3. (Heb 13.4)   God will judge the immoral and adulterous
    ____ 4. (Matt 27.24) Pilate...washed his hands
    ____ 5. (John 13.5)   began to wash the disciples' feet
    ____ 6. (Acts 22.16) be baptized and wash away your sins
    ____ 7. (1 Cor 6.11) you were washed, you were sanctified
____ 8. (Matt 8.14)   when Jesus entered Peter's house
____ 9. (Acts 7.42)   in the wilderness, O house of Israel
____10. (Luke 1.27)   Joseph, of the house of David
____11. (John 14.2)   in my Father's house are many rooms
____12. (Rom 16.5)   greet also the church in their house
____13. (1 Peter 2.5)   like living stones...built into a spiritual house
____14. (Heb 3.2)   Moses also was faithful in God's house

	15. (Matt 8.2)	make me clean
	16. (Acts 18.6 KJV)	your blood be upon your own heads; I am clean
	17. (Matt 10.1)	unclean spirits
	18. (Matt 27.59)	wrapped it in a clean linen shroud
	19. (Acts 15.9)	cleansed their hearts by faith
	20. (1 Cor 7.14)	otherwise, your children would be unclean
21. (Matt 10.8)		cast out demons
22. (Acts 27.38 KJV)		they...cast out the wheat into the sea
23. (Gal 4.30)		cast out the slave and her son
24. (John 9.34)		will you teach us?" And they cast him out
25. (Luke 20.15)		they cast him out of the vineyard
26. (Acts 27.19)		on the third day they cast out...the tackle of the ship
	27. (Luke 15.24 KJV)	for this my son was...lost
	28. (Luke 19.10)	came to seek and to save the lost
	29. (John 6.12)	gather up the fragments...that nothing may be lost
	30. (Mark 9.50)	if the salt has lost its saltness
	31. (Luke 15.11)	I have found the coin which I had lost
	32. (Matt 15.24)	only to the lost sheep of the house of Israel
	33. (Mark 2.22)	burst the skins and the wine is lost

F-2 Old Testament: Literal or Figurative? (Instructions as for Drill F-1)

	1. (Num 22.31)	the LORD opened the eyes of Balaam
	2. (2 Kgs 4.35)	and the child opened his eyes
	3. (Psa 119.18)	open my eyes, that I may behold
	4. (Deut 11.6)	how the earth opened its mouth
	5. (Judges 11.35)	I have opened my mouth to the LORD
	6. (Ezek 2.8)	open your mouth and eat what I give you
7. (Gen 4.1)		Adam knew Eve his wife
8. (Gen 31.32 KJV)		Jacob knew not that Rachel had stolen
9. (Exo 1.8 KJV)		a new king...which knew not Joseph
	10. (Micah 1.12)	but evil came down from the LORD
	11. (Exo 2.5)	daughter of Pharaoh came down to bathe
	12. (Exo 34.29)	as he came down from the mountain
13. (Exo 12.33)		we are all dead men
14. (2 Kgs 4.32)		the child lying dead
	15. (Gen 38.24)	your daughter-in-law has played the harlot
	16. (Exo 34.15)	when they play the harlot after their gods
17. (Gen 17.14)		any uncircumcised male...shall be cut off
18. (Exo 6.30)		I am of uncircumcised lips
	19. (Gen 27.1)	Isaac was old and his eyes were dim
	20. (Gen 31.40)	my sleep fled from my eyes
	21. (Josh 24.7)	your eyes saw what I did to Egypt
	22. (1 Sam 16.12)	he was ruddy, and had beautiful eyes
	23. (1 Kgs 1.20)	the eyes of all Israel are upon you
	24. (2 Kgs 4.35)	the child opened his eyes
	25. (2 Kgs 6.20)	the LORD opened their eyes and they saw
	26. (2 Kgs 25.7)	and put out the eyes of Zedekiah
	27. (Job 11.4)	I am clean in God's eyes
	28. (Isa 13.18)	their eyes will not pity children
	29. (Zech 1.18)	I lifted my eyes and saw

2. RECOGNIZING AND COUNTING FIGURES OF SPEECH

Purpose. Figurative language serves as an enrichment of the message, and since many figurative meanings are of necessity lost in translation, either because the original figure cannot be translated, or because there is no equivalent figure in the receptor language, new figures should be introduced elsewhere as replacements. Ideally we would like to keep the same ratio of figures in the translation as there are in the original. Generally this can be done if the translator is sufficiently aware of the total resources of his language.

Instructions. Study the following passages in the three translations quoted and in your own language. Mark all nonliteral usage by underlining. Once you have marked all four translations, count up the number of figures in each. See if there is any significant difference between translations. Does the difference in the number of figures change the impact of the translation?

Examples
2 Peter 2.14

RSV They have eyes full of adultery, insatiable for sin. They entice unsteady souls. They have hearts trained in greed. Accursed children!

Number of figures 7

TEV They want to look at nothing else but immoral women; their appetite for sin is never satisfied. They lead weak people into a trap. Their hearts are trained to be greedy. They are under God's curse!

Number of figures 4

NEB They have eyes for nothing but women, eyes never at rest from sin. They lure the unstable to their ruin; past masters in mercenery greed, God's curse is on them!

Number of figures 6

YL

Number of figures ___
   Evaluation:
RSV and NEB have 7 and 6 figures respectively; TEV has only 4. TEV is straight-forward, but lacks some of the "punch" of NEB. On the other hand, NEB's use of high-level language and specialized figures makes it harder to understand for readers for whom English is a second language.

---

1 Peter 5.2-4

RSV Tend the flock of God that is your charge, not by constraint but willingly, not for shameful gain but eagerly, not as domineering over those in your charge but being examples to the flock. And when the chief Shepherd is manifested you will obtain the unfading crown of glory.

Number of figures ___

TEV Be shepherds of the flock that God gave you, and look after it willingly as God wants you to, and not unwillingly. Do your work, not for mere pay, but from a real desire to serve. Do not try to rule over those who have been given into your care, but be examples to the flock. And when the Chief Shepherd appears, you will receive the glorious crown which will never lose its brightness.

Number of figures ___

Phps I urge you then to see that your "flock of God" is properly fed and cared for. Accept the responsibility of looking after them willingly and not because you feel you can't get out of it, doing your work not for what you can make, but because you are really concerned for their well-being. You should aim not at being "little tin gods" but as examples of Christian living in the eyes of the flock committed to your charge. And then, when the chief shepherd reveals himself you will receive that crown of glory which cannot fade. (Sixth printing, 1959)

Number of figures ___

YL

Number of figures ___

   Evaluation:

Isa 30.27-28

RSV Behold, the name of the LORD comes from far, burning with his anger, and in thick rising smoke; his lips are full of indignation, and his tongue is like a devouring fire; his breath is like an overflowing stream that reaches up to the neck; to sift the nations with the sieve of destruction, and to place on the jaws of the peoples a bridle that leads astray.

Number of figures ___

TEV The LORD's power and glory can be seen in the distance. Fire and smoke show his anger. He speaks, and his words burn like fire. He sends the wind in front of him like a flood that carries everything away. It sweeps nations to destruction and puts an end to their evil plans.

Number of figures ___

NEB See, the name of the LORD comes from afar, his anger blazing and his doom heavy. His lips are charged with wrath and his tongue is a devouring fire. His breath is like a torrent in spate, rising neck-high, a yoke to force the nations to their ruin, a bit in the mouth to guide the peoples astray.

Number of figures ___

YL

Number of figures ___

    Evaluation:

3. RECOGNIZING AND IDENTIFYING DIFFERENT KINDS OF FIGURES

    Purpose. In the previous drills we have been developing skills in recognizing figures of speech. In this drill section we not only want
    (a) to identify expressions as figures of speech, but we also want
    (b) to learn to recognize what kind of a figure of speech it is or what kind of special figurative function it has. Here now follows a partial listing of the kinds of figures of speech and figurative functions found in the Bible.

    (1) Simile: a simple comparison. Something is said to be like something else. The two things are compared because they are seen as sharing some quality or qualities; for example, in God is like a rock, God is seen as sharing certain qualities of a rock. Often the shared quality is indicated in the text, as in Our God is like a strong rock. The shared quality can be either an essential component, as in round as a ball; or even more frequently it is a conventionally accepted supplementary component that may be unique to a culture; for example, in Choco he is stupid as a tiger,

because a _tiger_ is considered to be big but stupid. Similes can usually be retained in translation, even if they are new, when the shared component is expressed.

(2) Metaphor: an abbreviated comparison. The _as_ or _like_ marker of the comparison has been left out, and one thing is said to be something else, for example, _Our God is a rock_. Again the shared quality may be expressed as in _Our God is a strong rock_. As in similes, the shared quality is usually a conventionally accepted supplementary component, as in Choco _he is a tiger_, where the Choco person will hear the quality _stupid_, but North Americans will hear the quality _aggressive_. Many metaphors can be kept in translation if they are changed to complete similes.

(3) Metonym: one word is replaced by another that is seen as associated with it in some way; for example, in _they fell by the sword_ the word _sword_ really replaces the word _war_. In actual fact they may have been speared or run over by a chariot, but because a _sword_ is an important weapon of war, it can be used as a metonym to replace the word _war_. Often the association is not obvious to everyone; that is why certain poems rich in metonyms are hard to understand. If a person cannot identify the association involved, he will have no way of knowing what the metonym means. Metonyms often can be retained in translation if the word replaced is also added, for example, _take this cup from me_ rendered as _take this cup of suffering from me_.

(4) Synecdoche: a special type of metonym. In a synecdoche the association between the words replaced is either a part-for-the-whole, for example, _my mouth praises the Lord_, for "I praise the Lord"; or a whole-for-a-part, as in Paul's admonition to Timothy, _drink no more water_, which means "don't drink only water"; or _everybody came to see him_, where everybody really means "many people." Every whole-for-a-part synecdoche is a hyperbole, an exaggeration. This latter kind of synecdoche can seldom be retained. The part-for-the-whole type can often be retained or replaced by a very similar part, for example, _my tongue praises the Lord_ can be rendered as _my mouth praises the Lord_.

(5) Idiom: an expression of two or more words whose unit meaning is different from the sum of the meaning of its parts, for example, _go jump in the lake_ meaning "go away, you are a nuisance," or the biblical _heap coals of fire on his head_ meaning "make him ashamed." Idioms are highly language-bound and must usually be translated only by their meaning or, if possible, by a different figure that is taken from the receptor language and that has the same meaning.

Special Usages of Metaphors and Metonyms. Metonyms, and in some cases, metaphors, can be used for a variety of special functions. Since these different special uses often require different treatment in translation, the translator needs to be able to identify them and to treat them correctly.

(i) Anthropomorphism: using human body parts, emotions, or actions to describe spiritual beings, for example, _the arm of the Lord_, _the devil said_, _the spirit grabbed him_, etc. Since most cultures speak of spirits in human terms, anthropomorphisms can usually be kept in the form of the original. There are some exceptions; for example, _the spirit entered his body_ may have to be rendered as _the spirit grabbed him_ or _took his soul_ if the culture in question does not view spirits as entering bodies.

(ii) Hylopsychism: ascribing human activities or functions to nonliving things, for example, _the earth opened its mouth and swallowed them_, or _the trees danced for joy_. Many languages have difficulty understanding such usage. The translation may have to say: _the earth split open, the people fell in and were covered up_, or even _the trees waved as if they were happy_.

(iii) Personification: addressing a thing, town, or mountain as if it were a person, for example, _Hear, O earth_, or _Woe to you Tyre and Sidon!_ Some languages do not permit such an address, and the word _people_ has to be added in the translation as in _Hear, O people of the earth_, or _Woe to you, people of Tyre and Sidon!_

(iv) Religious specialization: an ordinary word is used to describe religious or spiritual experiences, for example, _we were lost but now we are saved_, where both _lost_ and _saved_ are used for spiritual rather than physical experience; or _we are_

God's children, where children involves a spiritual rather than a biological relationship. Most languages can extend the meanings of ordinary words to cover spiritual experience, but great care needs to be taken to be sure the new spiritual usage is adequately marked; for example, the narrow way leads to life needs to be marked as the narrow way leads to eternal life. See also The Marking of Meaning, Drills C-11 to C-13.

(v) Word avoidance: sometimes words become taboo, that is, they are felt to be too dangerous to use. This means that they have become too holy, and therefore they are dangerous. The Hebrews felt that God's name was too holy for ordinary people to say, so they replaced it with other words such as the Almighty, the Creator, or even heaven, as in he who is in the heavens. Compare the New Testament usage I have sinned against heaven, where heaven really means "God." Likewise the Devil's name can be dangerous, so he is referred to as the evil one. Where such a replacement word is misleading, it may have to be changed, for example, I have sinned against God, not heaven. For a scholarly translation it might be wise to call attention to the word avoidance by means of a footnote.

(vi) Euphemism: when certain words become too heavily charged with negative emotions they are replaced by a substitute word or expression. This is especially true of words relating to sex, bodily functions, and death, for example, he knew her for "he had intercourse with her," or he passed away for "he died." All languages employ euphemisms wherever possible, but not necessarily the same ones. The translators must try to find local euphemisms wherever possible. As in common-language English, euphemisms may be tainted with negative feelings, and a straightforward expression must be used, for example, "they had sexual intercourse."

Rhetorical Figures. The following three kinds of nonliteral meaning are not figures of speech but rhetorical devices. However, since their meaning is not literal, we include them here.

(1) Hyperbole: an over- or understatement for purposes of emphasis or attracting attention (see also whole-for-a-part synecdoche), such as he knows everything or he knows nothing.

(2) Irony: using a statement in its opposite meaning, for example, how strong you are! meaning "you are really very weak!"

(3) Secret language: the meaning of secret language is known only to the one who understands the code. Secret language is usually marked in some way in the text, as in abomination of desolation (let the reader understand).

Instructions
(a) Underline the figurative expression(s) in the RSV or KJV substitute for the original language.

(b) Identify the kind of figure of speech or figurative usage and write its name in the blank marked (b).

(c) Compare the series of translations, including your own language, in order to see how the different translations have handled the above figures in translation. We want to ask such questions as: Has the original figure been kept? Has it been kept only in part? Has a different figure been substituted for the one in the text? Does the new figure introduce any strange components? Has the original figure been changed to a nonfigure? Write your evaluation in the space provided.

(d) Make a new meaningful translation of the passage into your own language on the line marked (d).

```
Example
Acts 2.30
KJV  fruit of his loins                    (b)  idiom, containing a metaphor
  Compare:                                       fruit and a metonym loins
TEV  one of David's descendants
BE   fruit of his body
NEB  one of his own direct descendants     (d)_____
LB   one of David's own descendants
YL   _____

   Evaluation:
BE retains the figure but changes loins to body, yet the meaning is not clear.
All the others replace the figure with a nonfigure and say descendant.
```

F-5 New Testament: What Kind of Figure of Speech?

1. Matt 3.8
    RSV   bear fruit that befits repentance   (b)_____
      Compare:
    TEV   do the things that will show that
            you have turned from your sins
    NEB   prove your repentance by the fruit   (d)_____
            it bears
    TNT   show by your conduct that you
            have truly repented
    Phps do something to show that your
            hearts are really changed
    YL   _____

      Evaluation:

2. Matt 3.16
    RSV   descending like a dove   (b)_____
      Compare:
    TEV   coming down like a dove
    LB   coming down in the form of a dove
    YL   _____   (d)_____

      Evaluation:

3. Matt 5.2   (b)_____
    RSV   he opened his mouth and taught
      Compare:
    TEV   he began to teach them
    JB   he began to speak   (d)_____
    Phps he began his teaching by saying
    NAS   opening his mouth He began to teach
    YL   _____

      Evaluation:

[190]

4. Matt 5.6
   RSV   hunger and thirst for righteousness   (b)_____
      Compare:
   TEV   whose greatest desire is to do what
            God requires
   TNT   who hunger and thirst for what is   (d_____
            right
   LB   who long to be just and good
   NEB   who hunger and thirst to see right
            prevail
   YL   _____

   Evaluation:

F-6 Old Testament: What Kind of Figure of Speech? (Instructions as for Drill F-5)

1. Gen 20.3
   RSV   you are a dead man   (b)_____
      Compare:
   TEV   you are going to die
   NEB   you shall die
   LB   you are a dead man   (d)_____
   JB   you are to die
   YL   _____

   Evaluation:

2. Gen 29.2
   RSV   the stone on the well's mouth was   (b)_____
            large
      Compare:
   TEV   a large stone over the opening
   NEB   over its mouth was a huge stone   (d)_____
   LB   a heavy stone covered the mouth
            of the well
   JB   the stone on the mouth of the well
            was a large one
   NAS   the stone on the mouth of the well
            was large
   YL   _____

   Evaluation:

3. Gen 30.2
   RSV   who has withheld from you the   (b)_____
         fruit of the womb
      Compare:
   TEV   he is the one who keeps you from
         having children   (d)_____
   NEB   God, who has denied you children
   LB   he is the one who is responsible
         for your barrenness
   JB   it is he who has refused you mother-
         hood
   NAS   God, who withheld from you the fruit
         of the womb
   YL   _____

      Evaluation:

4. Gen 30.22
   RSV   then God remembered Rachel   (b)_____
      Compare:
   TEV   then God remembered Rachel
   NEB   then God thought of Rachel
   LB   then God remembered about Rachel's   (d)_____
         plight
   JB   then God remembered Rachel
   YL   _____

      Evaluation:

4. SIMILES

Analyzing Complete Similes
        Purpose. We want to learn to recognize the four essential parts of a simple comparison, called a simile. We will give the following names to each of the four parts of the comparison. Note the abbreviations which we will use, given in [ ] before the name: [O] object (of the comparison)—the person or thing about which the statement is being made; [M] marker (of the comparison)—usually words like "as," "like," "similar to," etc. or "bigger/smaller than" with degree added; [I] image (of the comparison)—the thing to which the object is being compared; [B] basis (of the comparison)—the component of meaning on the basis of which the comparison is being made.
        Instructions. Study the biblical phrases presented in this drill and identify each of the four parts of the comparison. Write each part into the appropriate box on the drill sheet.

Examples

Isa 53.6   all we like sheep have gone astray

O	all we	M	like	I	sheep	B	have gone astray
	Object		Marker		Image		Basis

Isa 9.18   wickedness burns like fire...it consumes...it kindles

O	wickedness	M	like	I	fire	B	consumes, kindles
	Object		Marker		Image		Basis

F-7 New Testament: Complete Similes

1. Matt 9.36   [crowds] helpless like sheep without a shepherd

O		M		I		B	

2. Matt 10.16   so [you] be wise as serpents

O		M		I		B	

3. Matt 10.16   and innocent as doves

O		M		I		B	

4. Matt 17.2   his [Jesus'] garments became white as light

O		M		I		B	

5. Matt 28.3   his [the angel's] raiment white as snow

O		M		I		B	

6. Luke 3.22   the Holy Spirit descended upon him in bodily form as a dove

O		M		I		B	

7. Luke 12.24   of how much more value are you than the birds

O		M		I		B	

8. Luke 12.36   [you] be like men who are waiting for their master...so they may
open to him at once

O		M		I		B	

9. Luke 13.19   it [kingdom of God] is like a grain of mustard seed which a man took
and sowed in his garden; and it grew and became a tree

O		M	I		B	

F-8 Old Testament: Complete Similes (Instructions as for Drill F-7)

1. Gen 3.5   you...be like God, knowing good and evil

O		M	I		B	

2. Gen 25.25   all his body like a hairy mantle

O		M	I		B	

3. Gen 31.26   carried away my daughters like captives

O		M	I		B	

4. Gen 49.4   [Reuben] unstable as water

O		M	I		B	

5. Exo 15.10   they sank as lead

O		M	I		B	

6. Exo 15.16   they are as still as a stone

O		M	I		B	

7. Exo 19.18   [Mt. Sinai smoked] like the smoke of a kiln

O		M	I		B	

8. Exo 24.10   a pavement of sapphire stone, like the very heaven for clearness

O		M	I		B	

9. Exo 24.17   the glory of the LORD was like a devouring fire

O		M	I		B	

Translating Complete Similes

Purpose. In this exercise we want to demonstrate that complete similes can almost always be translated into another language. The exceptions are: (a) where the biblical image involves culturally unknown items, for example, snow in many tropical cultures; (b) where the image in the receptor's language has very different essential or supplementary components which contradict or obscure the message of the Bible; for example, if the word fox has a strong local supplementary component of "sex fiend," it may override the biblical component of "destructive" in the expression "Herod is a destructive fox." People will still "hear" that Herod was a sex fiend even though the biblical component of destructive is clearly expressed.[a]

Instructions

(a) Copy the appropriate phrases from your Bible or New Testament on the line marked YL.

(b) Now compare all the translations, including the one in your language, to see how the similes have been treated in the translation, and write your findings in the space marked "evaluation."

(c) Note any similes that cannot be translated into your language. Discuss the reasons why.

Example
Isa 53.6
RSV all we like sheep have gone astray
   Compare:
TEV all of us were like sheep that were lost
NEB we have all strayed like sheep
LB   we are the ones who strayed away like sheep
YL   _____

   Evaluation:
All of the translations listed keep the simile, but there are some differences of focus, emphasis, and language level.

---

[a]Many Western commentators still prefer the supplementary components conventional to European writings, namely, sly, deceitful; but in Third World countries the newer German exegesis cited above is finding wide acceptance.

F-9 New Testament: Translating Complete Similes

1. Matt 9.36
   RSV [crowds] helpless, like sheep without a shepherd
   Compare:
   TEV [crowds] helpless, like sheep without a shepherd
   LB   [crowds] didn't know...where to go for help. They were like sheep without a shepherd
   JB   [crowds] dejected, like sheep without a shepherd
   YL   _____

   Evaluation:

2. Matt 10.16
   RSV so be wise as serpents and innocent as doves
   Compare:
   TEV you must be as cautious as snakes and as gentle as doves
   JB   so you be cunning as serpents and yet as harmless as doves
   TNT therefore [you] like snakes be constantly on the alert and be as guileless as doves
   YL   _____

   Evaluation:

F-10 Old Testament: Translating Complete Similes (Instructions as for Drill F-9)

1. Gen 3.5
   RSV you will be like God knowing good and evil
   Compare:
   TEV you will be like God and know what is good and what is bad
   JB   you will be like gods, knowing good and evil
   LB   you will become like him [God]...you will be able to distinguish good from evil
   YL   _____

   Evaluation:

2. Gen 25.25
   RSV all his body like a hairy mantle
   Compare:
   TEV his skin was like a hairy robe
   NEB hairy all over like a hair-cloak
   LB   so covered with reddish hair one would think he was wearing a fur coat
   YL   _____

   Evaluation:

Analyzing Incomplete Similes

Instructions. The following similes are incomplete, that is, the supplementary component, on the basis of which the comparison is made, is missing. This usually means the comparison was so familiar in biblical times that everyone understood it even when the reason for the comparison was not expressed. Study the context from which the quotation is taken and identify what the missing ground of the comparison is. Write out the four parts of the comparison putting the implicit basis of the comparison in the dotted box on the right.

Examples

Exo 7.1   I make you as God to Pharaoh

Object	Marker	Image	Basis
O	you	M	as	I	God	B	who controls

or can do miracles

Luke 11.30 as Jonah became a sign to the men of Nineveh, so will the Son of man be to this generation

Object	Marker	Image	Basis
O	Son of man to	M	as—so	I	Jonah to the peo-	B	sign that it is

this generation   ple of Nineveh   time to repent

F-11 New Testament: Analyzing Incomplete Similes

1. Matt 10.16   send you out as sheep in the midst of wolves

| O | | M | | I | | B | |

2. Matt 17.20   faith as a grain of mustard seed

| O | | M | | I | | B | |

3. Matt 18.17   let him be to you as a Gentile and a tax collector

| O | | M | | I | | B | |

4. Matt 23.37   how often would I have gathered your children together as a hen gathers her brood

| O | | M | | I | | B | |

5. Matt 24.27   as the lightning comes...so will be the coming of the Son of man

| O | | M | | I | | B | |

6. Matt 24.37-38   as were the days of Noah, so will be the coming of the Son of
                   man...eating and drinking, marrying and given in marriage

O		M		I		B	

7. Matt 25.32   he will separate them...as a shepherd separates the sheep from the
                goats

O		M		I		B	

8. Matt 28.3   his appearance was like lightning

O		M		I		B	

9. Luke 11.44   you are like graves which are not seen

O		M		I		B	

F-12 Old Testament: Analyzing Incomplete Similes (Instructions as for Drill F-11)

1. Deut 32.2   my teaching [shall] drop as the rain

O		M		I		B	

2. Deut 32.10   he [God] kept him as the apple of his eye

O		M		I		B	

3. Deut 33.20   Gad couches like a lion

O		M		I		B	

4. Josh 7.5   [hearts of the people] became as water

O		M		I		B	

5. Job 13.12 (KJV)   your remembrances are like unto ashes

O		M		I		B	

6. Psa 18.33   he made my feet like hind's feet

O		M		I		B	

Translating Incomplete Similes

Purpose. In this drill we want to learn that incomplete similes can be kept in the receptor language if the comparisons are known to the speakers of the language. If they are not known, it still may be possible to retain them by expressing explicitly the implicit component of meaning on the basis of which the comparison is being made, in other words, by making it a complete simile.

Instructions

(a) Study the translations listed below, including your language, to see how they have handled the incomplete similes in translation. Discuss any positive or negative feature raised by specific translations. Write your findings in the space marked "evaluation."

(b) On the line marked (b) prepare a new translation for your language that expresses the meaning clearly.

Example
Matt 17.20
RSV   faith as a grain of mustard seed
    Compare:
TEV   faith as big as a mustard seed
NEB   faith no bigger even than a mustard seed
LB   faith even as small as a tiny mustard seed
YL   _____

    (b) _____

    Evaluation:
All of the translations except RSV make explicit the hidden component of meaning the size. NEB and LB emphasize the smallness.

F-13 New Testament: Translating Incomplete Similes

1. Matt 10.16
    RSV   send you out as sheep in the midst of wolves
        Compare:
    TEV   sending you just like sheep to a pack of wolves
    Phps   sending you out like sheep with wolves all around you
    *   sending you out like helpless sheep among fierce wolves
    YL   _____

        (b) _____

        Evaluation:

2. 1 Peter 1.24
   RSV   all flesh is like grass
      Compare:
   TEV   all men are like the wild grass
   NEB   all mortals are like grass
   TNT   all mankind is like grass
   JB   all flesh is grass
   *   all mankind is short-lived like grass
   YL   _____

   (b) _____

   Evaluation:

3. Rev 3.3
   RSV   I will come like a thief
      Compare:
   TEV   I will come upon you like a thief
   LB   I will come suddenly upon you, unexpected as a thief
   GeCL   *I will surprise you like a thief*
   YL   _____

   (b) _____

   Evaluation:

F-14 Old Testament: Translating Incomplete Similes (Instructions as for Drill F-13)

1. Exo 15.7
   RSV   the fury, it consumes them like stubble
      Compare:
   TEV   your anger...burns them up like straw
   JB   your fury...it devours them like stubble
   LB   your anger...consumed them as fire consumes straw
   NAS   Thy burning anger, and it consumes them as chaff
   YL   _____

   (b) _____

   Evaluation:

2. Psa 18.33
   RSV   he made my feet like hinds' feet
      Compare:
   TEV   he makes me sure-footed as a deer
   JB   who makes my feet like the hinds'
   NEB   who makes me swift as a hind
   Br   *he makes my foot nimble as that of a doe*
   LB   he gives me the surefootedness of a mountain goat upon the crags
   YL   _____

   (b) _____

   Evaluation:

5. METAPHORS

Analyzing Complete Metaphors

Purpose. In this drill we want to learn to recognize metaphors as abbreviated comparisons, that is, comparisons without as or like to signal that a comparison is being made. A full metaphor contains three parts: the object compared [O], the image with which the object is compared [I], and the meaning component(s), or the basis upon which the comparison is being made [B]. A metaphor lacks the marker of the comparison which is present in a full simile.

Instructions. Read the RSV quotations below and identify the three parts of the following full metaphors. Write each element into the corresponding box. Where there is more than one metaphor, use only the one underlined.

Example
Gen 49. 14   Issachar is a strong ass

O	Issachar		I	ass		B	strong
	Object			Image			Basis of comparison

F-15 New Testament: Complete Metaphors

1. Matt 10.6   go rather to the lost <u>sheep</u> of the house of Israel

O		I		B	

2. Matt 16.23   [Peter] get behind me <u>Satan</u>...you are not on the side of God

O		I		B	

3. John 6.48   I am the bread of life

O		I		B	

4. John 10.9   I am the door; if any one enters by me

O		I		B	

5. John 10.11   I am the <u>good shepherd</u>. The good shepherd lays down his life for the sheep

O		I		B	

6. Heb 2.17   he might become a merciful and faithful high priest

O		I		B	

7. 1 Peter 1.23 you have been born anew, not of perishable <u>seed</u> but of imperishable, through the living and abiding word of God

O		I		B	

8. 1 Peter 2.4 Come to him, to that living stone

O [   ] I [   ] B [   ]

9. 2 Peter 2.17 these [people] are waterless springs

O [   ] I [   ] B [   ]

10. Jude 13 [these people are] <u>wild waves of the sea</u>, casting up the foam of their own shame

O [   ] I [   ] B [   ]

F-16 Old Testament: Complete Metaphors (Instructions as for Drill F-15)

1. Gen 16.12 [Ishmael] a wild ass of a man

O [   ] I [   ] B [   ]

2. Gen 49.22 Joseph is a fruitful bough

O [   ] I [   ] B [   ]

3. Gen 49.27 Benjamin is a ravenous wolf

O [   ] I [   ] B [   ]

4. Deut 4.24 your God is a devouring fire

O [   ] I [   ] B [   ]

5. Deut 33.29 the LORD, the shield of your help

O [   ] I [   ] B [   ]

6. Song 1.13 my beloved is to me a bag of myrrh, that lies between my breasts

O [   ] I [   ] B [   ]

7. Isa 8.14 he will become...a rock of stumbling

O [   ] I [   ] B [   ]

8. Isa 23.16 [city of Tyre] O forgotten harlot

O [   ] I [   ] B [   ]

9. Isa 33.11 your breath is a fire that will consume you

O [   ] I [   ] B [   ]

Translating Complete Metaphors
Instructions
(a) Compare the various translations listed below, including your language, to see how they have handled the metaphor in translation. Has it been retained, modified, changed to a simile, etc.? Discuss the implications of the different solutions. Write your evaluation in the space provided.

(b) Make a new translation of the passage into your language, giving special attention to the metaphor. Can it be retained as a metaphor? Can it be retained as a full simile? Try to translate it with a figure of speech rather than as a nonfigure. Write your translation on the line marked (b).

Example
Matt 10.6
RSV   but go rather to the lost sheep of the house of Israel
     Compare:
TEV   instead, go to the lost sheep of the people of Israel
LB   but only to the people of Israel, God's lost sheep
GeCL   *but rather go to the lost among the people of Israel*
*   go instead to those people of Israel who are like lost sheep
YL   _____

   (b) _____

     Evaluation:
TEV   keeps the metaphor and only changes house to people
LB   tries to clarify the metaphor by using it in appositive position
GeCL   drops the sheep part of the metaphor
*   changes the metaphor into a simile

F-17 New Testament: Complete Metaphors

1. Matt 16.23
    RSV   get behind me, Satan!...you are not on the side of God, but of men
      Compare:
    TEV   get away from me, Satan! You are an obstacle in my way, because these
                thoughts of yours are men's thoughts, not God's
    NIV   get out of my sight, Satan!...you do not have in mind the things of God,
                but the things of men
    YL   _____

      (b) _____

      Evaluation:

2. John 6.48
    RSV   I am the bread of life
       Compare:
    TEV   I am the bread of life
    GeCL   *I am the bread that gives life*
    YL   _____

      (b) _____

      Evaluation:

1. Gen 16.12
   RSV   [Ishmael] shall be a wild ass of a man
      Compare:
   TEV   your son will live like a wild donkey
   NEB   he shall be a man like the wild ass
   JB   a wild ass of a man he will be
   LB   will be a wild one—free and untamed as a wild ass
   YL   _____

   (b)   _____

   Evaluation:

2. Deut 4.24
   RSV   the LORD your God is a devouring fire
      Compare:
   TEV   the LORD your God is like a flaming fire
   NEB   the LORD your God is a devouring fire
   JB   Yahweh your God is a consuming fire
   LB   he is a devouring fire
   YL   _____

   (b)   _____

   Evaluation:

Metaphors with Missing Basis of Comparison

   Purpose. In this drill we want to learn to recognize and to understand metaphors when the component of meaning, on the basis of which the comparison is being
made, has not been stated. Usually this means that the metaphor was well known to all
the people in the original language; they understood it even when the ground of the
comparison was left implicit.

   Instructions. Study the context and try to identify the missing component,
then write all three parts of the comparison into the blanks provided. The missing
basis of the comparison goes into the dotted box on the right.

Example
Isa 1.22   your silver has become dross

O	your silver		I	dross		B	useless, worthless
	Object			Image			Basis

F-19 New Testament: Metaphors with Missing Basis

1. Matt 3.7   you brood of vipers

   O [   ]   I [   ]   B [   ]

2. Matt 5.13   you are the salt of the earth

   O [   ]   I [   ]   B [   ]

3. Matt 23.24   you blind guides

   O [   ]   I [   ]   B [   ]

4. Luke 11.34   your eye is the lamp of your body

   O [   ]   I [   ]   B [   ]

5. Luke 13.32   go and tell that fox

   O [   ]   I [   ]   B [   ]

6. John 8.12   I am the light of the world

   O [   ]   I [   ]   B [   ]

7. Acts 2.20   the moon [turned] into blood

   O [   ]   I [   ]   B [   ]

8. Rom 3.13   their throat is an open grave

   O [   ]   I [   ]   B [   ]

9. Col 1.18   he [Christ] is the <u>head</u> of the <u>body</u>, the church

   O [   ]   I [   ]   B [   ]

   O [   ]   I [   ]   B [   ]

10. James 3.6   the tongue is a fire

   O [   ]   I [   ]   B [   ]

11. 2 Peter 2.13 they are blots and blemishes

   O [   ]   I [   ]   B [   ]

1. Gen 15.1   I am your shield

    | O | | I | | B | |

2. Gen 18.27   I who am but dust and ashes

    | O | | I | | B | |

3. Gen 45.8   he has made me a father to Pharaoh

    | O | | I | | B | |

4. Gen 49.9   Judah is a lion's whelp

    | O | | I | | B | |

5. Deut 7.16   [their gods] would be a snare to you

    | O | | I | | B | |

6. Deut 28.24   the LORD will make the rain of your land powder and dust

    | O | | I | | B | |

7. Psa 18.2   the LORD is my rock

    | O | | I | | B | |

8. Prov 20.27   the spirit of man is the lamp of the LORD

    | O | | I | | B | |

9. Prov 22.14   the mouth of a loose woman is a deep pit

    | O | | I | | B | |

10. Amos 4.1   hear this word, you cows of Bashan

    | O | | I | | B | |

11. Hab 1.12   O LORD...and thou, O Rock

    | O | | I | | B | |

12. Zech 9.13   I have made Ephraim its arrow

    | O | | I | | B | |

<u>Translating Metaphors with Missing Basis of Comparison</u>
      <u>Instructions</u>
      (a) Compare the various translations listed below, including your language, in order to see how they have handled the metaphors whose basis of comparison is not explicit in the text, and write your evaluation.

      (b) Make a translation for your language on the basis of the insights you have now gained on metaphors of this type. Write your translation on the line marked (b).

Example   Evaluation:
Matt 3.7   TEV has kept the metaphor but abbreviated
RSV   you brood of vipers   it to only <u>snakes</u>. LB has tried to make
    Compare: it into a <u>sort of</u> swearword on the model
TEV   you snakes   of the English son-of-a-gun / bitch ex-
LB   you sons of snakes   pressions. NEB/Phps have retained the
NEB   you vipers' brood   metaphor and only changed the expression
Phps   you serpent's brood   into a possessive by word order. RV has
RV   ye offspring of vipers   used <u>offspring</u> for <u>brood</u> but it amounts
PCL   *you breed of poisonous snakes*   to the same metaphor. PCL makes explicit
YL   _____   the poisonous quality implicit in <u>vipers</u>,
    (b) _____ but also retains the metaphor.

<u>F-21 New Testament: Metaphors with Missing Basis</u>

1. Matt 5.13
   RSV   you are the salt of the earth   Evaluation:
    Compare:
   TEV   you are like salt for all mankind
   NEB   you are salt to the world
   Phps   you are the earth's salt
   NIV   you are the salt of the earth
   Zink   *you are the salt of the earth.*
            (...to preserve it from rot)
   YL   _____
    (b)   _____

2. Luke 11.34
   RSV   your eye is the lamp of your body   Evaluation:
    Compare:
   TEV   your eyes are like a lamp for the
            body
   LB   your eyes light up your inward be-
            ing
   NEB   the lamp of your body is the eye
   NAS   the lamp of your body is your eye
   TNT   your eye is the lamp of your body
   YL   _____
    (b)   _____

1. Gen 15.1
   RSV   I am your shield   Evaluation:
       Compare:
   TEV   I will shield you from danger
   LB   I will defend you
   NAS   I am a shield to you
   Knox   I am here to protect you
   *   I will shield you
   YL   _____

   (b)   _____

2. Gen 45.8
   RSV   he has made me a father to Pharaoh   Evaluation:
       Compare:
   TEV   he has made me the king's highest
           official
   LB   he has made me a counselor to
           Pharaoh
   JB   he has made me father to Pharaoh
   Br   *he has made me "father" to Pharaoh*
   YL   _____

   (b)   _____

Analyzing Incomplete Metaphors

    Purpose. In this drill we want to sharpen our capacity to recognize incomplete metaphors. Unlike the previous drill, however, in which the metaphors lacked the component on which the comparison was based, here almost any part of the metaphor can be missing.

    Instructions. Study the RSV quotations and try to develop full metaphors. Then write out the three parts in the boxes provided. Dotted lines for all boxes mean any part of the comparison can be missing. If the statement contains more than one metaphor, analyze the underlined one. If two are underlined, use two sets of boxes to make your analysis.

Examples
John 21.16 tend my sheep

| O | my followers | | I | sheep | | B | are dependent on me |

Col 2.2   they are knit together in love

| O | people in the church | | I | something knitted | | B | closely linked with each other |

F-23 New Testament: Incomplete Metaphors

1. Matt 5.6   blessed are those who hunger and thirst for righteousness

   | O | | I | | B |

2. Matt 7.6   do not throw your pearls before swine

   | O | | I | | B |

   | O | | I | | B |

3. Matt 7.13   enter by the narrow gate

   | O | | I | | B |

4. Matt 9.37   the harvest is plentiful, but the laborers are few

   | O | | I | | B |

   | O | | I | | B |

5. Matt 16.6   beware of the leaven of the Pharisees

   | O | | I | | B |

6. Mark 1.3   prepare the way of the Lord

   | O | | I | | B |

7. Mark 4.17   have no root in themselves

   | O | | I | | B |

8. Luke 11.52   you have taken away the key of knowledge

   | O | | I | | B |

9. John 1.29   [saw Jesus] behold the Lamb of God

   | O | | I | | B |

10. 1 Thes 5.19 do not quench the Spirit

   | O | | I | | B |

F-24 Old Testament: Incomplete Metaphors (Instructions as for Drill F-23)

1. Isa 10.2   that widows may be their spoil

   | O | | I | | B | |

2. Isa 14.29   the rod which smote you is broken

   | O | | I | | B | |

3. Isa 21.10   O [Babylon] my threshed and winnowed one

   | O | | I | | B | |

4. Isa 27.6   Israel shall blossom and put forth shoots

   | O | | I | | B | |

5. Isa 30.27   the LORD comes from afar burning with his anger

   | O | | I | | B | |

6. Isa 33.11   you conceive chaff, you bring forth stubble

   | O | | I | | B | |

   | O | | I | | B | |

7. Isa 41.14   fear not, you worm Jacob

   | O | | I | | B | |

8. Jer 6.28   they are bronze and iron

   | O | | I | | B | |

9. Hos 12.1   Ephraim herds the wind

   | O | | I | | B | |

10. Joel 3.16   the LORD roars from Zion

   | O | | I | | B | |

Translating Incomplete Metaphors

Instructions

(a) Compare the various translations listed below, including your language, and note how they have handled the incomplete metaphors in translation. Obviously some have been more successful than others. Write your findings in the space marked "evaluation."

(b) On the line marked (b) make a new translation of the passage into your language with a fully adequate treatment of the metaphor.

Example

Matt 5.6

RSV   blessed are those who hunger and thirst for righteousness

   Compare:

TEV   happy are those whose greatest desire is to do what God requires

NEB   how blest are those who hunger and thirst to see right prevail

JB   happy those who hunger and thirst for what is right

TNT   happy are those who hunger and thirst for what is right

Phps   happy are those who are hungry and thirsty for true goodness

*   happy are those people whose desire for righteousness is as strong as
          their hunger and thirst

YL   _____

  (b) _____

   Evaluation:

TEV has changed the metaphor to a nonfigure and given only the meaning: <u>whose
      greatest desire is</u>.

NEB/JB/TNT have kept the incomplete metaphor as in the RSV.

Phps has made adjectives out of the verbs, but basically kept the incomplete met-
      aphor.

* has changed the incomplete metaphor into a complete simile.

Also note that the NEB follows a different exegesis.

Col 2.2

RSV   they are <u>knit together</u> in love

   Compare:

TEV   they may be drawn together in love

JB   to bind you together in love

NEB   in the unity of love

Phps   how strong are the bonds of Christian love

LB   knit together by strong ties of love

Brc   I want you to be wedded together in love

YL   _____

  (b) _____

   Evaluation:

TEV has only a weak reflection of the metaphor.

JB shifts the image from <u>knitting</u> to <u>binding</u>.

Phps follows JB in a more generic way.

LB keeps the figure and emphasizes <u>strong ties</u> as the basis for the comparison.

NEB is entirely abstract.

Brc shifts the figure to <u>wedded</u> and probably uses <u>strength and permanence</u> as the
      basis.

F-25 New Testament: Incomplete Metaphors

1. Matt 7.13
   RSV   enter by the narrow gate
      Compare:
   TEV   go in through the narrow gate
   LB   heaven can be entered only through the narrow gate
   *   enter God's kingdom one by one, as squeezing through a narrow gate
   YL   _____

   (b) _____

   Evaluation:

2. Matt 9.37
   RSV   the harvest is plentiful, but the laborers are few
      Compare:
   TEV   there is a large harvest, but few workers to gather it in
   NEB   the crop is heavy, but labourers are scarce
   TNT   the harvest indeed is great, but the workers are few
   JB   the harvest is rich but the laborers are few
   *   the many people ready to accept the Good News are like a great field ready
             to harvest and the disciples are too few to do the harvesting
   YL   _____

   (b) _____

   Evaluation:

F-26 Old Testament: Incomplete Metaphors (Instructions as for Drill F-25)

1. Gen 27.40
   RSV   break his yoke from your neck
      Compare:
   TEV   you will break away from his control
   NEB   break off his yoke from your neck
   LB   you will finally shake loose from him and be free
   *   you will break away from his control like an ox that breaks its yoke
   YL   _____

   (b) _____

   Evaluation:

2. Deut 31.16
   RSV   play the harlot after the strange gods
      Compare:
   TEV   [the people] will become unfaithful to me
   KJV   go a whoring after the gods of the strangers
   NEB   will go wantonly after their gods
   LB   [these people] will begin worshiping foreign gods
   JB   [this people] will start playing the harlot, following the alien gods
   *   like wives being prostitutes, so this people will be unfaithful to God
   YL   _____

   (b)   _____

   Evaluation:

6. METONYMS

Recognizing Metonyms and Translating Their Meanings

   Purpose. In these drills we want to learn to recognize and to translate metonyms. The word metonym means a name given to one thing which is really the name of
something else. This "something else" is always associated with the word replaced in
some way or other. Usually there is a conventionally accepted association on the
basis of which the word interchange is made; but in some kinds of writing, especially
poetry, the association between the two words is not readily recognized by a reader
or hearer who does not share the poet's experience. The important difference between
a metaphor and a metonym is that the former is formed on the basis of a supplementary
component while a metonym is based on an association between two words. In some cases
it is possible to interpret a figure either as a metaphor or as a metonym, such as
forgive us our debts. Debts as a metaphor would be rendered as: "our sins are debts";
while as a metonym debts would replace the word sins, because both are held against
a person and must be paid. When a figure can be interpreted either as a metaphor or
as a metonym, use the rendering that most fits the receptor language.
   For translating metonyms, the translator must first of all recognize the metonym for what it is; next, he must identify the associated word that it replaces;
then he must decide whether the receptor language can maintain the metonym or whether
its meaning must be clearly given in the translation. Stating the meaning clearly
could involve the loss of the metonym, as when I came to bring a sword is rendered as
I came to bring war. Sometimes it is possible "to cross the translation river twice"
by retaining the metonym and adding the meaning by means of an of-phrase, as in I
came to bring the sword of war.
   For the translator, an easy way to distinguish between a metaphor and a metonym is on the basis of the following two questions:
   (a) Can it be easily changed into a complete simile? For example, He is an ox
can be readily changed into He is strong as an ox. This shows that ox is a metaphor.
If it cannot be changed into a simile it is a metonym. For example, in I came to
bring a sword, sword cannot be changed into a simile. To say I came to bring war
which is like a sword is nonsense.
   (b) Can the meaning easily be added by an of-phrase? For example, I came to
bring a sword can readily be restated as I came to bring the sword of war.

Instructions

(a) Study the RSV or KJV substitute for the original language and identify and underline the metonym.

(b) On the line marked (b) supply the word that is being replaced.

(c) Compare the translations listed, including your own language, to see how the metonyms have been handled. Write your findings in the space marked "evaluation."

(d) If the translation in your language is not adequate, make one that is easily understood and write it on the line marked (d).

Example
Luke 22.42

RSV	remove this <u>cup</u> from me	(b) suffering

Compare:

TEV	take this cup of suffering away from me
JB/NEB	take this cup away from me
LB	please take away this cup of horror from me
TNT	remove this cup from me
YL	_____

(d)   _____

Evaluation:
TEV and LB have crossed the "river twice," but LB's use of <u>horror</u> is not emotively accurate. All the rest have merely retained the metonym.

Luke 1.71

RSV	from the <u>hand</u> of all who hate us	(b) power

Compare:

TEV	from the power of all those who hate us
JB	from the hands of all who hate us
NEB	out of the hands of all who hate us
LB	from all who hate us
Beck	from the power of all who hate us
Brc	from the power of those who hate us
YL	_____

(d)   _____

Evaluation:
TEV, Beck, and Brc replace the metonym by its meaning. JB and NEB retain the metonym without clarification, and LB leaves it out altogether.

1. Matt 3.5
   RSV   then went out to him Jerusalem   (b)_____

   Compare:
   TEV   people came to him from Jerusalem
   NEB   they flocked to him from Jerusalem
   JB   then Jerusalem...made their way to
              him
   NIV   people went out to him from Jeru-
              salem
   TNT   people of Jerusalem...went out to
              him
   YL   _____

   (d)   _____

   Evaluation:

2. Matt 3.7
   RSV   to flee from the wrath to come   (b)_____

   Compare:
   TEV   you could escape from the punish-
              ment God is about to send
   NEB   to escape from the coming retribu-
              tion
   JB   to fly from the retribution that
              is coming
   LB   could escape the coming wrath of
              God
   TNT   to flee from the coming wrath
   YL   _____

   (d)   _____

   Evaluation:

3. Matt 6.12
   RSV   forgive us our debts   (b)_____

   Compare:
   TEV   forgive us the wrongs that we
              have done
   NEB   forgive us the wrong we have done
   JB   forgive us our debts
   LB   forgive us our sins
   TNT   forgive us our debts
   YL   _____

   (d)   _____

   Evaluation:

[215]

4. Matt 10.34
   RSV   I have not come to bring peace,   (b)_____
                  but a sword
      Compare:
   TEV   I did not come to bring peace, but
                  a sword
   NEB   I have not come to bring peace,
                  but a sword
   JB   it is not peace I have come to
                  bring, but a sword
   LB   [don't imagine] I came to bring
                  peace to the earth! No, rather,
                  a sword
   GeCL   *I have not come to bring peace,*
                  but strife
   YL   _____

      (d)   _____

      Evaluation:

5. John 8.23
   RSV   I am from above   (b)_____
      Compare:
   TEV   I come from above
   NEB   I [belong] to the world above
   TNT/JB/LB   I am from above
   BE   I am from heaven
   YL   _____

      (d)   _____

      Evaluation:

F-28 Old Testament: Metonyms (Instructions as for Drill F-27)

1. Gen 1.2
   RSV   upon the face of the deep   (b)_____
      Compare:
   TEV   the raging ocean that covered
                  everything
   NEB   over the face of the abyss
   JB   over the deep
   LB   [missing, see footnote]
   NAS   over the surface of the deep
   YL   _____

      (d)   _____

      Evaluation:

2. Gen 3.19

RSV   you shall eat bread   (b)_____

   Compare:

TEV   to make the soil produce anything
NEB   you shall gain your bread
JB   shall you eat your bread
LB   to master it [the soil]
NAS   you shall eat bread
YL   _____

   (d)   _____

   Evaluation:

3. Gen 4.25

KJV   [God] hath appointed me another   (b)_____
                seed

   Compare:

TEV   God has given me a son
NEB/LB   God has granted me another son
JB   God has granted me another off-
                spring
NAS   God has appointed me another
                offspring
YL   _____

   (d)   _____

   Evaluation:

7. SYNECDOCHES

Recognizing and Translating Synecdoches

     Purpose. Here we want to learn to recognize and to translate synecdoches. Synecdoches are a special kind of metonym. They also represent the replacement of one word by another associated with it; but in the case of synecdoches, the association involves either a part-for-the-whole or a whole-for-a-part relationship between the words being exchanged. For example, in my mouth praises God, the word mouth is used as a part-for-the whole synecdoche replacing the whole person I; or in everybody in New York came to see the president, the everybody is a whole-for-a-part synecdoche. Obviously not every person came, but very many people came. The whole-for-a-part synecdoches always involve overstatements called hyperboles. In translating synecdoches, great care must be exercised to ascertain the usage of the receptor language because it is usually not possible to "cross the translation river twice." We can either use the synecdoche or we cannot use it. In a few cases, however, when the parts-for-the-whole are closely related, such closely related parts are acceptable as replacements; for example, for my mouth praises God it may be possible to say my lips praise God or my tongue praises God.

(a) Study the RSV or KJV substitute for the original language, and identify the synecdoche and underline it.

(b) On the line marked (b) write the word for which the synecdoche stands and classify it as P (part-for-the-whole) or W (whole-for-a-part) respectively.

(c) Study the translations listed below, including your language, to see how they have treated the synecdoches in translation. Write your evaluation in the space provided. If your translation needs improvement, try to do it.

Examples
Matt 22.17

KJV   is it lawful to give tribute unto <u>Caesar</u>?

(b) <u>Roman government</u>   P

Compare:

TEV   is it against our Law to pay taxes to the Roman Emperor?

NEB   are we...permitted to pay taxes to the Roman Emperor?

JB   is it permissible to pay taxes to Caesar?

LB   is it right to pay taxes to the Roman government?

YL   _____

Evaluation:

Only LB does not continue with the synecdoche and uses <u>Roman government</u>; all the rest retain the synecdoche.

1 Tim 5.23

KJV   drink no longer <u>water</u>

(b) <u>not only water</u>   W

Compare:

TEV   do not drink water only

JB   you should give up drinking only water

NEB   stop drinking nothing but water

NAS   no longer drink water exclusively

RV   be no longer a drinker of water

YL   _____

Evaluation:

All except RV have removed the whole-for-a-part synecdoche.

F-29 New Testament: Synecdoches

1. Matt 13.16

RSV   blessed are your eyes, for they see

(b)_____

Compare:

TEV   how fortunate you are! Your eyes see

NEB   happy are your eyes because they see

JB   happy are your eyes because they see

NIV   blessed are your eyes because they see

LB   blessed are your eyes, for they see

Phps   how fortunate you are to have eyes that see

YL   _____

Evaluation:

2. Matt 26.38

RSV   my soul is very sorrowful, even to   (b)_____
         death

   Compare:

TEV   the sorrow in my heart is so great that
         it almost crushes me

NEB   my heart is ready to break with grief

JB   my soul is sorrowful to the point of
         death

Beck   my soul is so full of sorrow I am
         almost dying

TNT   I am in mortal agony

YL   _____

   Evaluation:

3. Mark 6.5

RSV   he could do no mighty work there, ex-   (b)_____
         cept that he laid his hands upon a
         few sick people and healed them

   Compare:

TEV   he was not able to perform any miracles
         there, except that he placed his hands
         on a few sick people and healed them

NEB   he could work no miracle there, except
         that he put his hands on a few sick
         people and healed them

JB   he could work no miracle there, though
         he cured a few sick people by laying
         his hands on them

NIV   he could not do any miracles there, ex-
         cept lay his hands on a few sick peo-
         ple and heal them

LB   he couldn't do any mighty miracles among
         them except to place his hands on a
         few sick people and heal them

Phps   he could do nothing miraculous there apart
         from laying his hands on a few sick
         people and healing them

YL   _____

   Evaluation:

F-30 <u>Old Testament: Synecdoches</u> (Instructions as for Drill F-29)

1. Gen 3.19
   RSV   in the sweat of your face   (b)_____
        Compare:
   TEV   you will have to work hard and sweat
   JB   with sweat on your brow
   LB   all your life you will sweat
   NEB   by the sweat of your brow
   NAS   by the sweat of your face
   YL   _____

   Evaluation:

2. Gen 4.23
   RSV   hear my voice [you wives of Lamech]   (b)_____
        Compare:
   TEV   listen to me
   JB   hear my voice
   NEB/LB   listen to me
   Beck   hear what I say
   YL   _____

   Evaluation:

3. Gen 4.26
   RSV   began to call upon the name of the   (b)_____
               LORD
        Compare:
   TEV   began using the LORD's holy name in
               worship
   JB   invoke the name of Yahweh
   LB   began to call themselves "the Lord's
               people"
   NEB   began to invoke the LORD by name
   NAS   began to call upon the name of the LORD
   YL   _____

   Evaluation:

4. Gen 8.9
   KJV   found no rest for the sole of her   (b)_____
               foot
        Compare:
   TEV   did not find a place to light
   JB   finding nowhere to perch
   LB   found no place to light
   NEB   found no place where she could settle
   NAS   found no resting place for the sole of
               her foot
   YL   _____

   Evaluation:

8. EUPHEMISMS

Purpose. All languages find that certain words acquire very dangerous connotations. Such words are felt to be too dirty, too dangerous, too holy, or otherwise to be avoided. When a word becomes taboo, the language develops an indirect way of referring to the idea expressed by the dirty or dangerous word. This is called a euphemism. The Hebrews called euphemisms clean talk.

While all languages seem to develop euphemisms, they may not necessarily do so for the same concepts. Fairly widespread taboos can be found in regard to the ideas of death and sex. But even euphemisms, once they are established, seem to pick up the negative components again, and so they in turn are abandoned. For example, in English the avoidance of the word death is strong. For some time those dealing with dead bodies were referred to as undertakers, that is, people who undertook to take care of the dead on behalf of the bereaved. Then undertaker began to carry too many of the negative components of death itself, so other euphemisms developed like funeral parlor, mortician (the latter is very interesting because it is built on the Latin word death which English speakers did not recognize as such), etc.

For the translator the use of euphemisms in culturally sensitive areas is important. However, he also needs to be warned that many euphemisms tend to be short-lived. If this happens to expressions used in the translation, its usefulness may be limited.

Instructions

(a) Study the following biblical quotations and underline the euphemisms they contain.

(b) Write the actual meaning in English on the line marked (b).

(c) If your language also uses a euphemism to express the idea, write it on the line marked YL.

Examples

he gave up his ghost (Mark 15.37 KJV)

(b) he died _____ YL _____

he had forced [Hb: humbled, afflicted] his sister (2 Sam 13.22)

(b) he raped _____ YL _____

there is not a man on earth to come in to us after the manner of all the earth
  (Gen 19.31)

(b) to have sexual intercourse for the YL _____
      purpose of having children

F-31 New Testament: Euphemisms

1. [Joseph] knew her not until she had borne a son (Matt 1.25)

   (b)_____ YL _____

2. cast him into the outer darkness (Matt 22.13)[a]

   (b)_____ YL _____

[a]See note with number 14. It probably is a euphemism for hell, but commentators vary.

3. Jesus cried again in a loud voice and yielded up his spirit (Matt 27.50)

   (b)_____ YL_____

4. are you the Christ, the Son of the Blessed? (Mark 14.61)

   (b)_____ YL_____

5. Jesus uttered a loud cry and breathed his last (Mark 15.37)

   (b)_____ YL_____

6. how shall this be, seeing that I know not a man? (Luke 1.34 KJV)

   (b)_____ YL_____

7. a woman of the city, who was a sinner (Luke 7.37)[a]

   (b)_____ YL_____

   [a]sinner here is obviously not used in its literal meaning, but is a euphemism
   for a prostitute.

8. I have sinned against heaven (Luke 15.18)

   (b)_____ YL_____

9. [Ananias] fell down and gave up the ghost (Acts 5.5 KJV)

   (b)_____ YL_____

10. men likewise gave up natural relations with women (Rom 1.27)

    (b)_____ YL_____

11. men committing shameless acts with men (Rom 1.27)

    (b)_____ YL_____

12. it is well for a man not to touch a woman (1 Cor 7.1)

    (b)_____ YL_____

13. let the marriage bed be undefiled (Heb 13.4)

    (b)_____ YL_____

14. for them the nether gloom of darkness has been reserved (2 Peter 2.17)[b]

    (b)_____ YL_____

    [b]Ancient Hebrews visualized the world as having a dark place deep underneath
    the earth. But since it was a place of punishment, it functions as a euphemism
    for hell.

15. giving themselves over to fornication, and going after strange flesh (Jude 7
    KJV)

    (b)_____ YL_____

F-32 Old Testament: Euphemisms (Instructions as for Drill F-31)

1. till you return to the ground (Gen 3.19)

   (b)_____ YL_____

2. saw the nakedness of his father (Gen 9.22)

   (b)_____ YL_____

3. go in to my maid (Gen 16.2)

   (b)_____ YL_____

4. I gave my maid to your embrace (Gen 16.5)

   (b)_____ YL_____

5. it had ceased to be with Sarah after the manner of women (Gen 18.11)

   (b)_____ YL_____

6. put your hand under my thigh (Gen 24.2)

   (b)_____ YL_____

7. a virgin, whom no man had known (Gen 24.16)

   (b)_____ YL_____

8. the way of women is upon me (Gen 31.35)

   (b)_____ YL_____

9. saw her, he seized her and lay with her and humbled her (Gen 34.3)

   (b)_____ YL_____

10. perform the duty of a brother-in-law to her (Gen 38.8)

   (b)_____ YL_____

11. he spilled the seed on the ground (Gen 38.9 KJV)[a]

   (b)_____ YL_____

   [a]The Hebrew actually says only: he spilled on the ground.

12. Joseph's hand shall close your eyes (Gen 46.4)

   (b)_____ YL_____

13. [Reuben] went up to his father's bed (Gen 49.4)

   (b)_____ YL_____

14. I am to be gathered to my people (Gen 49.29)

   (b)_____ YL_____

15. Saul went in to cover his feet (1 Sam 24.3 KJV)

   (b)_____ YL_____

16. David slept with his fathers (1 Kgs 2.10)

   (b)_____ YL_____

[223]

9. CHANGING NONFIGURES TO FIGURES OF SPEECH

Purpose. In this drill section we want to become aware of the fact that many nonfigurative expressions have figurative equivalents. This is important to remember, because in the process of translation many of the figures of speech in the original will be lost. The reason for this is that there are no equivalents in the receptor language. We will therefore have to change many nonfigurative expressions into figures of speech so as to retain about the same ratio of figures to nonfigures as in the original. In order to sharpen our awareness we will take English translations and mark nonfigurative expressions and then try to render them as figures of speech. Obviously not all figures will fit into a given context, but for the purpose of practice let's make as many figurative renderings as possible.

Instructions

(a) In the first column write down equivalent figurative expressions for the nonfigurative ones underlined in the following passages from the TEV. If you can find more than one figure of speech, so much the better. For example, for number 1 below he begged for help, one could say he cried his heart out calling for help or he said: "Please, lend me a hand" or "Please, lend me your help" or "Please, don't close your ears to my call for help," etc.

(b) In the second column write the figurative equivalents from your own language. Again, try to find as many figures as possible and discuss the different connotations they carry.

F-33 New Testament: Changing Nonfigures to Figures of Speech

1. A leper came to Jesus, knelt down, and (1) begged him for help. (2) "If you want to," he said, "you can make me clean." Jesus was (3) filled with pity, and reached out and (4) touched him. "I do want to," he answered. "Be clean!" At once the (5) leprosy left the man and he was clean. Then Jesus (6) spoke harshly with him and (7) sent him away at once. "Listen," he said, "don't (8) tell this to anyone. But go straight to the priest and (9) let him examine you; then (10) offer the sacrifice that Moses ordered, to (11) prove to everyone that you are now clean" (Mark 1.40-45 TEV, third edition).

1.	1.
2.	2.
3.	3.
4.	4.
5.	5.
6.	6.
7.	7.
8.	8.
9.	9.
10.	10.
11.	11.

"When I came to the well today, (1) I prayed, 'LORD, God of my master Abraham, please (2) give me success in what I am doing. Here I am at the well. When a young woman comes out to get water, (3) I will ask her to (4) give me a drink of water from her jar. (5) If she agrees and also offers to bring water for my camels, may she be the one that you have chosen as the wife for my master's son.' Before I had finished my silent prayer, Rebecca came with a water jar on her shoulder and (6) went down to the well to get water. I said to her, 'Please give me a drink.' She quickly (7) lowered her jar from her shoulder and said, 'Drink, and I will also (8) water your camels.' So I drank, and she watered the camels. I asked her, 'Who is your father?' And she answered, 'My father is Bethuel son of Nahor and Milcah.' Then I put the ring in her nose and the (9) bracelets on her arms. I knelt down and worshiped the LORD, (10) I praised the LORD, the God of my master Abraham, who had (11) led me straight to my master's relative, where I found his daughter for my master's son" (Gen 24.42-48 TEV).

1.	1.
2.	2.
3.	3.
4.	4.
5.	5.
6.	6.
7.	7.
8.	8.
9.	9.
10.	10.
11.	11.

10. FIGURATIVE MEANING IN THE RECEPTOR LANGUAGE

Purpose. In this drill we want to focus our attention on the many figurative meanings that are used in our own languages. Whether your language is English, Zulu, or whatever, your language has many figures of speech, but often people are not conscious of them. Study and discuss the following examples.

Examples

In English the word "fish" can be used figuratively or as a part of an idiom in the following ways:

(a) slippery: slippery as a fish
(b) coldness: cold as a fish
(c) other interests or concerns: I have plenty of other fish to fry (said by a girl about a boy who no longer likes her)
(d) getting mixed up in other people's business: I will teach you not to fish in my pond!
(e) to retrieve: fish out the anchor!
(f) social rejection: he's a queer fish
(g) misfit: he is neither fish nor fowl
(h) reinforcement: a fishplate for the mast
(i) archery: a single fish arrow has only one V notch
(j) using difficulties of others: to fish in troubled waters
(k) to force a choice: fish or cut the bait!
(l) exhausted: it's all fished out

The Lengua of Paraguay have many figurative expressions based on -vahloc "innermost." Here is a partial list:

(a) to love: the innermost dissolves
(b) to be happy: the innermost spreads
(c) to meditate: the innermost searches
(d) to hope: the innermost waits
(e) to be greedy: the innermost demands
(f) to be frightened: the innermost jumps
(g) to fear: the innermost trembles
(h) to be cooperative: the innermost is gentle
(i) to be selfish: the innermost is locked up, closed up
(j) to be sick: the innermost is unclean, bad, rotten
(k) to be converted: to change one's innermost
(l) to be healthy/at peace: the innermost is clean or at rest
(m) to be bewitched: the innermost has been known by someone
(n) to hate: the innermost hardens
(o) to think, thank: the innermost mentions
(p) to be afraid: the innermost falls, stumbles
(q) to be excited: the innermost works hard
(r) to worry: the innermost keeps on mentioning
(s) to be kind: the innermost receives, accepts
(t) to be sympathetic: the innermost is open, wide open
(u) to be proud: the innermost mentions itself again and again
(v) to be upset: the innermost is wavy, turbulent
(w) to become well: the innermost is restored, becomes clear
(x) to comfort: to refresh the innermost, to cool the innermost

F-35 Figurative Meaning in the Receptor Language: Psychological and Mental States

Instructions. In the space provided, list all the figurative meanings and usages you can think of in your language for each of the following adjectives and nouns. Discuss the contributions of each member of the class and write down any additional figurative uses that come to mind during the discussion.

1. brave

2. cowardly

3. confident

4. fearful

5. proud

6. humble

7. angry

8. loving

9. hopeful

10. discouraged

F-36 Figurative Meaning in the Receptor Language: Colors and Objects, Etc. (Instructions as for Drill F-35)

1. red

2. black

3. yellow

4. green

5. white

6. bird

7. ox

8. bull

9. lion

10. dog

F-37 Figurative Meaning in the Receptor Language: Event Words (Instructions as for Drill F-35)

1. to die

2. to be born

3. to love

4. to redeem

5. to kill

6. to cheat someone

F-38 Counting Figures of Speech in the Receptor Language

Instructions. Select two paragraphs or two short stories written in your own language by different people and mark all nonliteral meanings and any culturally significant acts which carry implicit meaning.

F-39 Comparing the Bible and Literature in Your Language as to Figurative Usage

Instructions. Select a story from your culture that is well-told and see if you can match it with a similar story from the Bible. For example, many languages have a flood story and this can be matched with the biblical account. Count the number of figures in both stories. If one is longer than the other, establish a ratio by counting the words or lines and see how they compare as to number and kinds of figures of speech.

11. FIGURATIVE ACTIONS

Purpose. Related to figures of speech are actions which express "nonliteral" meanings. Like figures of speech, the meaning of such actions is understood only in the cultural settings in which the same meanings are attached to these actions. Other cultures might view the actions as accidental or as meaning whatever their own culture says such an action means. The problem for the translator is that these actions are actual history—the people did just what it says. Thus the translator must of necessity try to "cross the translation river twice"—once with the form of the action, but also a second time with its meaning.

This double approach is usually possible if the gesture in question carries little or no meaning, or if it has a different meaning when such a meaning is not charged with strong negative emotions in the receptor language. For example, in East Africa putting branches on the road before a visitor may seem strange, but when the biblical meaning is also expressed in the translation, the form creates no difficulty. In some parts of West Africa, however, putting branches before a visitor is a strong insult. In such cases the strength of the negative feeling must be carefully considered. If the feelings are very strong, it may be necessary to put only the meaning in the text. However, the biblical form and the differences in cultural meaning are then given in a footnote. There are cases, however, where certain gestures are considered so lewd that even a footnote indicating the biblical form would be offensive. In such cases only the meaning should be given in the text.

The translator should also be aware that both in the Bible and in his own culture the same gesture can have different meanings in different settings. This is one of the reasons why there is such a wide difference between translations in their treatment of gestures.

Luckily we have a number of contexts in which the meaning of the figurative action is indicated. So we will begin our study with those contexts in which the original marks the meaning of the action, and then proceed to contexts in which the meaning is left unmarked.

Instructions. The following biblical quotations contain gestures or actions that carry meanings.

(a) Study the context and identify the gesture or action and its meaning.

(b) Compare the various translations, including your own language, to see whether the relationship between gesture or action and its meaning marker is clear.

Example
1 Sam 24.8
RSV David bowed with his face to the earth and did obeisance

Gesture bowed low _____   Meaning to show respect _____

Compare:
TEV David bowed down to the ground in respect
NEB David prostrated himself in obeisance
JB   David bowed to the ground and did homage
LB   David bowed low before him
NAS David bowed with his face to the ground and prostrated himself
YL   _____

Figurative Actions or Gestures in Marked Contexts

F-40 New Testament: Figurative Actions or Gestures and Their Meanings in Marked Contexts

1. Mark 6.11
   RSV   shake off the dust that is on your feet for a testimony against them

   Gesture_____ Meaning_____

   Compare:
   TEV   shake the dust off your feet. This will be a warning to them
   JB   shake off the dust from under your feet as a sign to them
   NEB   shake the dust off your feet...as a warning to them
   Phps shake the dust off your feet as a protest against them
   LB   shake off the dust from your feet...it is a sign that you have abandoned it
          to its fate
   YL   _____

2. Matt 11.21
   RSV   they would have repented long ago in sackcloth and ashes

   Action_____ Meaning_____

   Compare:
   TEV   the people there would have put on sackcloth, and sprinkled ashes on them-
          selves to show that they had turned from their sins
   NEB   they would have repented long ago in sackcloth and ashes
   LB   their people would have repented long ago in shame and humility
   TNT   their inhabitants would long ago have put on sackcloth and thrown ashes
          over their heads as a sign that they had repented
   YL   _____

F-41 Old Testament: Figurative Actions or Gestures and Their Meanings in Marked Contexts (Instructions as for Drill F-40)

1. Num 24.10
   RSV   Balak's anger was kindled against Balaam, and he struck his hands together

   Gesture:_____ Meaning_____

   Compare:
   TEV   Balak clenched his fists in anger
   NEB   Balak was very angry with Balaam, beat his hands together
   LB   Balak was livid with rage...striking his hands together in anger
   JB   Balak flew into a rage...he beat his hands together
   NAS   Balak's anger burned against Balaam, and he struck his hands together
   YL   _____

2. Isa 13.2
   RSV   wave the hand for them to enter

   Gesture:_____ Meaning_____

   Compare:
   TEV   raise your arm as a signal for them to attack the gates
   NEB   beckon with arm upraised to the advance
   JB   beckon them to come to the Noble Gate
   LB   wave them on as they march against Babylon
   NAS   wave the hand that they may enter the doors
   YL   _____

[230]

F-42 New Testament: Figurative Actions or Gestures and Their Meanings in Unmarked Contexts (Instructions as for Drill F-40)

1. Matt 10.14
   RSV   shake off the dust from your feet

   Action_____ Meaning_____

      Compare:
   TEV   shake the dust off your feet
   NEB   shake the dust of it [town] off your feet
   JB   shake the dust from your feet
   NIV   shake the dust off your feet
   Phps/LB   shake off the dust of that place from your feet
   *   show your complete break with them by shaking even the dust off your
                   feet
   YL   _____

2. Matt 21.7
   RSV   they brought the ass...and he [Jesus] sat thereon

   Action_____ Meaning_____

      Compare:
   TEV   they brought the donkey...and Jesus got on
   NEB   brought the donkey...and Jesus mounted
   JB   they brought the donkey...and he sat on them [cloaks]
   NIV   they brought the donkey...and Jesus sat on them [cloaks]
   LB   brought the animals to him...for him to ride on
   Phps   they brought the donkey...and Jesus took his seat upon them [cloaks]
   *   they brought the donkey, the traditional mount of Israel's kings...and
                   Jesus got on
   YL   _____

3. Matt 22.11
   RSV   a man who had no wedding garment

   Action_____ Meaning_____

      Compare:
   TEV   a man who was not wearing wedding clothes
   NEB   one man who was not dressed for a wedding
   JB   one man who was not wearing a wedding garment
   NIV   a man there who was not wearing wedding clothes
   LB   a man who wasn't wearing the wedding robe [provided] for him (brackets
   Phps   a man not dressed for a wedding   in LB)
   YL   _____

4. Mark 7.25
   RSV   [a woman] came and fell down at his feet

   Action_____ Meaning_____

      Compare:
   TEV   came...and fell at his feet
   NEB   came in, and fell at his feet
   LB/NIV/JB   came and fell at his feet
   Phps   arrived and prostrated herself before him
   YL   _____

1. Gen 18.2
   RSV   bowed himself to the earth

   Action_____ Meaning_____

   Compare:
   TEV   bowing down with his face touching the ground
   NEB   bowed low to the ground
   JB   bowed to the ground
   NAS   bowed himself to the earth
   LB   welcomed them
   YL   _____

2. Gen 24.65
   RSV   she took her veil and covered herself

   Action:_____ Meaning_____

   Compare:
   TEV   she took her scarf and covered her face
   NEB   she took her veil and covered herself
   JB   she took her veil and hid her face
   LB   she covered her face with her veil
   *   she took her scarf and covered her face as a modest young woman should
   YL   _____

3. Gen 29.11
   RSV   Jacob kissed Rachel

   Action:_____ Meaning_____

   Compare:
   TEV   then he kissed her
   NEB   he kissed Rachel
   JB/LB   Jacob kissed Rachel
   *   Jacob greeted Rachel with a kiss
   YL   _____

4. Gen 33.3
   RSV   [Jacob] bowed himself to the ground seven times

   Action_____ Meaning_____

   Compare:
   TEV   [Jacob] bowed down to the ground seven times
   JB   he himself went ahead of them and bowed to the ground seven times
   LB   he bowed low seven times
   NEB   bowing low to the ground seven times
   NAS   bowed down to the ground seven times
   YL   _____

G. DISCOURSE ANALYSIS

1. ACTOR-ACTION LINES

Purpose. All languages have standard patterns for introducing background information, moving the action in a story, introducing new characters, referring to previously mentioned persons or events, etc. In this drill we want to practice a very simple kind of discourse diagraming in order to become aware of some of these features of discourse structure. In the process we hope that the translator will recognize that there are places where English and the original languages do not correspond. He must also realize that in his translation he can follow neither the English pattern nor that of the original language, but must follow the patterns of his own language.

Instructions

(a) Study the discourse structure of the assigned passage and make a discourse analysis of the version indicated according to the example of RSV Luke 10.29-37 on the following pages. Note how changes of actors or focus are made and how new actors are brought onto the stage. Note that the actors are referred to by name, pronoun, or "#" in successive sentences. (The sign "#" indicates that the actor is implicit, not mentioned.) Is this correct? Now look at the action line. Which verb forms mark forward movement in the story, and which signal background information? Now study the connector line. Are sentence and paragraph links properly marked? Finally, check how this story fits into the larger context from which it is taken. Are the verbs in the first verse in the proper form when you look at the larger context?

(b) After you have made your analysis, compare it with the other version given. Are there any specific differences? Discuss them. Are there any ambiguities which a modern reader could misinterpret?

(c) What differences of discourse structure do you note between English and your language?

Compare:

Luke 10.29-37

KJV But he, willing to justify himself, said unto Jesus, And who is my neighbor? And Jesus answering said, A certain man went down from Jerusalem to Jericho, and fell among thieves, which stripped him of his raiment, and wounded him, and departed, leaving him half dead. And by chance there came down a certain priest that way; and when he saw him, he passed by on the other side. And likewise a Levite, when he was at the place, came and looked on him, and passed by on the other side. But a certain Samaritan, as he journeyed, came where he was; and when he saw him, he had compassion on him, and went to him, and bound up his wounds, pouring in oil and wine, and set him on his own beast, and brought him to an inn, and took care of him. And on the morrow when he departed, he took out two pence, and gave them to the host, and said unto him, Take care of him: and whatsoever thou spendest more, when I come again, I will repay thee. Which now of these three, thinkest thou, was neighbor unto him that fell among the thieves? And he said, He that showed mercy on him. Then said Jesus unto him, Go, and do thou likewise.

Example
A simplified discourse analysis of Luke 10.29-37 RSV

LINK	ACTOR	ACTION	BACKGROUND (setting, items not in focus, content of speeches, etc.)
but	he (lawyer)		desiring to justify
			himself
	#	said	who is my neighbor
	Jesus	replied	(story in reply)
	a man		was going from Jerusalem
and	he	fell among robbers	
	who	stripped him	
and	#	beat him	
and	#	departed	leaving him half dead
now by chance	a priest		was going down that road
and when	he	saw him	
	he	passed by on the	
		other side	
so likewise	a Levite		when he came to the place
	he	saw him	
and	he	passed by on the	
		other side	
but	a Samaritan		as he journeyed
	#	came	to where he was
when	he	saw him	
	he	had compassion	

LINK	ACTOR	ACTION	BACKGROUND
and	#	went to him	
and	#	bound up his wounds	
then	he	set him on his own beast	
and	#	brought him to an inn	
and	#	took care of him	
and the next day	he	took out two denarii	
and	#	gave them to the inn-keeper	saying, Take care...
(implicit: now)	(he)	(asked)	which of these...
and	he	said (answered)	the one who
and	Jesus	said to him	go and do...

G-1 New Testament: Discourse Analysis of Luke 19.1-10

NEB   Entering Jericho he made his way through the city. There was a man there named Zacchaeus; he was superintendent of taxes and very rich. He was eager to see what Jesus looked like; but, being a little man, he could not see him for the crowd. So he ran on ahead and climbed a sycomore-tree in order to see him, for he was to pass that way. When Jesus came to the place, he looked up and said, 'Zacchaeus, be quick and come down; I must come and stay with you today.' He climbed down as fast as he could and welcomed him gladly. At this there was a general murmur of disapproval. 'He has gone in', they said, 'to be the guest of a sinner.' But Zacchaeus stood there and said to the Lord, 'Here and now, sir, I give half my possessions to charity; and if I have cheated anyone, I am ready to repay him four times over.' Jesus said to him, 'Salvation has come to this house today!—for this man too is a son of Abraham, and the Son of Man has come to seek and to save what is lost.'

Compare:

KJV And Jesus entered and passed through Jericho. And, behold, there was a man named
Zaccheus, which was the chief among the publicans, and he was rich. And he sought
to see Jesus who he was; and could not for the press, because he was little of
stature. And he ran before, and climbed up into a sycamore tree to see him; for
he was to pass that way. And when Jesus came to the place, he looked up, and saw
him, and said unto him, Zaccheus, make haste, and come down; for to-day I must
abide at thy house. And he made haste, and came down, and received him joyfully.
And when they saw it, they all murmured, saying, That he was gone to be guest
with a man that is a sinner. And Zaccheus stood, and said unto the Lord; Behold,
Lord, the half of my goods I give to the poor; and if I have taken any thing from
any man by false accusation, I restore him fourfold. And Jesus said unto him,
This day is salvation come to this house, forasmuch as he also is a son of Abraham. For the Son of man is come to seek and to save that which was lost.

LINK	ACTOR	ACTION	BACKGROUND

(Draw similar dotted lines on your own lined notepaper to continue the analysis)

TEV   Now the snake was the most cunning animal that the LORD God had made. The snake asked the woman, "Did God really tell you not to eat fruit from any tree in the garden?" "We may eat the fruit of any tree in the garden," the woman answered, "except the tree in the middle of it. God told us not to eat the fruit of that tree or even touch it; if we do, we will die." The snake replied, "That's not true; you will not die. God said that because he knows that when you eat it, you will be like God and know what is good and what is bad." The woman saw how beautiful the tree was and how good its fruit would be to eat, and she thought how wonderful it would be to become wise. So she took some of the fruit and ate it. Then she gave some to her husband, and he also ate it. As soon as they had eaten it, they were given understanding and realized that they were naked; so they sewed fig leaves together and covered themselves. That evening they heard the LORD God walking in the garden, and they hid from him among the trees. But the LORD God called out to the man, "Where are you?" He answered, "I heard you in the garden; I was afraid and hid from you, because I was naked." "Who told you that you were naked?" God asked. "Did you eat the fruit that I told you not to eat?"

   Compare:

RSV   Now the serpent was more subtle than any other wild creature that the LORD God had made. He said to the woman, "Did God say, 'You shall not eat of any tree of the garden'?" And the woman said to the serpent, "We may eat of the fruit of the trees of the garden; but God said, 'You shall not eat of the fruit of the tree which is in the midst of the garden, neither shall you touch it, lest you die.'" But the serpent said to the woman, "You will not die. For God knows that when you eat of it your eyes will be opened, and you will be like God, knowing good and evil." So when the woman saw that the tree was good for food, and that it was a delight to the eyes, and that the tree was to be desired to make one wise, she took of its fruit and ate; and she also gave some to her husband, and he ate. Then the eyes of both were opened, and they knew that they were naked; and they sewed fig leaves together and made themselves aprons. And they heard the sound of the LORD God walking in the garden in the cool of the day, and the man and his wife hid themselves from the presence of the LORD God among the trees of the garden. But the LORD God called to the man, and said to him, "Where are you?" And he said, "I heard the sound of thee in the garden, and I was afraid, because I was naked; and I hid myself." He said, "Who told you that you were naked? Have you eaten of the tree of which I commanded you not to eat?"

LINK	ACTOR	ACTION	BACKGROUND

(Draw similar dotted lines on your own lined notepaper to continue the analysis)

2. REFERENCE LINES IN DISCOURSE

Purpose. While all languages can potentially tell the same story, each language has its own way of doing it. One of the frequent areas of difference between languages is the way a person (or persons) is referred to once he has been introduced. English, for example, has both he and she as third person singular pronouns. If both a previously introduced male and female are referred to in a story, how is the reference to them kept clear? Or if several characters move on and off the stage at different times in the narrative, when must the full identification or name be used instead of just he or she? In these drills we want to become aware of the fact that even Greek and English differ in this regard. Therefore a good English translation will not follow the Greek or Hebrew pattern of referring to a character, but will follow the requirements of English. If Greek and English, which both belong to the Indo-European language family, differ, how much more will languages from completely different language families differ? Regardless of how much they differ, however, the translator must follow the natural pattern of the receptor language, and not that of the text from which the translation is made.

Instructions

(a) In parentheses below the blank the character(s) referred to in the narrative has been provided. Sometimes English requires the full identification, sometimes only a pronoun, and sometimes some other reference, or even no reference at all. Study the context and write the proper English reference into the blank above the word in parentheses. Use the symbol # to indicate that no visible reference marker is required in the context.

(b) Have different members of the class read their versions. Discuss any differences.

(c) Now compare your version with the TEV from which the passage has been taken.

(d) Now compare your version with the RSV.

(e) Now compare the version in your language and note any differences.

Example
Acts 10.21-23

TEV So *Peter* went down and. **#** said to *the men,* "**I** am *the man*
(Peter)　　　　　　(Peter)　　　　　　(men)　(Peter)　(Peter)

you are looking for. Why have *you* come?" "*Captain Cornelius* sent
(men)　　　　　　　　　　　(men)　　　(Captain Cornelius)

us," *they* answered. "*He* is a good *man*
(men)　(men)　　　　　(Captain Cornelius)　　　(Captain Cornelius)

who worships *God* and **#** is highly
(Captain Cornelius)　　　(God)　　(Captain Cornelius)

respected by all *the Jewish people.* *He* was told by *one*
(Jewish people)　　(Captain Cornelius)　　　(angel)

of *God's* *angels* to invite *you* to *his* house, so
(God)　(angels)　　　(Peter)　(Captain Cornelius')

that *he* could hear what *you* had to say." *Peter*
(Captain Cornelius)　　(Peter)　　　(Peter)

invited *the men* in and **#** had *them* spend the night there.
(men)　　(Peter)　(men)

RSV   And Peter went down to the men and said, "I am the one you are looking for;
      what is the reason for your coming?" And they said, "Cornelius, a centurion,
      an upright and God-fearing man, who is well spoken of by the whole Jewish
      nation, was directed by a holy angel to send for you to come to his house,
      and to hear what you have to say." So he called them in to be his guests.

      The only ambiguous reference that violates the English pattern in the RSV oc-
      curs in verse 23 where it says: "So he called them in." Since Captain Cornelius
      was the last person referred to, he would normally refer to him.
YL
───

G-3 New Testament: Reference Lines of Matt 2.13

TEV   After _____ had left, _____ of _____ appeared in a dream to
             (wise men)   (angel)   (God)

      _____ and said _____, " _____, get up, _____ take _____
      (Joseph)   (to Joseph)   (Joseph)   (Joseph)   (Jesus)

      and _____ _____ and _____ run away to Egypt, and _____ stay
          (Jesus)   (Mary)   (Joseph)   (Joseph)

      there until _____ tell _____ to leave.
                  (angel of the Lord)   (Joseph)

      Compare:
RSV   Now when they had departed, behold, an angel of the Lord appeared to Joseph in
      a dream and said, "Rise, take the child and his mother, and flee to Egypt, and
      remain there till I tell you...
YL
───

G-4 Old Testament: Reference Lines of Gen 4.8-9   (Instructions as for Drill G-3)

RSV   _____ said to _____ _____ _____, "Let _____ go out to
      (Cain)   (Abel) (Cain) (Abel)   (Cain and Abel)

      the field." And when _____ were in the field, _____ rose up
                           (Cain and Abel)   (Cain)

      against _____ _____ _____, and _____ killed _____. Then _____
              (Cain) (Abel) (Abel)   (Cain)   (Abel)   (God)

      said to _____, "Where is _____ _____ _____?" _____ said, " _____
              (Cain)   (Abel) (Cain) (Abel)   (Cain)   (Cain)

      do not know; am _____ _____ _____ _____?"
                      (Cain) (Cain) (Abel) (Cain)

      Compare:
TEV   Then Cain said to his brother Abel, "Let's go out in the fields." When they were
      out in the fields, Cain turned on his brother and killed him. The LORD asked
      Cain, "Where is your brother Abel?" He answered, "I don't know. Am I supposed to
      take care of my brother?"
YL
───

3. VERB TENSE SEQUENCES IN DISCOURSE

Purpose. In these drills we want to become aware of the patterns of verb sequences which different languages use in telling stories. English has its patterns, but the receptor language also has its patterns and the two need not be the same. In South American Indian languages, for example, the introduction to a story is set in space and time, but the rest of the story is told in the neutral tense, as in "Long ago in X country there lived a man who liked to hunt. One day as he is going into the forest he hears..." In these lessons the translator will become aware of the tense patterns in English, but he cannot necessarily follow them in his own language. He must use those patterns that are natural for his language.

Instructions
(a) In the blanks provided in the English biblical stories below, fill in the proper tense for the verb which appears in infinitive form under the blank.

(b) When you have filled in the blanks, compare your version with the TEV. Discuss any differences with the help of the teacher.

(c) Now compare the TEV version with your language. Note any differences between the usage of English and that of your own language.

Example
Mark 3.31-35
Then Jesus' mother and brothers _arrived_ . They _stood_ outside the
                                  (to arrive)   (to stand)

house and _sent_ in a message, _asking_ for him. A crowd _was sitting_
          (to send)   (to ask)   (to sit)

around Jesus, and they _said_ to him, _"Look_ , your mother and your bro-
                        (to say)   (to look)

thers and sisters _are_ outside, and they _want_ you." Jesus _answered_ ,
                  (to be)   (to want)   (to answer)

"Who _is_ my mother? Who _are_ my brothers?" He _looked_ at the people
     (to be)   (to be)   (to look)

sitting around him and _said_ , _"Look_ ! Here _are_ my mother and my
(to sit)   (to say) (to look)   (to be)

brothers! Whoever _does_ what God _wants_ him _to do_ _is_ my bro-
                  (to do)   (to want)   (to do) (to be)

ther, my sister, my mother."

Evaluation:
Past tense is used to indicate the movement of events in the story: arrived, stood, sent, told, answered, looked, said. Present participle asking is used to indicate the content of the message sent. Past continuative was sitting is used to indicate background information. Imperative Look! calls attention in direct speech. Present tense is used in the direct quotations.

YL _____

G-5 New Testament: Verb Tense Sequences of Matt 2.13-15

NEB   After they _____, an angel of the Lord _____ to Joseph in a dream,
               (to go)   (to appear)

and _____ to him, '_____ up, _____ the child and his mother
    (to say)   (to rise)   (to take)

and _____ with them to Egypt, and _____ there until I _____
    (to escape)   (to stay)   (to tell)

you; for Herod _____ _____ for the child _____ away with him.'
             (to go)   (to search)   (to do)

So Joseph _____ from sleep, and _____ mother and child by night he
        (to rise)   (to take)

_____ away with them to Egypt, and there he _____ till Herod's
(to go)   (to stay)

_____.
(to die)

    Compare:
TEV   After they had left, an angel of the Lord appeared in a dream to Joseph and
said, "Get up, take the child and his mother and run away to Egypt, and stay
there until I tell you to leave. Herod will be looking for the child to kill
him." Joseph got up, took the child and his mother, and left during the night
for Egypt, where he stayed until Herod died.

YL   _____

G-6 Old Testament: Verb Tense Sequences of Exo 2.11-12 (Instructions as for Drill
    G-5)

RSV   One day, when Moses _____ up, he _____ out to his people and _____
                (to grow)   (to go)   (to look)

on their burdens; and he _____ an Egyptian _____ a Hebrew, one of
                (to see)   (to beat)

his people. He _____ this way and that, and _____ no one he _____
          (to look)   (to see)   (to kill)

the Egyptian and _____ him in the sand.
         (to hide)

    Compare:
TEV   When Moses had grown up, he went out to visit his people, the Hebrews, and he
saw how they were forced to do hard labor. He even saw an Egyptian kill a Hebrew, one of Moses' own people. Moses looked all around, and when he saw that
no one was watching, he killed the Egyptian and hid his body in the sand.

YL   _____

4. FOCUS, BACKGROUND, FOREGROUND, ETC.

Purpose. In this series of drills we want to sharpen our awareness of how a story develops. We have already learned some things when we made our first discourse analysis in Drills G-10 to G-13; but now we want to pay attention to some of the things that were not treated in that analysis. It is important for the translator to be aware of what is in focus and what describes the background, so that he can treat the various kinds of information according to the usage of the receptor language. All too often what was background gets treated as ongoing story in a translation, and this causes confusion for the reader.

Instructions

(a) Study the RSV story in the column on the left. On the line marked (a) classify the information in the numbered phrases as: background, ongoing event in the main line of the story, additional information emphasizing a point already made, introduction of a new character, foregrounding a character or an event, etc.

(b) Once you have classified the kind of information, try to decide what its function is and write it on the line marked (b).

(c) Now read the TEV rendering on the right and see if the information has been handled differently from the RSV. Are there any improvements?

(d) Now study your Bible version of the passage and see whether the information and focus have been handled properly.

Example
Mark 11.12-14

RSV	Kind of Information	TEV
(1) On the following day, (2) when they came from Bethany, (3) he was hungry. (4) And seeing in the distance a fig tree in leaf, he (5) went to see if he could find anything on it. (6) When he came to it, (7) he found nothing but leaves, (8) for it was not the season for figs. (9) And he said to it, (10) "May no one ever eat fruit from you again." (11) And his disciples heard it.	1(a) setting of text (b) time setting ?(a) background (b) setting of event 3(a) background (b) condition of actor 4(a) first event (b) starts movement 5(a) second event (b) moves story 6(a) third event (b) setting for next E 7(a) fourth event (b) moves story 8(a) background (b) reason for fourth E 9(a) fifth event (b) introduces speech 10(a) detail of fifth E (b) content of speech 11(a) last event (b) introduces witnesses from background	The next day, as they were coming back from Bethany, Jesus was hungry. He saw in the distance a fig tree covered with leaves, so he went to see if he could find any figs on it; but when he came to it, he found only leaves, because it was not the right time for figs. Jesus said to the fig tree, "No one shall ever eat figs from you again!" And his disciples heard him.

YL _____

RSV	Kind of Information	TEV

RSV

(1) When the day of Pentecost had come, (2) they
were all together in one
place. (3) And suddenly
a sound came from heaven
like the rush of a mighty
wind, (4) and it filled
all the house where they
were sitting. (5) And
there appeared to them
tongues as of fire,
(6) distributed and
resting on each one of
them. (7) And they were
all filled with the Holy
Spirit (8) and began to
speak in other tongues,
as the Spirit gave them
utterance. (9) Now there
were dwelling in Jerusa-
lem Jews, (10) devout
men from every nation
under heaven. (11) And
at this sound the multi-
tude came together,
(12) and they were be-
wildered, (13) because
each one heard them
speaking in his own
language. (14) And they
were amazed and wondered,
(15) saying, "Are not
all these who are speak-
ing Galileans? (16) And
how is it that we hear,
each of us in his own
native language?
(17) Parthians and Medes
and Elamites

Kind of Information

1(a)_____
(b)_____
2(a)_____
(b)_____
3(a)_____
(b)_____
4(a)_____
(b)_____
5(a)_____
(b)_____
6(a)_____
(b)_____
7(a)_____
(b)_____
8(a)_____
(b)_____
9(a)_____
(b)_____
10(a)_____
(b)_____
11(a)_____
(b)_____
12(a)_____
(b)_____
13(a)_____
(b)_____
14(a)_____
(b)_____
15(a)_____
(b)_____
16(a)_____
(b)_____
17(a)_____
(b)_____

TEV

When the day of Pentecost
came, all the believers
were gathered together in
one place. Suddenly there
was a noise from the sky
which sounded like a strong
wind blowing, and it filled
the whole house where they
were sitting. Then they saw
what looked like tongues of
fire which spread out and
touched each person there.
They were all filled with
the Holy Spirit and began to
talk in other languages, as
the Spirit enabled them to
speak. There were Jews living in Jerusalem, religious
men who had come from every
country in the world. When
they heard this noise, a
large crowd gathered. They
were all excited, because
each one of them heard the
believers talking in his own
language. In amazement and
wonder they exclaimed,
"These people who are talking like this are Galileans!
How is it, then, that all of
us hear them speaking in our
own native languages? We are
from Parthia, Media, and Elam;

YL _____

RSV

(1) One day, when Moses had grown up, (2) he went out to his people and looked on their burdens; (3) and he saw an Egyptian beating a Hebrew, (4) one of his people. (5) He looked this way and that, (6) and seeing no one he killed the Egyptian and hid him in the sand. (7) When he went out the next day, (8) behold, two Hebrews were struggling together; (9) and he said to the man that did the wrong, "Why do you strike your fellow?" (10) He answered, "Who made you a prince and a judge over us? (11) Do you mean to kill me as you killed the Egyptian?" (12) Then Moses was afraid, (13) and thought, "Surely the thing is known." (14) When Pharaoh heard of it, (15) he sought to kill Moses. (16) But Moses fled from Pharaoh, (17) and stayed in the land of Midian;

Kind of Information

1(a)_____

(b)_____

2(a)_____

(b)_____

3(a)_____

(b)_____

4(a)_____

(b)_____

5(a)_____

(b)_____

6(a)_____

(b)_____

7(a)_____

(b)_____

8(a)_____

(b)_____

9(a)_____

(b)_____

10(a)_____

(b)_____

11(a)_____

(b)_____

12(a)_____

(b)_____

13(a)_____

(b)_____

14(a)_____

(b)_____

15(a)_____

(b)_____

16(a)_____

(b)_____

17(a)_____

(b)_____

TEV

When Moses had grown up, he went out to visit his people, the Hebrews, and he saw how they were forced to do hard labor. He even saw an Egyptian kill a Hebrew, one of Moses' own people. Moses looked all around, and when he saw that no one was watching, he killed the Egyptian and hid his body in the sand. The next day he went back and saw two Hebrew men fighting. He said to the one who was in the wrong, "Why are you beating up a fellow Hebrew?" The man answered, "Who made you our ruler and judge? Are you going to kill me just as you killed that Egyptian?" Then Moses was afraid and said to himself, "People have found out what I have done." When the king heard about what had happened, he tried to have Moses killed, but Moses fled and went to live in the land of Midian.

YL_____

5. FLASHBACKS

   Purpose. In these drills we want to learn to identify flashback material within an ongoing story. We tried to learn how to reorder kernels for languages that cannot handle flashbacks in Drill E-5. However, even when a language permits flashbacks, it usually has special ways of handling or marking them. The translator needs to recognize flashbacks, first of all; and then he must know how to handle them properly in translation.

   Instructions

   (a) Read the following selections from the RSV on the left and identify which material represents flashbacks.

   (b) Write the flashbacks into the lines provided in the middle of the page.

   (c) Now study the TEV rendering of the passage on the right and see how flashback material has been handled.

   (d) Now study the passage in your language to see how it has handled flashback material. If it has not been handled correctly, make the necessary corrections.

Example
John 21.1-4

RSV	Flashbacks	TEV
1 After this Jesus revealed himself again to the disciples by the Sea of Tiberias; and he revealed himself in this way. 2 Simon Peter, Thomas called the Twin, Nathanael of Cana in Galilee, the sons of Zebedee, and two others of his disciples were together. 3 Simon Peter said to them, "I am going fishing." They said to him, "We will go with you." They went out and got into the boat; but that night they caught nothing. 4 Just as day was breaking, Jesus stood on the beach; yet the disciples did not know that it was Jesus.	Verses 2 and 3 represent a flashback which eventually leads into the story. In TEV the first part of the account is treated as a sort of title. The flashback is then introduced by "This is how it happened."	1 After this, Jesus appeared once more to his disciples at Lake Tiberias. This is how it happened. 2 Simon Peter, Thomas (called the Twin), Nathanael (the one from Cana in Galilee), the sons of Zebedee, and two other disciples of Jesus were all together. 3 Simon Peter said to the others, "I am going fishing." "We will come with you," they told him. So they went out in a boat, but all that night they did not catch a thing. 4 As the sun was rising, Jesus stood at the water's edge, but the disciples did not know that it was Jesus.

YL _____

RSV	Flashbacks	TEV

RSV

At that time Herod the tetrarch heard about the fame of Jesus; and he said to his servants, "This is John the Baptist, he has been raised from the dead; that is why these powers are at work in him." For Herod had seized John and bound him and put him in prison, for the sake of Herodias, his brother Philip's wife; because John said to him, "It is not lawful for you to have her." And though he wanted to put him to death, he feared the people, because they held him to be a prophet. But when Herod's birthday came, the daughter of Herodias danced before the company, and pleased Herod, so that he promised with an oath to give her whatever she might ask. Prompted by her mother, she said, "Give me the head of John the Baptist here on a platter." And the king was sorry; but because of his oaths and his guests he commanded it to be given; he sent and had John beheaded in the prison, and his head was brought on a platter and given to the girl, and she brought it to her mother. And his disciples came and took the body and buried it; and they went and told Jesus.

YL _____

TEV

At that time Herod, the ruler of Galilee, heard about Jesus. "He is really John the Baptist, who has come back to life," he told his officials. "That is why he has this power to perform miracles." For Herod had earlier ordered John's arrest, and he had him tied up and put in prison. He had done this because of Herodias, his brother Philip's wife. For some time John the Baptist had told Herod, "It isn't right for you to be married to Herodias!" Herod wanted to kill him, but he was afraid of the Jewish people, because they considered John to be a prophet. On Herod's birthday the daughter of Herodias danced in front of the whole group. Herod was so pleased that he promised her, "I swear that I will give you anything you ask for!" At her mother's suggestion she asked him, "Give me here and now the head of John the Baptist on a plate!" The king was sad, but because of the promise he had made in front of all his guests he gave orders that her wish be granted. So he had John beheaded in prison. The head was brought in on a plate and given to the girl, who took it to her mother. John's disciples came, carried away his body, and buried it; then they went and told Jesus.

RSV	Flashbacks	TEV
Now when David and his men came to Ziklag on the third day, the Amalekites had made a raid upon the Negeb and upon Ziklag. They had overcome Ziklag, and burned it with fire, and taken captive the women and all who were in it, both small and great; they killed no one, but carried them off, and went their way. And when David and his men came to the city, they found it burned with fire, and their wives and sons and daughters taken captive. Then David and the people who were with him raised their voices and wept, until they had no more strength to weep. David's two wives also had been taken captive, Ahinoam of Jezreel, and Abigail the widow of Nabal of Carmel. And David was greatly distressed; for the people spoke of stoning him, because all the people were bitter in soul, each for his sons and daughters. But David strengthened himself in the LORD his God.		Two days later David and his men arrived back at Ziklag. The Amalekites had raided southern Judah and attacked Ziklag. They had burned down the town and captured all the women; they had not killed anyone, but had taken everyone with them when they left. When David and his men arrived, they found that the town had been burned down and that their wives, sons, and daughters had been carried away. David and his men started crying and did not stop until they were completely exhausted. Even David's two wives, Ahinoam and Abigail, had been taken away. David was now in great trouble, because his men were all very bitter about losing their children, and they were threatening to stone him; but the LORD his God gave him courage.

6. STUDYING THE DISCOURSE PATTERNS OF YOUR OWN LANGUAGE

Purpose. In order to produce a natural translation in your own language, you must be aware of its patterns. In this section we want to make the same analyses in your language as we have been making for English in Drills G-1 to G-10.

Instructions. Select two fairly short stories in your own language and make the following analyses on each:

G-11 and G-12 Actor-Action Line. Analyze the stories as in Drills G-1 and G-2.

G-13 and G-14 Reference Line. Analyze the stories as in Drills G-3 and G-4.

G-15 and G-16 Tense Sequence. Analyze the stories as in Drills G-5 and G-6.

G-17 and G-18 Focus, Foregrounding, Backgrounding, Etc. Now study the story and identify the focus of each sentence. Note what is background information and how characters are moved from background into the foreground, or how a new character is introduced. Follow the instructions for Drills G-7 and G-8.

G-19 and G-20 Flashbacks. If there are no flashbacks in the stories you have analyzed, find two stories that contain them and see how they are handled. See Drills G-9 and G-10.

7. WRITING IN YOUR OWN LANGUAGE

Purpose. In order to gain experience in using the patterns of one's own language consciously, it often is good to try to do some creative writing. Such writings should be reviewed by competent people and the good and poor points analyzed. In this way one can learn how to avoid poor style and learn to use the best patterns.

G-21 Writing an Account of an Experience

Instructions

(a) In your own language write down an experience, such as a trip, a hunting experience, an accident, a wedding, etc. Be sure to include all the significant events in the experience.

(b) Duplicate (or write on the blackboard) several stories prepared by class members choosing the best and the worst, and discuss the problems and good points of each.

Example story

Our Trip to the Translator Training Workshop

My name is John Mumbwa. I live in Tenga Village. Mr. Chirumba also lives in my village. Mr. Chirumba and I were both invited to come to the translator training workshop at Kabwe. We were very happy. Mr. Chirumba has a car. We went together in Mr. Chirumba's car. We left Tenga Village at six o'clock in the morning on Monday. We drove all day. We drove south on the Great North Road. We arrived at Kabwe at four o'clock in the afternoon. There were many holes in the road. We also had some trouble finding petrol. We saw some impala and some warthogs. We had two punctured tires. Another trouble we had was that the car would not start when we wanted to leave so the people had to push us.

Analysis:
This story is just a series of events listed one after the other. In fact, the last sentence does not even occur in the chronological order of events. There are no paragraphs. One could almost say each sentence functions like a separate paragraph. There are very few connectors between kernel sentences. It is not an interesting story.

G-22 Writing a Story with a Positive Highlight

Instructions

(a) Read the example story provided and discuss its good and poor points. Are the paragraphs correct? What about the links between the sentences? What carries the positive tone? What improvements can you suggest?

(b) Now rewrite your story from Drill G-21 in a similar way. Try to make the story interesting and at the same time try to leave the reader with a positive feeling.

Example story

The bright sun was just beginning to look over the top of the mountains into our valley to chase away the cold of the night, when Mr. Chirumba arrived with his car to make the trip to the translators' training workshop at Kabwe.

Everybody in Tenga Village was excited, and my wife had been up long before five o'clock to prepare food for our breakfast and for our trip. I had been packing the last things and was eagerly waiting for Mr. Chirumba to come.

Now that he had arrived we arranged our baggage in the boot of the car, said good-bye to our families, and to many villagers who had come to see us off, and got into the car. But the car was stubborn. It didn't want to start. The people had to push us to get it started. On the way we found plenty of bad holes, but Mr. Chirumba was a good driver. He always saw them in time to slow down or to go around them. The trees along the road were just getting new leaves, so the hillsides were covered with red, yellow and orange-colored trees. It was a beautiful sight. Several impala ran across the road in front of us. It was exciting to see them jump high over the ditch beside the road and then disappear into the bush. We also saw several herds of warthogs. When the noise of the car frightened them they ran off in a cloud of dust. We had to laugh because all we could see besides the dust were their tails sticking straight up into the air like little radio aerials.

We had been worried about finding petrol, but our worries were unnecessary. Well before our petrol was finished we found some at Mpika. When we arrived at Kabwe at five o'clock in the evening, I just couldn't believe that we had been driving eleven hours. There were so many beautiful things to see and so much to enjoy that the hours had just hurried by. Even the two punctured tires on the way had seemed more like rest periods rather than like trouble.

G-23 Writing a Story with a Negative Highlight

Instructions
(a) Read the story below and discuss its good and bad points. Is it properly paragraphed? Does it have good transitions within paragraphs and between paragraphs? What is it that carries the negative tone in the story? What improvements can you suggest?

(b) Now rewrite your story from Drill G-22 with a negative highlight.

Example story

It was one of those Monday mornings. We had been up early and had been waiting and waiting when Mr. Chirumba finally arrived with his car. Even though we were in a hurry, almost everybody in Tenga Village came to say good-bye. With everybody talking and trying to help, it was a nightmare to get our baggage packed into the boot. When we finally got into the car, the beast wouldn't start. Mr. Chirumba tried and tried, but the car remained stubborn and would not start. Even the sun seemed to laugh at us when it looked over the top of the hill into the valley. Instead of sympathizing with us the people just laughed and laughed. Finally they agreed to try and push us. When they came it was almost as if a horde of noisy hyenas had fallen on us, but with their pushing the car finally coughed and started. What a start! The road from Tenga Village to Great North Road seemed rough, but it was smooth compared to the big road. There were holes, and more holes, everywhere! It seemed as if someone had damaged the road just before we came along. Mr. Chirumba constantly had to slow down and crawl through the big holes, or he had to swerve sharply to go around the little ones. Since I had nothing to hold on to, I was swinging forward when he braked and then backward as he started up again. When he was trying to dodge the holes I was sliding left to right as a clock pendulum until every bone in my body ached.

Before long our petrol indicator began to warn us that we needed to get more fuel. We tried to get some, but in town after town there was no petrol, no petrol, no petrol. Finally, just when we were running out, we found some at Mpika. What a trip! When it wasn't the potholes and the sandpits in the road, it was the impala and the warthogs that made us slow down. Then to top it all off, we had several punctures. When we finally arrived at Kabwe after eleven long hours of driving, I felt like a bag of aching bones.

G-24 Writing a Story to Highlight a Character

Instructions
(a) Study the example story below and try to identify all the things that help give us a negative impression about Mr. Chirumba. What do you think the shift from using Mr. Chirumba to the driver implies? Would the story have been as effective if it had been written as indirect discourse? Are the transitions between clauses and paragraphs adequate? Can you suggest any improvements?

(b) Rewrite your story from Drill G-23 and make one character bad (or good). Remember, you may not say he is bad (or good); you have to make the reader feel it without directly saying it.

I had never driven with Mr. Chirumba before, but I was excitedly looking forward to a pleasant trip to the translators' workshop at Kabwe. I was already waiting, when Mr. Chirumba drove up, but he didn't even greet me. Just like a *mzungu* (a white man), he just growled: "Hurry up with your baggage. We can't wait here all day!" I tried to put my things into the boot as quickly as I could, but he grabbed them out of my hand impatiently and snapped: "Don't you even know how to put *katundu* (baggage) into the boot of a car?" Almost everybody from Tenga Village was there trying to say good-bye. I saw Mr. Chirumba's heart getting hotter and hotter. I was already afraid his anger would erupt on the people like hot lava from a volcano. But luckily it didn't erupt with the people—it erupted when the car wouldn't start. The harder the driver tried to start it, the more stubborn the car seemed to be. "You stupid car! I spend all my money trying to keep you fixed up, and here you still won't even start. I should get a hammer and smash you."

Then he rolled down his window and yelled to the people: "All of you people, make yourselves useful and push!" When the people came running and wanted to push, he literally screamed: "Be careful! Don't be like vultures attacking the carcass of a dead ox!" He was still boiling with anger over the careless people, when the sun looked over the mountain and shone brightly onto the windscreen of the car. It must have blinded the driver because he exploded again: "That stupid sun! I can't see a thing!" Luckily just then the car coughed and off we were.

I began to relax, thinking that once we were on the Great North Road the driver would also relax. But I was wrong—dead wrong. He fumed over potholes, he growled at the sandpits, he snarled at the warthogs and the impala that ran across the road, he even complained about the many leaves on the trees, because they hindered him from seeing what was around the curve.

Then we had one puncture, and another puncture. They certainly didn't help his patience any; but when our petrol began to finish and we couldn't find any in town after town, his anger reached such fierceness that my pen just refuses to write it down.

Finally we arrived at Kabwe. I was just sighing with relief when his voice thundered: "Can't you see that we've arrived? Get your junk out of the car so we won't be late for supper!"

G-25 Writing a Story with Flashbacks

Instructions

(a) Study the story below and try to identify all the flashbacks. Is there more than one layer of flashback? Can your language use flashbacks? Several layers of flashbacks? How does the section about the Old Testament differ from that about the New Testament?

(b) Now rewrite your original story in your own language with a series of flashbacks. If possible, use several layers of flashbacks.

(c) Study the various stories written by members of the class and see what improvements you can suggest for them.

Today my co-worker Mr. Chirumba and I gave the completed manuscript of the translation of the New Testament into our language to our translations consultant. It was a happy ending to three years of hard work; but it was a wiser happiness from that which I felt when Mr. Chirumba and I first arrived at Kabwe after an eleven-hour trip along the Great North Road to attend the translator training workshop. I was tired when we arrived, and happy, happy to have arrived, but even happier that I had been chosen to learn to do this important work of Bible translating.

Our three years were not without difficulties. My co-worker's temper showed itself every now and then, just like the morning when we were planning to leave for Kabwe and the car wouldn't start. I still remember how he shouted at the people: "Make yourselves useful and push!" And then when they rushed to do what he had ordered, how he screamed: "Be careful! Don't be like vultures attacking the carcass of a dead ox!"

The New Testament is now completed, but the Old Testament is still to be done. It will be an even longer road than the New Testament, and like the Great North Road, on which we travelled when we went for our training, there will be plenty of deep potholes, blind curves, and warthogs blocking the way. But I am confident that by the help of God we shall overcome all our problems, just like the impala we saw on that first trip jumping over the wide ditch beside the road with graceful ease.

I am sure there will also be moments when our reviewers' comments will puncture our pride just like the punctured tires we experienced on that trip to Kabwe; but I am confident that just as our first trip ended well, so the long trip of completing the Bible in our language will end well.

The examples given here are by no means the only possible ways of rewriting the original story. For example, we could have written the material as a make-believe story; it could have been rewritten with more characters—contrasting a good character with a bad character; the story could have been told from the driver's point of view; it could have been told from the point of view of what the various people in the car were thinking while the events of the story were taking place, and so on.

At one workshop different content stories were used for each section. While this gave us more variety, it did not provide the same clear-cut examples of good and bad points as rewriting the same content in different ways does.

Usually translators-in-training find this part of their training very exciting. At one program people stayed up all hours of the night reading the interesting parts of their stories to each other and enjoying them.

Of course the purpose in training translators to write well in their own language is to make them into better translators. And the training that has been described here should help in a number of ways:

(a) It should help the translator to look at the text to see from what point of view the story has been told.

(b) It should make him aware of the focus and the purpose of the biblical writer.

(c) It should make him aware of the literary devices used in the source text.

(d) It should make him aware of and give him experience in using the literary patterns of his own language.

(e) It should help him to make a translation that will read more like an original production in his own language, rather than an obviously stilted translation which merely copies the forms of the source language.

H. TESTING THE TRANSLATION

1. GENERAL TESTS BY TRANSLATORS

Purpose. In this section we want to point out the importance of adequately checking and testing every new translation. The translations consultant, the manuscript examiner, and the copy editor will, of course, do a lot of professional checking, but over and above these checks there are a series of tests which each translation team can and should do. Careful testing and checking should help the translators eliminate many "little foxes" that can do serious damage to the impact of their efforts.

Reading aloud. Hearing a translation read aloud often makes people aware of rough spots left in it. Such reading can take several forms:

1. reading aloud by one member of the team while other members each follow in a different version to check for inaccuracies, missing fragments, and wrong interpretations.

2. reading aloud by one member of the team while other members merely listen. This is to discover any ambiguous, strange or rough renderings that need to be improved.

3. reading aloud to various kinds of audiences—women, children, illiterates, church audiences, etc. The reading should be complete units and the listeners should then be encouraged to discuss and ask questions about the text. Also prepared content questions can be asked to check the receptors' comprehension. Any concerns expressed by hearers should be carefully considered. A variant form, using a prerecorded reading, is useful because it can be replayed just as it was heard the first time, to locate problem spots.

4. loud reading by various people not connected with the project. This should include children, women, new literates, etc. All hesitations, false starts, errors, substitutions, etc., should be noted. Making a tape recording of the reading is useful to assure a record of all the problems. If several people have the same problem, the text probably needs to be adjusted. Perhaps it does not flow smoothly or the expressions put together don't really fit in with each other. A variant is to have a person not connected with the translation read a passage to a church audience. The translation team should note audience reactions and the reader's problems. A discussion led by the reader can be helpful to check on ambiguities and other problems.

Publishing preliminary versions.

1. Several teams have found it very helpful to send problem verses to churches in mimeographed form, often with several alternative versions, or at least alternative words at certain points. Churches are then asked to pray with the team: "Lord how would you have said this if you had spoken our language in the first place?" This creates churchwide involvement in the translation process.

2. It has been useful to publish some chapters or a short book in preliminary but printed form with requests for reactions on problem spots. Preliminary editions have sometimes even included variants to make sure readers came to grips with crucial questions. Several teams have promised a new clean book to any reader who will mark his own book with corrections and return it to the team.

2. CHECKING FIDELITY IN THE ORIGINAL

Purpose. A translation should be as faithful a representative of the original as possible, including both form and meaning. Obviously, for a dynamic-equivalent-style translation, the meaning is always the first consideration.

For common language translations there is a second consideration, namely, the clarity and simplicity of the translation.

In this drill we now want to compare translations and see if they are (1) accurate, and (2) easily understood. It should be remembered that Drills H-1 to H-10 are merely samples of the kind of tests that should be performed. The actual passages used in the test may vary from language to language.

Instructions

(a) Study the RSV and TEV as the original text, remembering that the RSV gives priority to the form and the TEV gives priority to the meaning. For difficult passages, do not trust your own judgment, but consult a good Bible commentary.

(b) Compare the translations to be tested, including your language to see (1) whether both form and meaning have been translated, (2) whether the meaning is a faithful representation of the original, and (3) whether the way in which it has been said is easy to understand.

Example
Matt 6.22
RSV   so, if your eye is sound, your whole body will be full of light
TEV   if your eyes are clear, your whole body will be full of light
   Compare:
NEB   if your eyes are sound, you will have light for your whole body
JB   it follows that if your eye is sound, your whole body will be filled with light
LB   if your eye is pure, there will be sunshine in your soul
TNT   if your eye is in good condition your whole body will be full of light
Knox so that if thy eye is clear, the whole of thy body will be lit up
BE   if then your eye is true, all your body will be full of light
Phps if your eye is sound, your whole body will be full of light
NAB   if your eyes are good, your body will be filled with light
NAS   if therefore your eye is clear, your whole body will be full of light
YL

Evaluation:
There is some difference between sound meaning "healthy" or "good condition," and pure in LB. But there is a sharp difference between body meaning "whole being" and soul in LB. Finally, the expression full of light, meaning "without darkness or unsoundness," is a much more serious expression than sunshine in your soul in LB. The use of clear for sound in Knox and NAS sounds strange in common-language English.

H-1 New Testament: Fidelity to the Original

Matt 5.29

RSV   if your right eye causes you to sin, pluck it out and throw it away; it is better that you lose one of your members than that your whole body be thrown into hell

TEV   so if your right eye causes you to sin, take it out and throw it away! It is much better for you to lose a part of your body than to have your whole body thrown into hell

Compare:

NEB   if your right eye is your undoing, tear it out and fling it away; it is better for you to lose one part of your body than for the whole of it to be thrown into hell

JB   if your right eye should cause you to sin, tear it out and throw it away; for it will do you less harm to lose one part of you than to have your whole body thrown into hell

LB   so if your eye—even if it is your best eye!—causes you to lust, gouge it out and throw it away. Better for part of you to be destroyed than for all of you to be cast into hell

TNT   if your right eye causes you to fall away, take it out and throw it away, for it is better for you that one part of your body should perish than that your whole body should be thrown into hell

BE   and if your right eye is a cause of trouble to you, take it out and put it away from you; because it is better to undergo the loss of one part, than for all of your body to go into hell

YL   _____

Evaluation:

H-2 Old Testament: Fidelity to the Original (Instructions as for Drill H-1)

Gen 6.11

RSV   now the earth was corrupt in God's sight, and the earth was filled with violence

TEV   but everyone else was evil in God's sight, and violence had spread everywhere

Compare:

NEB   now God saw that the whole world was corrupt and full of violence

JB   the earth grew corrupt in God's sight, and filled with violence

LB   meanwhile, the crime rate was rising rapidly across the earth, and, as seen by God, the world was rotten to the core

NAS   now the earth was corrupt in the sight of God, and the earth was filled with violence

AB   the earth was depraved and putrid in God's sight, and the land was filled with violence (desecration, infringement, outrage, assault, and lust for power)

YL   _____

Evaluation:

Purpose. One of the important limitations governing the adjustment of the biblical form in translation is that the adjusted form should never misrepresent biblical history or culture.

Instructions. Read the translations presented, including your language, noting especially all cultural and historical information. Do any of the translations presented contain any information which you feel misrepresents either biblical history or culture? Write your findings in the space provided. How could you avoid the misrepresentation and still be fully meaningful? Make the adjustment in YL, if necessary.

Example
1 Cor 16.20
RSV   greet one another with a holy kiss
    Compare:
TEV   greet one another with a brotherly kiss
NEB   greet one another with the kiss of peace
LB   give each other a loving handshake when you meet
Phps   shake hands all round as a sign of Christian love
TNT   greet one another with a holy kiss
YL   _____

    Evaluation:
Kissing as a greeting is a problem in many cultures. LB and Phps use handshake but that misrepresents biblical culture—they did not shake hands. For cultural situations in which the biblical form creates problems one could translate greet each other warmly as members of the Christian family. This leaves the form implicit. The biblical form could then be given in a footnote with the cultural explanation.

H-3 New Testament: Historical and Cultural Fidelity

1. Luke 13.11
    RSV   and there was a woman who had had a spirit of infirmity for eighteen years
        Compare:
    TEV   a woman there had an evil spirit in her that had kept her sick for eighteen years
    NEB   and there was a woman there possessed by a spirit that had crippled her for eighteen years
    LB   he saw a seriously handicapped woman who had been bent double for eighteen years
    Phps   in the congregation was a woman who for eighteen years had been ill from some psychological cause
    TNT   a woman was there who for eighteen years had had a spirit which made her weak
    YL   _____

        Evaluation:

2. Matt 22.4
   RSV   Again he sent other servants, saying, "Tell those who are invited, Behold,
          I have made ready my dinner, my oxen and my fat calves are killed, and
          everything is ready; come to the marriage feast."
   Compare:
   TEV   So he sent other servants with the message: "Tell the guests, 'My feast is
          ready now; my steers and prize calves have been butchered, and every-
          thing is ready. Come to the wedding feast!'"
   NEB   He sent others again, telling them to say to the guests, "See now! I have
          prepared this feast for you. I have had my bullocks and fatted beasts
          slaughtered; everything is ready; come to the wedding at once."
   LB   So he sent other servants to tell them, "Everything is ready and the roast
          is in the oven. Hurry!"
   Phps   He sent some more servants, saying to them: "Tell those who have been in-
          vited, 'Here is my wedding breakfast all ready, my bullocks and fat
          cattle have been slaughtered and everything is prepared. Come along to
          the festivities.'"
   YL   _____

   Evaluation:

H-4 Old Testament: Historical and Cultural Fidelity (Instructions as for Drill H-3)

1. Hab 2.2
   RSV   And the LORD answered me: "Write the vision; make it plain upon tablets, so
          he may run who reads it."
   Compare:
   TEV   The LORD gave me this answer: "Write down clearly on tablets what I reveal
          to you, so that it can be read at a glance."
   NEB   Then the LORD made answer: Write down the vision, inscribe it on tablets,
          ready for a herald to carry it with speed...
   LB   And the Lord said to me, "Write my answer on a billboard, large and clear,
          so that anyone can read it at a glance and rush to tell the others."
   JB   Then Yahweh answered and said, "Write the vision down, inscribe it on tab-
          lets to be easily read, since this vision is for its own time only..."
   YL   _____

   Evaluation:

2. Zech 2.1
   RSV   And I lifted my eyes and saw, and behold, a man with a measuring line in
          his hand!
   Compare:
   TEV   In another vision I saw a man with a measuring line in his hand.
   NEB   I lifted my eyes and there I saw a man carrying a measuring-line.
   LB   When I looked around me again, I saw a man carrying a yardstick in his hand.
   JB   Then, raising my eyes, I saw a vision. It was this: there was a man with a
          measuring line in his hand.

   YL   _____

   Evaluation:

[257]

Checking a Translation for Theological Bias

Purpose. Most translators try hard to make an accurate translation. However, sometimes quite unconsciously their doctrine, or their political or social outlook, begins to influence the translation. This is bias, and it represents inaccuracy of the worst kind, since it bends the translation to support the bias. For example, when a translator wants to retain the plural in Genesis 1.26, "let us make man," because he regards it as the first reference to the Trinity, he is letting a New Testament teaching influence his translation of the Old Testament. Or a translator may want to retain the singular "seed" in Genesis 3.15 to preserve the reference to Jesus Christ. Again, he may want to correct the text as the KJV (following Textus Receptus) did in Mark 1.2, "as it is written in the prophets," because Mark quotes both Malachi and Isaiah; but the recognized original text clearly says, as in the RSV, "as it is written in Isaiah the prophet." Or he may translate demon possession with "psychiatric problems." All such adjustments are to be avoided because they represent bias and do not accurately reflect the values and the presuppositions which underlie the biblical text.

Instructions

(a) Compare the translations presented and see if they are significantly different from the RSV. Do you detect any possible bias?

(b) Write your evaluation of the different translations in the space provided.

Example

Matt 1.17

RSV   so all the generations from Abraham to David were fourteen generations

Compare:

TEV   so then, there were fourteen generations from Abraham to David

NEB   there were thus fourteen generations in all from Abraham to David

LB   these are fourteen of the generations from Abraham to King David

YL   _____

Evaluation:

LB tries to leave the door open for more generations between Abraham and David because it is aware that other genealogies differ; but this makes it unfaithful to what Matthew says. The translator will often face the temptation to harmonize contradictory renderings, but he must avoid the temptation. His task is to translate faithfully what the given text says.

H-5 New Testament: Checking for Theological Bias

1. Matt 2.9

RSV   the star which they had seen in the East went before them

Compare:

TEV   they saw the same star they had seen in the east...it went ahead of them

NEB   the star which they had seen at its rising went ahead of them

LB   the star appeared to them again, standing over Bethlehem

Phps the star, which they had seen in the east, went in front of them

YL   _____

Evaluation:

2. Matt 13.52
   RSV   every scribe who has been trained for the kingdom of heaven is like a house-
         holder who brings out of his treasure what is new and what is old
      Compare:
   TEV   every teacher of the Law who becomes a disciple of the Kingdom of heaven is
         like a homeowner who takes new and old things out of his storage
         room
   NEB   a teacher of the law has become a learner in the kingdom of Heaven, he is
         like a householder who can produce from his store both the new and the
         old
   LB   those experts in Jewish law who are now my disciples have double treasures—
         from the Old Testament as well as from the New
   YL   _____

      Evaluation:

H-6 Old Testament: Checking for Theological Bias (Instructions as for Drill H-5)

1. Gen 1.4-5
   RSV   and God saw that the light was good; and God separated the light from the
         darkness. God called the light Day, and the darkness he called Night. And
         there was evening and there was morning, one day
      Compare:
   TEV   God was pleased with what he saw. Then he separated the light from the dark-
         ness, and he named the light "Day" and the darkness "Night." Evening
         passed and morning came—that was the first day
   NEB   and God saw that the light was good, and he separated the light from the
         darkness. He called the light day and the darkness night. So evening
         came, and morning came, the first day
   LB   and God was pleased with it, and divided the light from darkness. So he let
         it shine for awhile, and then there was darkness again. He called the
         light "daytime," and the darkness "nighttime." Together they formed the
         first day
   YL   _____

      Evaluation:

2. Isa 7.14
   RSV   behold, a young woman shall conceive and bear a son
      Compare:
   TEV   a young woman who is pregnant will have a son
   NEB   a young woman is with child and she will bear a son
   JB   the maiden is with child and will soon give birth to a son
   LB   a child shall be born to a virgin
   AB   behold, the young woman who is unmarried and a virgin shall conceive and
         bear a son
   YL   _____

      Evaluation:

Checking a Translation for Emotive Accuracy

Purpose. A good translation not only is accurate in regard to the information contained in the original, but it also tries to maintain emotive equivalence. On the whole, a translation should not be blander than the original, and in fact it should be at least 20 percent more emotive than the RSV (or the text that you are using as a substitute for the Greek and Hebrew) because the RSV is a formal correspondent rather than a dynamic equivalent translation, and as such hides a good part of the emotive force of the original.

Instructions

(a) Study the numbered and underlined expressions in the RSV and identify the equivalent expressions in the other translations presented, including your language.

(b) Rank the equivalent expression in each translation as emotively the same (S), emotively higher (H), or emotively lower (L) than the RSV.

(c) Write your decisions on the summary lines provided and see which translations are consistently higher or lower than the RSV. If you would like to see an example, see Drill C-19.

H-7 New Testament: Emotive Accuracy

1. Matt 2.18
   RSV   (1) a voice was heard in Ramah, (2) wailing and loud lamentation
      Compare:
   TEV   a sound is heard in Ramah, the sound of bitter crying and weeping
   LB   screams of anguish come from Ramah, weeping unrestrained
   NEB   a voice was heard in Rama, wailing and loud laments
   JB   a voice was heard in Ramah, sobbing and loud lamenting
   YL   _____

      Summary:
   TEV   (1) ____   (2) ____
   LB   ____   ____
   NEB   ____   ____
   JB   ____   ____
   YL   ____   ____

2. Matt 4.6
   RSV   lest you (1) strike your foot against a stone
      Compare:
   TEV   so that not even your feet will be hurt on the stones
   LB   prevent you from smashing on the rocks below
   NEB   for fear you should strike your foot against a stone
   JB   in case you hurt your foot against a stone
   YL   _____

      Summary:
   TEV   (1) ____
   LB   ____
   NEB   ____
   JB   ____
   YL   ____

1. Gen 19.13
   RSV   because (1) <u>the outcry</u> against its people (2) <u>has become great</u> before the
            LORD
      Compare:
   TEV   the LORD has heard the terrible accusations against these people
   LB   the stench of the place has reached to heaven
   NEB   the outcry against it has been so great that the LORD...
   JB   for there is a great outcry against them, and it has reached Yahweh
   YL   _____

      Summary:
   TEV   (1) ____   (2) ____
   LB   ____   ____
   NEB   ____   ____
   JB   ____   ____
   YL   ____   ____

2. Gen 30.2
   RSV   (1) Jacob's anger was <u>kindled</u> against Rachel, and he said, (2) <u>"Am I in the</u>
            <u>place of God...?"</u>
      Compare:
   TEV   Jacob became angry with Rachel and said, "I can't take the place of God"
   LB   Jacob flew into a rage. "Am I God?" he flared
   NEB   Jacob said angrily to Rachel, "Can I take the place of God...?"
   JB   this made Jacob angry with Rachel, and he retorted, "Am I in God's place?"
   YL   _____

      Summary:
   TEV   (1) ____   (2) ____
   LB   ____   ____
   NEB   ____   ____
   JB   ____   ____
   YL   ____   ____

3. 1 Sam 25.36
   RSV   he was (1) <u>very drunk</u>
      Compare:
   TEV   he was drunk
   LB   he was roaring drunk
   NEB   became very drunk
   JB   he was very drunk
   YL   _____

      Summary:
   TEV   (1) ____
   LB   ____
   NEB   ____
   JB   ____
   YL   ____

3. CHECKING THE OVERALL IMPACT OF A TRANSLATION

Purpose. Language has three communicative functions: conveying information, expressing and stirring emotions, and moving receptors to action. In this drill we want to try and make people aware of how these factors work together for an overall impact.

Instructions. Compare the translations of Matthew 4.1-11 listed in parallel columns with the RSV "original" in regard to the following:

(a) Accuracy: Does the translation represent a faithful rendering of the meaning of the original?

(b) Understandability: Which translation(s) is/are most readily understandable for a person for whom English is a second language and who has only primary school education?

(c) Emotive force: We are here again concerned with faithfulness to the original and ask: Is the emotive force of the translation the same as the original, or is it higher or lower?

(d) Overall impact: If we accept that the purpose of a translation is to move its receptors to positive response, we need to ask: What is the overall impact of this translation? Will its message motivate people to act or will it leave them unmoved?

(e) On a separate sheet, evaluate your own language translation in the same way.

H-9   New Testament: Overall Impact of a Translation

1. Mark 4.1

RSV	TEV	LB
Again he began to teach beside the sea. And a very large crowd gathered about him, so that he got into a boat and sat in it on the sea; and the whole crowd was beside the sea on the land.	Again Jesus began to teach beside Lake Galilee. The crowd that gathered around him was so large that he got into a boat and sat in it. The boat was out in the water, and the crowd stood on the shore at the water's edge.	Once again an immense crowd gathered around him on the beach as he was teaching, so he got into a boat and sat down and talked from there.

Evaluation:
Accuracy:
    (good/fair/poor)   _____   _____
Understandability:
    (same/easier/harder)   _____   _____
Emotive force:
    (same/lower/higher)   _____   _____
Overall impact:
    (same/less/greater)   _____   _____

2. Mark 4.5

RSV	TEV	NEB
Other seed fell on rocky ground, where it had not much soil, and immediately it sprang up, since it had no depth of soil	Some of it fell on rocky ground, where there was little soil. The seeds soon sprouted, because the soil wasn't deep	Some seed fell on rocky ground, where it had little soil, and it sprouted quickly because it had no depth of earth

Evaluation:
Accuracy:
   (good/fair/poor)   _____   _____
Understandability:
   (same/easier/harder)   _____   _____
Emotive force:
   (same/lower/higher)   _____   _____
Overall impact:
   (same/less/greater)   _____   _____

H-10 Old Testament: Overall Impact of a Translation (Instructions as for Drill H-9)

Gen 16.4-6

RSV	TEV	NEB
And he went in to Hagar, and she conceived; and when she saw that she had conceived, she looked with contempt on her mistress. And Sarai said to Abram, "May the wrong done to me be on you! I gave my maid to your embrace, and when she saw that she had conceived, she looked on me with contempt. May the LORD judge between you and me!"	Abram had intercourse with Hagar, and she became pregnant. When she found out that she was pregnant, she became proud and despised Sarai. Then Sarai said to Abram, "It's your fault that Hagar despises me. I myself gave her to you, and ever since she found out that she was pregnant, she has despised me. May the LORD judge which of us is right, you or me!"	He lay with Hagar and she conceived; and when she knew that she was with child, she despised her mistress. Sarai said to Abram, 'I have been wronged and you must answer for it. It was I who gave my slave-girl into your arms, but since she has known that she is with child, she has despised me. May the LORD see justice done between you and me.'

Evaluation:
Accuracy:
   (good/fair/poor)   _____   _____
Understandability:
   (same/easier/harder)   _____   _____
Emotive force:
   (same/lower/higher)   _____   _____
Overall impact:
   (same/less/greater)   _____   _____